AF607872

Collective Preventive Diplomacy

SUNY series in Global Politics

James N. Rosenau, editor

Collective Preventive Diplomacy

A Study in International Conflict Management

Barry H. Steiner

State University of New York Press

Published by
State University of New York Press, Albany

Printed in the United States of America

For information, address State University of New York Press, Albany, NY
www.sunypress.edu

Production by Michael Haggett
Marketing by Susan M. Petrie

Library of Congress Cataloguing-in-Publication Data

Steiner, Barry H. (Barry Howard), 1942–
Collective preventive diplomacy : a study in international conflict management / Barry H. Steiner.
p. cm. — (SUNY series in global politics)
Includes bibliographical references and index.
ISBN 978-0-7914-5988-1 (pb. alk. paper)—ISBN 978-0-7914-5987-4 (hc. alk. paper)
1. Diplomatic negotiations in international disputes—Case studies. 2. Diplomacy. 3. Conflict management. I. Title. II. Series.

JZ6045.S74 2004
327.1'72—dc22

2004041674

10 9 8 7 6 5 4 3 2 1

This Book is Dedicated to my Mother

And to the Memory of my Father (ע״ה)

Contents

Tables and Illustrations

Tables

Figure

Cartoons

Acknowledgments

This study was made possible by a solicited grant from the United States Institute of Peace in September 1994. I would like to thank the Institute for its support and patience.

Greg Rasmussen carried out research on half of the cases examined in this study—Belgium, the first Bosnia case, the Memel, and Cyprus—and he also critiqued profiles that I subsequently prepared on the first three of these cases. In late 1994 and early 1995 Rasmussen was a virtual collaborator on this study, and it is a pleasure to recall the great stimulation I received in working with him.

Richard Betts, Alexander George, and I. William Zartman kindly provided comments and critiques on earlier drafts of this study. I alone am responsible for the result.

From the beginning of this project, Nancy St. Martin has translated my rough drafts into clean copy with enormous efficiency and unfailing good cheer.

The Bildarchiv Preussischer Kulturbesitz in Berlin has kindly permitted me to reproduce on the cover of this study a 1881 painting by Anton von Werner, "The Congress of Berlin." I would like to thank Klaus Goken for photographing the painting, and Ulla Harmsen for makng the reproduction available for my use.

Two cartoons by Bill Mauldin used here ("Well, Gentlemen . . . Time to Be at Each Other's Throats" (1946); and "I'm Merely Withdrawing My Congo Support" (1961)) have been provided from the Mauldin Collection in the Prints and Photographs Division of the Library of Congress, Washington, D.C. (LC-USZ62, CD-1/Mauldin, nos. 267 and 713). A third Mauldin cartoon ("Good Heavens! I'd Swear I Heard One of the Pieces

Groan!" has been taken from a Mauldin book, *Back Home* (New York: William Sloane, 1947), page 296.

These three cartoons are copyright 1946, 1961, and 1947, respectively, by Bill Mauldin. They are reproduced with permission for this publication in this medium only. Copying or reproduction without written permission of the Estate of William H. Mauldin is prohibited. Jonathan M. Gordon and Valerie Verdugo facilitated use of these cartoons on behalf of the Estate of Bill Mauldin.

Portions of chapter 9 of this study were published earlier in different form in the journal *Global Society*.

I am grateful to the Canadian Defense College for the opportunity to present ideas in this study and to receive feedback.

Finally, my wife JoAnn, and my children Mitzi and Benjamin, backed this project with plenty of emotional support.

Part I

Framework and Concepts

Chapter 1

Introduction

Divisions within small states have in recent years been the most important cause of war.[1] This study focuses on violence or threat of violence induced by small-state ethnic conflict as a collective great-power agenda issue. Its interests are both empirical and prescriptive. Empirically, it uses contemporary and historical cases to understand the opportunities and limitations for major states coping with conflict between small-state ethnic communities. At present, the great powers lack agreement about attainable conflict reduction objectives when foreign domestic antagonists, such as those recently encountered in Somalia and Bosnia-Herzegovina, are unwilling or unable to practice restraint. Prescriptively, the study seeks to enlarge the ability of those states to plan for and to defuse such conflict. It is guided by the assumption that the major states cannot easily reject involvement when intrastate small-power conflict is increasingly perceived as an international-order problem. The great powers have traditionally exercised responsibility for maintaining world order because of their distinctive role in the hierarchy of states.[2]

While collective great-power intervention in small-state ethnic conflict dates from the nineteenth century, scholarly and public concern about it came about only after the Soviet-American Cold War ended in the early 1990s.[3] As several new UN peacekeeping programs were then initiated, UN Secretary-General Boutros Boutros-Ghali argued strongly for collective international intervention in small-state domestic conflict. Boutros-Ghali maintained that such intervention should be designed to facilitate "preventive diplomacy" (PD), which he defined as "action to prevent disputes from arising between parties, to prevent existing disputes from escalating into conflicts and to limit the spread of the latter when they occur."[4] Arguing that the United Nations should widen its role in heading off violence within and between states before it happened, he implied that the major powers would work to support this vision, which depended upon major-state resources. However, he did not discuss how great-power support would be forthcoming.

Eight years later, a UN panel on peace operations headed by Lakhdar Brahimi noted the need for great-power action to counter states that instigate and support conflict within their neighbors, and referred by implication to the major states when it observed, "If a [UN] operation is given a mandate to protect civilians, . . . it also must be given the specific resources to carry out that mandate."[5] The major states have the necessary capabilities to provide for such a mandate, and thus have a veto over providing it, but they have often in the past tolerated a mismatch of UN capabilities with UN objectives. The Brahimi panel report did not show how the great powers can be persuaded to allocate to UN peace operations the priority they deserve.

Michael Lund, specifically addressing PD requirements, has called for "explicitly multilateral and multilevel" norms and procedures to provide for "more regularized [and] widely established arrangements" so as to "preempt crises rather than wait for them to erupt."[6] Comprehensive capabilities for early warning of potential crises would be put into place and applied as needed in particular disputes to keep response time between warnings and preventive action as short as possible.[7] But Lund noted that great-power action to sustain a PD regime was in doubt: "[T]he task of galvanizing and maintaining resolve behind . . . coherent . . . [preventive] action is perhaps harder today than during the Cold War, especially if the action contemplated is likely to be multilateral. In an era of scattered, local conflicts, major powers appear to see few reasons to intervene in conflicts that do not *yet* greatly affect their national interests."[8] To deal with this problem, Lund recommended "downloading" prevention responsibilities from the major powers to the UN Security Council and to local actors within particular regions.[9]

This study attempts to fill in the gap in present-day understanding of the linkage between great-power action and commonly understood PD requirements. Sympathetic to the contemporary need for great-power-inspired PD, the study is particularly concerned with *collective* great-power PD action as an alternative to PD initiated independently by any single great power. It argues that collectively initiated PD is a potential enhancer of PD effectiveness in relation to small-state antagonists, and an underappreciated instrument of great-power leadership in this area.

This introductory chapter spells out this study's distinctive preoccupations, its key issues, and its "focused comparison" methodology.

Focus of the Study

The purpose of the present study is to better understand the roles and potential of the major states, working together and supported where possible by international organizations such as the UN, in the practice of PD. It provides a context to understand how the great powers affect PD practice, and to reconcile the stature and role of the great powers with PD requirements. It defines PD as the application of international values to a dispute that is local or regional but which has substantial international implications.

Specifically, the study breaks new ground in four ways. First, it explicitly takes account of great-power relationships, tracing how they affect major-state will and capability to defuse small-state conflict. Given the prominence of the great powers in the international system, this study in effect probes the international system as a causal variable upon internal small-state conflict.[10] The focus is on the impact that international conditions, including the hierarchy of states, the international balance of power, and the concert of major states, have upon the parties to small-state domestic ethnic conflict.[11] Although the study also traces the effect of small-state behavior on the large powers, it was undertaken in the expectation that international values would be primarily promoted in the world by the major states; that their strength and influence would preponderate; and that international value promoters therefore require study.[12]

Second, the chief conceptual contribution made in this study is to distinguish two distinct PD functions in relation to small-state conflict. Collective *intervention* is directed to defusing conflict between the primary antagonists in conciliatory or coercive fashion. Intervention supplies the potential for negotiation and communication between the primary antagonists when, as often happens, channels are otherwise lacking for these purposes. Collective *insulation,* unrelated in itself to the needs of the primary antagonists, defuses the conflict as an irritant to great-power relations. Insulation heads off unilateral great-power action that, by opportunistically supporting one antagonist or another in the local dispute, interferes with the ability of the great powers to bring collective influence to bear upon them. It also creates a great-power consensus about the terms to be offered to the primary antagonists. Intervention and insulation comprise the international values in the definition of PD adopted here. The definition is broad enough to allow for both elements, but it also invites disaggregating them.

Third, in examining the interplay between the great powers and small-state antagonists, the study anticipates changing great-power relationships and motivations toward the local conflict as that conflict evolves. Because great-power orientations can change, the diffidence commonly shown by the major states in the early stages of local conflict should not be accepted as a constant; that is to say, aggravated local conflict can energize collective great-power PD in a manner that factions in local conflict may not have anticipated.[13] This in turn opens up potential for later great-power intervention in aggravated, violent, and polarized local conflict. From this point of view, PD is not "do or die": even if they initially fail, great-power efforts at intervention and insulation persist. Those efforts should become more effective over time as the major states learn from their mistakes. The PD definition adopted here thus raises the issue of contrasting the effectiveness of later as against earlier great-power intervention in local conflict.

Finally, this study aims at strengthening those who would apply international values in the contemporary period. It does so by seeking diagnoses of policy problems encountered in a variety of PD experiences, so that developments giving rise to those problems can be better appreciated and anticipated. The focus of these diagnoses is the gap between what Alexander George has termed "gross capabilities" and the "usable options" of states[14] in defusing small-power intrastate ethnic conflict. What were the reasons why the great powers were not able to apply their gross capabilities in the most effective way? What enabled them eventually to mobilize usable resources? What problems in their own relations and in their relationship with the primary antagonists did they have to overcome before they succeeded in interventionist PD? The study also strives to offer policy prescriptions linked to different types of collective great-power PD. Extended comparison of cases, taking into account international and local conflict conditions, PD techniques employed by the great powers, and divergences in the case material, underpin the study's diagnoses and prescriptions. While such analysis can hardly assure PD success under every condition, it can identify circumstances in which advance planning and a more refined menu of choice is likely to make a difference.

Collective Great-Power Action

PD can be exercised by great powers singly or together, by regional states, by international organizations, or by international civil servants such as the

UN secretary general. The focus here upon collective great-power activity is prompted by (1) the frequent link between great-power intervention in small-state disputes and the depth of great-power unity; (2) the presumption that collective action is likely to have a greater impact upon the local antagonists than major states acting individually; and (3) the recent decline in the willingness of specific major states to intervene independently in small-state disputes.

First, the link between great-power collective intervention in small-power disputes and the depth of great-power unity takes different forms. Major-state *unity* is an obstacle to intervention if the great powers give other issues greater weight and are determined to react to local ethnic conflict in slow, plodding fashion. Alternatively, great-power *disunity* can be the problem, the major states being unable to deal with the local problem in concerted fashion. Or the disunity impels the major states to find a consensus in order to prevent a breach in their own relationship that could lead to hostilities. Together, these possibilities highlight how great-power unity depends either on reaching a common position toward small-state problems, or else upon the belief that only such unity can create a solution for the small-state difficulties.

Second, collective great-power action increases major-state leverage upon the primary antagonists while reducing the incentives for opportunistic unilateral major-state action in support of one or another of them. As already suggested, successful PD requires bringing the superior power of the major states to bear upon the weaker ones. In recent years, the potential for exerting this power has on balance been increased by the weakness of political institutions and the low level of internal unity in many small-states. As Barry Buzan has pointed out, weak states are most distinguished by a "high level of concern with domestically generated threats to the security of the government," and, as a result, "large-scale use of force [is] a major and continuing element in the domestic political life of the nation."[15] This condition creates an *objective* weak-state dependence upon outside patrons, and also a *subjective* dependence that varies according to the insecurity of the leaders. As intrastate conflict in such countries intensifies, the major states are likely to be prime candidates to provide assistance, and whether they respond separately or collectively can make a significant difference for weak-state conditions. Should the major states respond separately, they will invite the weak-state regime and its challengers to compete for allies, with the weak state becoming then a contending issue among the major states.[16] If the great powers respond collectively, they are better positioned to limit military assistance so that the domestic conflict is not intensified and, on the other hand, to expose the primary antagonists to alternatives to violence. In general, prospects for effective PD seem enhanced when collective great-power action permits encouraging and if necessary imposing restraint on weak-state primary antagonists.

Finally, the focus upon collective great-power action is supported by the growing reluctance of individual major states in the post–Cold War period to intervene unilaterally in deep-seated small-power intrastate disputes. This development increases individual major-state incentives to seek collective responsibility for intervening, and to apply more stringent intervention criteria. The May 1994 American Presidential Decision Directive on reforming multilateral peace operations reflects this trend, tightening as it did conditions under which the United States would participate, either with or without American combat troops, in multilateral military action. Although originally envisioned as a grant of authority to the UN to substitute for unilateral American military action, the directive was sharply revised following the death of eighteen American soldiers in a peacekeeping mission in Somalia, and the turning away by armed Haitian demonstrators of ships carrying American and Canadian peacekeepers prepared to land in Haiti. As Madeleine K. Albright, then American ambassador to the UN, put it in May 1994, "The U.N. has not yet demonstrated the ability to respond effectively when the risk of combat is high and the level of local cooperation is low."[17]

Since many weak states can threaten to fight outside forces while downplaying a willingness to cooperate with them, and since the use of force will often be indispensable for outside influence upon the primary antagonists, it is not surprising that the strong states are highly skeptical about PD. However, assuming that military operations launched from outside remain *objectively* important if intrastate problems are to be surmounted, and assuming, as seems reasonable, that anticipating intervention and insulation problems ahead of time can assist collective great-power planning, the focus on collective great-power action remains timely. Collective action appears to be a precondition for overriding strong American skepticism about multilateral peacekeeping operations. Because of the link, already referred to, between such operations and PD in difficult cases, great-power consensus is likely to be indispensable for PD, whether or not it is directed through the UN.

The Great Powers and Small-Power Intrastate Conflict

Intrastate conflicts that have been objects of great-power concerns include, according to one listing, "violent civilian power struggles, military coups, militarized ideological campaigns, insurgencies, civil wars, and revolutions."[18] These are all widespread; cause great suffering; affect and involve neighboring states through refugee flows, outside military assistance and bases, hot-pursuit operations, and outside instigation of internal conflict; engage the interests of major states and international organizations; and are major agenda items for the international community.[19] Collective great-power interests and agendas can be immediately affected by small-state internal conflict, or by the prospect of it, or they could be affected by it in delayed fashion, after the conflict is played out for a time. The great powers often internationalize local conflict, exporting international values to, and widening concerns about, local disputes. They also localize and particularize international concerns, connecting major states and diplomatic frameworks to specific disputes.

When international interests and agendas are linked to small-state internal conflict, the scope of great-power activity depends upon four considerations: (1) the will and capability of the major states; (2) relations between major states and the primary antagonists; (3) international norms of outside intervention in domestic conflict; and (4) the timing of international engagement in local conflict. First, the major states tend to be much less concerned about the intrastate small-power conflict than about relationships among themselves, shaped by their respective international needs. For this reason, insulating the small-power problem as a great-power issue usually receives higher major-state priority than intervention in the dispute. Collective intervention is often delayed until after the emergence of local conflict, as the major states slowly establish common positions, and it depends heavily on the consent of the primary antagonists. However, though the great powers usually have low intrinsic concerns for the intrastate small-power issues, they can have strong extrinsic ones if some major states are perceived to be independently willing and able to intervene in them, to the detriment of those who do not. Great powers otherwise inclined to intervene unilaterally are offered inducements to join with other major states to ensure that the conflict remains insulated. Insulation is also promoted by rapid collective intervention in those cases, dampening the chances of unilateral action. On the other hand, failure to insulate the conflict can be very problematic for the major states. Great-power persistence in intervening unilaterally or in remaining outside the great-power coalition usually leads to increased international tensions and to the threat of great-power war.

When major states perceive that international stability depends directly on a local problem, they will attach high priority to it. International impacts upon the local conflict will then tend to be considerable relative to local or noninternational ones. That is, even if local conflict is aggravated and protracted and the local antagonists polarized, the great powers will tend to collectively intervene more forcefully, and be more strongly motivated to exert influence upon the primary antagonists. On the other hand, when international stability does not appear to depend on the local problem, collective intervention will tend to be weaker and less effective. Noninternational causes of local ethnic conflict will tend to be much more important relative to international ones, and the low priority attached by the major states to the small-state conflict weakens their leverage to affect the behavior of the primary antagonists.[20]

Second, primary antagonists in local conflict are not internationally inactive: they can oppose, delay, stir controversy, and act as spoilers, blunting the effect of interventionist PD and causing it to fail when it depends on the antagonists' consent. The primary antagonists are also usually much more strongly motivated toward each other and toward outside states than the latter are toward them. A difference in perspective about the intrastate conflict also characterizes the primary antagonists, on one hand, and interested outside states and organizations, on the other. The former view their conflict "inside out," giving importance to external actors only insofar as the latter provide assistance with sustaining the positions and strengths of the primary antagonists. Obtaining outside assistance—in the form of material aid to combatants, humanitarian assistance to civilians, and political support in the form of recognition or influence upon the adversary—is essential when, as is often the case, no one primary antagonist is able to dominate its opponent. The major powers and international organizations, by contrast, view the intrastate conflict "outside in," treating it as significant only in light of its effect upon international stability and order.

Of the primary antagonists, the central regime as the recognized government often has larger resources to resist and impede outside intervention and to affect and benefit from it than does its challenger, giving it leverage upon the major states that the challenger usually does not possess. The constituted government ordinarily has greater standing to request international intervention, and it can make the request anticipating that intervention will enhance its ability to suppress its opposition; when the government no longer feels this purpose is being served, it is better positioned to oppose, retard, or systematically interfere with external efforts, even when publicly favoring them.

Paradoxically, the leverage of the central regime upon the great powers increases when it is most vulnerable to its challenger, and when the regime is highly valued by the international community. In such a case, weakness and formal independence give it enormous bargaining advantages. (This condition is often linked to what may be termed "fictitious" borders, which the central regime cannot police and the challenging group can consequently capitalize upon to reap full benefits from neighboring state assistance.) Although the central regime then lacks actual independence, the international community's determination to prevent it from being overrun enables the regime to inject its own demands into international negotiations.

Third, international norms of nonintervention in the domestic affairs of states have a mixed effect upon international responses to intrastate conflict. On one hand, the norms provide a defense for regimes defending their prerogatives—that is, to be supreme within their territorial jurisdiction. They are repeatedly cited to protect states against great-power interference, and even more to protect peoples within a state against domination from outside. "[T]he norm of nonintervention," Lori Fisler Damrosch has written, "aims at securing the rights of people within a state to exercise political freedoms without external domination. [The] values of conflict containment and autonomy are at the heart of the international legal system's commitment to a norm against external involvement in internal affairs."[21]

Nonintervention norms and sovereign prerogatives reinforce the disinclination of the major states to intervene in intrastate small-power disputes, and when the great powers do intervene, norms and prerogatives incline them to move slowly and deliberately and to rely upon the consent of the primary antagonists. On the other hand, the scope of domestic jurisdiction is generally believed to have narrowed in recent years, partly because international organizations have intruded into the national life of states, and partly because governments at times have seriously damaged the security concerns of their peoples.[22] Political challengers have also contributed to this shift by trampling upon the rights of individuals with the aid of neighboring states.

Finally, two questions of timing affect the scope of international engagement in local conflict: first, whether intervention occurs prior to violence and polarization between the antagonists, and second, whether with the onset of polarization the antagonists perceive a hurting stalemate that they could not resolve in any other way.[23] Receptivity of the primary antagonists to outside mediation is often diminished once violence sets in because the ensuing civil strife hardens outlooks and divisions. Prompt outside intervention is justified by the difficulty of negotiating an end to civil wars, a problem reflected in the apparent rarity of negotiated settlements to such wars. As Michael E. Brown has argued, "[I]f distant powers or international organizations are going to take action to manage conflicts, they should act sooner rather than later; probabilities of success are higher and costs are lower."[24] Intervention can be most efficacious prior to local confrontation, before positions have hardened. It has also been argued, however, that intrastate conflict is most ripe for settlement only following the onset of local stalemate, when civil strife aids international mediation in the later stages of the conflict. Since each of these ideas is logically compelling, no optimum point for international intervention can be identified.

Internal Ethnic Conflict

This study is limited to concerted great-power intervention in small-power intrastate ethnic conflict, a condition defined by Michael E. Brown as "a dispute about important political, economic, social, cultural, or territorial issues between two or more ethnic communities."[25] Ethnic conflict is conceptualized here as occurring between communities of people whose culture-centered attitudes, associated with ideas of historical descent, are awakened and strengthened vis-à-vis other cultural communities and foster a particular sense of identity. It is a cultural manifestation of an unsatisfactory relationship between politically stronger forces controlling the central institutions and politically weaker ones which do not.[26] Culture-centered attitudes are particularly strengthened when ethnic groupings are subjected to political and economic inequality, and have long-standing historical grievances. The focus upon PD in the 1990s was stimulated by a sharp increase in intrastate ethnic conflict. A 1994 study cited an "explosion of ethnopolitical conflicts since the end of the Cold War [that] is, in fact, a continuation of a trend that began as early as the 1960s. It is a manifestation of the enduring tension between states that want to consolidate and expand their power and ethnic groups that want to defend and promote their collective identity and interests."[27]

The scope of ethnic conflict, however, varies considerably. Economic issues and cultural suppression are a source of antagonism in some ethnic conflicts, but not in others. Complaints against some central regimes stimulate ethnic challengers to secede from a state, while elsewhere they do not. Ethnic conflict can grow out of deprivation sensed by the weaker antagonist in relation to the stronger, or out of the determination of the stronger antagonist to crush or annihilate the weaker. Such conflict can feature political consciousness, or nationalism, on the part of the cultural groupings; alternatively, political consciousness might be low even as cultural consciousness, from interaction with other cultural groups, is high. As Walker Connor has noted, "[I]n the less modern states, . . . cultural consciousness precedes political consciousness, and . . . cultural consciousness presupposes an awareness of other cultures."[28]

Selecting ethnic conflict as a focus for intrastate disunity permits more detailed comparisons between cases than does a more mixed domestic conflict sample. However, conflict between ethnic communities is particularly volatile domestic conflict and hence especially problematic for great-power PD. In the present study, the volatility is reflected in each of the measures affecting the scope of great-power PD discussed in the last section. First, the boundaries of ethnic communities do not coincide with the boundaries of states, but commonly spill across them. Neighboring states can therefore instigate and strengthen the revolt, at times militarily intervening in support of it. Great powers can also become sympathetically involved in intrastate ethnic conflict, transforming it from a low-priority to a high-priority question for other major states anxious to block them from obtaining unilateral advantages. When the local conflict leads to acute tensions between great powers, the major states often quickly act together to prevent the conflict from widening, as has been noted.

Second, intrastate ethnic conflict complicates the relationship between great powers and primary antagonists in two ways. It stresses the weakest points of weak states by challenging the integrity of central institutions. When the central regime is, as often happens in premodern societies, already weak prior to the onset of ethnic confrontation, it is poorly able to protect itself when confrontation occurs and necessarily becomes dependent upon international assistance. That is to say, if the state's institutions are to be strengthened, outside assistance is often required to advise on and even perform basic governmental needs. The problem is particularly acute when outside states support a revolt against a central regime that militarily cannot protect itself or subdue an opposition that capitalizes upon poorly policed borders. Survival of the regime is then in doubt, and the international community is called upon to provide lifeline assistance.

Ethnic conflict also paradoxically strengthens weak central regimes by contributing to popular hatreds of other cultural groupings. Members of the dominant culture increasingly depend upon elites to resist internal challengers and outside intervention that does not envision clear-cut governmental superiority over its challenger.[29] As elites take advantage of unstable domestic conditions for narrow purposes, they have less incentive to make concessions to the opposing group or to international mediators. Their bargaining position in relation to mediators is enhanced as they manipulate their dependence upon international assistance to demand far-reaching safeguards and protection.

Third, controversies associated with international norms are accentuated by intrastate ethnic conflict. Rising ethnic hatreds and the inability of ethnic communities to bridge political differences stimulate the use of military force to suppress ethnic opposition. Central regimes then cite the international norm of noninterference to effectuate such hard-line effort, claiming the widest prerogative to act as they see fit. Yet excessive suppression has eroded the norm of nonintervention over the longer term and encouraged the international community to demarcate the moral and legal obligation to defend ethnic challengers deprived of rights.

Fourth, volatile relations between ethnic communities importantly affect the timing of effective international mediation. Such conflict is more conducive to violence than other types of intrastate conflict, and also to the polarization, mistrust, and security dilemma brought about by violence.[30] Ethnic conflict also tends to bring violence quickly, without plan or strategy but as a reaction to a sense of deprivation, before international mediation can be mobilized. It therefore narrows the window for receiving early warning of confrontation between ethnic groups and for useful early great-power intervention upon warning. Once violence occurs, stopping the fighting becomes a precondition for any other negotiating progress.[31] Finally, the depth of antagonism and mistrust between the ethnic communities makes it difficult to persuade the antagonists to stop fighting for more than short respites, and to accept a hurtful stalemate. Diminishing the opportunity for early collective intervention in the dispute, ethnic violence thus also appears to diminish the opportunity for later intervention.

Comparative Case Study

This study concentrates on the interplay between the major states and ethnic antagonists in multiethnic states in eight selected cases, employing comparative analysis of these cases (table 1.1). The burden of the study is that comparative analysis of cases can uncover generalizations. Its method, structured, focused comparison, employs case study as part of a set of questions directed to understanding a problem broader in scope than any single case. While study of one case could, according to Alexander George, be "a means of stimulating the imagination in order to discern important *new* general problems, identify possible theoretical solutions, and formulate potentially generalizable relations that were not previously apparent,"[32] many cases directed to the same problem can have cumulative effect and theoretical value. "[O]ne might consider," George has written, "how a *series* of heuristic and plausibility probe case studies might be employed in order to achieve cumulation. By viewing heuristic cases and plausibility probes within the framework of the strategy of controlled comparison it may be possible to cumulate the findings and to employ them as an admittedly weak, but still useful, form of hypothesis assessment that falls short of rigorous hypothesis testing."[33]

Focused comparison serves three purposes in this study. First, it highlights within circumscribed conditions important great-power motives for collective PD, the range of feasible collective diplomatic action, and the consequences of such diplomacy, each reflected across case lines and suggestive of broader tendencies that are subject to further testing. Second, it suggests limits to the generalizations, while also establishing commonalities. Third, it assists policy interests by allowing an inquiry into what might have induced more effective great-power action.

TABLE 1.1
Cases Studied in This Project

(1)	Belgian Revolution (1830–1838)
(2)	Greek Revolution (1821–1832)
(3)	Bosnian Revolution (1875–1878) (Bosnia I)
(4)	Armenian Unrest in the Ottoman Empire (1878–1914)
(5)	German/Lithuanian Conflict in the Memel (1918–1939)
(6)	Belgian Congo Conflict (1960–1964)
(7)	Cyprus Conflict (1960–present)
(8)	Croat/Muslim/Serb Conflict in Bosnia-Herzegovina (1992–1995) (Bosnia II)

Deriving generalizations from the case material requires operationalizing independent and dependent variables at the outset.[34] The variable to be explained—the dependent variable here—is the primary antagonist decision to accept or not accept great-power PD proposals. For primary antagonists to accept PD, either their attitudes, positions, and relationships need to change, or incentives must be provided to reconcile them to PD proposals. The effectiveness of great-power PD directed to local conflict cannot be discussed without referring to primary antagonist attitudes, positions, and relationships.

The causal factor bearing upon the primary antagonist decision—the independent variable in this analysis—is the collective major-state motivation to intervene in the local conflict. This motivation generates cooperative action between great powers to consult, act, and plan together in relation to the local conflict.[35] The motivation can be stronger or weaker, depending on the interests of the major states. If their collective motivation to act is low, the major great powers are reluctant to cooperate, mutually suspicious, and intent on preserving their prerogatives to act independently; if their motivation is high, they will be more disposed to cooperate, overcome their mutual suspicions, and be sympathetic to multilateral action. The study does not explicitly compare collective and independently initiated PD, and thus cannot prove that collective PD is more effective than its counterpart. However, it is driven by the commonsense assumption that collective action has larger potential to influence the primary antagonists than does unilateral PD effort. That is, associations between highly motivated great powers are presumed to enhance the chances that a framework mutually acceptable to the primary antagonists can be produced to satisfactorily manage local ethnic conflict.

This study was not conceived on the basis of any well-developed theoretical framework, hypotheses linking collective great-power activity and the primary antagonists not being yet available when this project began. The present study, as far as is known, is the first to investigate it empirically.[36] It has been motivated by the increasing policy attention great-power PD has received, in light of the proliferation of small-state ethnic conflict, and the much-commented-upon difficulties experienced by the major states in dealing with such conflict. In short, the policy importance of PD has justified proceeding with this study despite the absence of theoretical insight into it.

To move from the particular to general, independent and dependent variables must vary and their variance be given full play. However, specifying independent and dependent variables even in their most simplified, two-option form has analytical utility. The combination between them in this form yields a four-fold matrix (table 1.2).

The absence of a general theory of PD must be kept in mind when examining this matrix. The preconditions and reasons for reaching one combination rather than another are issues for the present study, but no claim is made that the study will yield a general theory. Rather than establish universally preponderating tendencies, case analysis is designed to highlight divergent patterns forming the building blocks for contingent, situationally grounded generalizations. As George has observed, the user of the controlled comparison method "seeks to identify the *conditions under which each distinctive type of causal pattern occurs* rather than attempting to address the question of *how often* each outcome and/or causal pattern does occur or can be expected to occur."[37]

The matrix addresses options associated with PD as a process whereby the major states seek to prevail upon the primary antagonists to change their behavior. These options anticipate much of the drama of the case analysis to follow. The matrix displays the contrast between a coercive-minded and a conciliatory-minded great-power coalition, a contrast reflecting strong and weak motivations to intervene, respectively. It displays how great-power influence efforts by no means invariably dominate

TABLE 1.2
A Simplified Model of Independent and Dependent Variables

		Dependent Variable: Receptivity of Primary Antagonists	
		Acceptance	*Nonacceptance*
Independent Variable: Great-Power Motivation	Strong	Successful coercive intervention	Misperception between primary antagonist and great-power coalition in aggravated local conflict
	Weak	Successful conciliatory intervention	PD provides force-dampening but no reconciliation

primary antagonist thinking. And it invites explanations for the failure of PD intervention initiatives. PD may fail because the great powers rival each other more than they cooperate. It may fail because one or more major states persist in independently taking sides in the local conflict, bolstering primary-antagonist will or ability to reject collective great-power PD. And it may fail because of the depth of suspicion of the primary antagonists toward each other or the great powers. Collective PD may fail even if great-power motivation to intervene is strong, as a primary antagonist in aggravated local conflict misjudges the depth of major-state commitment. And collective PD may at times succeed even if great-power motivation is weak, depending on the relationship and interests of the primary antagonists. These possibilities, which might otherwise be neglected, point to the need for careful whole-case analysis that can distinguish ultimate PD success from prior failure.

The Cases

Finding generalizations about the PD process is difficult not only because PD is delicate and complex, but also because of the considerable variation between and within PD cases. First, the present study is designed to escape the limitation of large multicase comparisons, which is that they "[do] not capture the details and nuances of each particular communal group's traits, grievances, and conflicts."[38] In-depth study of eight cases reported upon here is ideal for combining "details and nuances" with generalizations.[39]

Second, the study strives for more diversity in the case sample than is commonly allowed for, because it employs historical and contemporary cases. The logic for doing so is threefold. First, older cases—even if largely forgotten today—are usually better documented than widely-known recent ones. Second, the cultural awareness of peoples that shaped ethnic conflict was already facilitated by social communication within and across ethnic lines in nineteenth-century Europe. And third, the major states were as busy coping with these conflicts in the nineteenth as in the twentieth century; while many fewer cases of small-state ethnic conflict arose prior to 1945 than afterward, a larger proportion of the former occasioned international attention because they challenged major-state territorial empire, the building and maintaining of which were more widespread prior to 1945 than afterward. Ethnic conflict in the earlier period at times directly affected the actual and potential balance of power between the major states.

To be sure, the research task would have remained the same whatever the PD cases selected, namely, abstracting from apparently idiosyncratic elements of the cases and uncovering patterns applicable to the contemporary period. Further, it is difficult to establish the representativeness of any sample of eight cases. For his part, George has argued that controlled comparison remains an important analytical method even if the cases are not representative of the general universe of instances of interest. "The desideratum that guides selection of cases in the controlled comparison approach," he has written, "is not numbers but *variety*. . . . [T]he investigator in designing the study will either seek cases in which the outcome of the dependent variable differed or cases having the same outcome but a different explanation for it."[40]

A third source of diversity is the enormous variability of the PD process, even within cases. For example, great powers can change their level of engagement in the local dispute. When PD requirements are greater than the level of mobilization of their resources, the major states must either deepen their commitment to reach a settlement in the local conflict, or else withdraw. Their choice between persuasion and coercion as PD techniques, which reflects their level of PD commitment, is also changeable. They can employ only one of these techniques to achieve both a military and political settlement, or vary their use of the techniques when dealing with military and political questions. The choice of techniques depends on whether the primary antagonists agree on separating or continuing to be part of the same state, on whether their relationship is violent, and on whether certain transition effects of the local conflict—including neighboring states' involvement, byproduct effects upon civilians, and primary-antagonist challenges to major-state pacification efforts—intrude to stimulate sharpened major-state involvement in the local conflict. Much of the PD drama is in deepening great-power involvement in the local conflict.

The primary antagonists also illustrate variability within cases, seeking on a competitive basis to influence the great powers to intervene on their behalf. Indeed, the onset of great-power intervention typically occurs because the central regime or its ethnic challenger demonstrates sufficient influence with the major states to cause them to intervene. This involvement is always linked to an important discontinuity in the relationship between the primary ethnic antagonists—that is, to the onset of more severe conflict or confrontation between them.

Moving from the particular to the general, the present study focuses upon three issues of interest in all the cases: (1) how the great powers come

TABLE 1.3
Core Empirical Questions

1. What significant early warning signs of domestic unrest appeared in the cases?
2. Were these signs perceived by great-power leaders?
3. How did information at the disposal of policymakers about these and other indicators affect international intervention?
4. What problems for the great powers in gaining important information were presented in the cases?
5. How strong was the political will of great-power leaders to deal with the problem of civil strife?
6. How important were differences among the great powers in forging a collective response to the unrest?
7. How important were these differences and informational shortcomings for the success or failure of intervention?

to be collectively engaged in the small-state ethnic conflict and how their engagement deepens; (2) how and why the primary antagonists accept or reject PD proposals from the major states; and (3) whether the great powers are warned, or could have been warned, about impending confrontation between the local ethnic antagonists in time to defuse it before it becomes critical.

An interest in controlled comparison guides the preparation of profiles for each of the cases selected for study here. Core empirical questions are asked of each of these cases (table 1.3). Analysis of the cases is also controlled. First, to derive generalizations in spite of the case variety, analysis repeatedly highlights apparently important distinctions between the cases, often by using typologies. Commonalities within these distinctions are then made explicit, and hypotheses are derived in the course of probing the distinctions and the commonalities.

Outline of This Study

The remainder of this chapter summarizes the content of this study. Chapter 2 spells out the distinction between insulation and intervention as forms of PD. It outlines a PD typology based upon the motivation of the major powers to intervene in local ethnic conflict; this motivation may be high or low or shift from low to high. Chapter 3 argues that great-power relationships in different eras can be fruitfully compared on the basis of long-standing, empirically verified efforts of the major states to collectively address small-state conflict. The chapter shows how PD diplomacy is shaped by Tight Concert, Loose Concert, and Prevailing Opposition patterns of great-power relationships. In each of these patterns, great-power PD directed to local ethnic conflict is a consequence of "outside in" calculations by the major states.

Profiles of each of the eight PD cases analyzed in this study are provided in chapter 4. They focus upon the core empirical questions listed in this chapter. Chapters 5 through 9 focus on the interplay between the great powers and the primary antagonists over the entire local conflict cycle. On the great-power side, the focus is especially on the changeable, collectively perceived interests shaping PD. When addressing the primary antagonists, the study gives heavy attention to their relationship and to their dependence upon outside states.

Chapter 5 concentrates on the emergence of local ethnic conflict and the local consequences of great-power PD. It shows how primary antagonist calculations contribute to such diplomacy. It argues that political grievances of the ethnic challenger are a much more important stimulator of ethnic conflict in our cases than nationalism, making the challenger group more dependent upon the major powers. Chapter 6, on the shaping of collective PD agendas, discusses insulation and intervention as PD objectives, and also the timing of great-power initiatives. It argues that insulation has been easier for the great powers to realize than intervention, and that insulationist PD shapes interventionist PD.

Chapters 7 and 8 focus on alternate PD techniques. Chapter 7 considers conciliation as a tool of great-power influence for reconciling the antagonists and for tension-reducing, force-dampening efforts. It concludes that collective conciliation in the cases is generally of limited utility, but that force dampening is more significant than are reconciliation efforts. Intensification of local ethnic conflict stimulates conciliatory crisis management measures. Chapter 8 deals with coercive PD. It points out that, in contrast to conciliatory great-power responses, coercive measures are usually delayed and therefore more subject to transitional developments that deepen great-power involvement, including humanitarian emergency, military intervention by secondary states, and, where international forces intervene in the local conflict arena, provocations by one of the primary antagonists against those forces. The chapter emphasizes how great-power relationships endure in spite of shifts and complications in relations between the major states and the primary antagonists.

Chapter 9 deals with the PD endgame, and especially how great-power initiatives come to be successfully implemented. It distinguishes between political and military aspects of settlements, and between conciliatory and coercive techniques, and it argues that applications of coercive PD depend importantly on whether great-power vital interests are present.

Chapter 10 recapitulates the most important arguments of the study and applies them to the needs of contemporary policy officials and planners. The chapter distinguishes between first-cut general conclusions and more important second-cut contingent conclusions. The first of these assist policy officials in diagnosing PD policy problems, while the second—following the PD typology outlined in chapter 2—help in diagnosis and in policy prescription.

Chapter 2

Insulation and Intervention

A Conceptual Overview

Insulation, neglected in the PD literature, commonly takes precedence as a great power objective over intervention and conditions the scope and will of the major states to become involved in intrastate local conflict. That conclusion, and the discussion of the problems—for the major states as well as for the primary antagonists—flowing from it, is based on the assumption that the major states are capable of independently taking whatever collective position on the local conflict that they choose. They can remain relatively aloof, rejecting enforcement action and even nonmilitary techniques for reconciling the local antagonists. They can accept nonmilitary or military modes of influencing the antagonists. They can vary these in the life cycle of the local conflict. Whatever they choose to do, they are capable of making an independent impact on the conflict as a consequence of their special strength and legitimacy in world politics.

This chapter provides a framework for conceptualizing about PD.[1] It distinguishes between insulation and intervention as PD policy preoccupations, and between PD based on high and on low motivations, and argues that they are indispensable for understanding the variability of great-power PD experience and for developing PD policy guidance. The chapter then sets forth a typology and a checklist of policymaking concerns that emphasize the variability of PD experience, the importance of insulation as a PD objective, and the tension between great-power and local antagonist interests. Finally, it discusses the problem of small-state antagonist resistance to great-power objectives and what can be done to overcome it.

The framework developed here is designed to provide a more informed basis for policy decision and to extend the ability of the great powers to defuse small-state antagonism. It will do so if it sensitizes policymakers, intelligence staffs, and policy planners to variations in great-power PD experience.

Insulation and Great-Power Motivations

The central conceptual contribution of this study is that insulation and intervention constitute equally important PD policymaking preoccupations. Agreement between the major states on insulating the local conflict as an issue among themselves is a prerequisite to collective great-power intervention in the local dispute, but tensions often exist between the two, especially when, as in cases studied here, great power intervention is collective rather than unilateral. These tensions complicate the PD policy problem, and if they are not appreciated and anticipated, the effectiveness of PD initiatives is likely to be reduced.

Collective major-state action greatly increases the potential for persuading the local antagonists to accept a peaceful framework between themselves, compared to the influence that can be mobilized by any one great power acting alone. However, the value to great powers of striving for such action is not a constant. It will be relatively low if no major state would be inclined to intervene unilaterally in the local conflict; it will be higher, conversely, if some major states are inclined to intervene on their own and others wish to restrain them. Two scenarios can be distinguished. One is when all great powers are reticent about becoming involved in small-state intrastate conflict, and only agreement among themselves can permit them to intervene. Such agreement is not ordinarily reached in time to facilitate collective intervention in the early stage of local conflict. On the other hand, the need for early collective agreement is lessened by the absence of any likelihood of individual major states intervening on their own. A second scenario is where one or more major states are strongly motivated to intervene unilaterally and the others are strongly impelled to prevent it.[2] Insulation is far more delicate in this scenario than in the first, and is usually coupled with a plan for collective intervention.

The distinction between weakly and strongly motivated great powers does not merely set off one case from another, but it often applies to transformation in great-power postures within particular cases. Recent cases of small-state civil strife in Bosnia-Herzegovina, Somalia, and Kosovo have underscored how great-power activity in relation to small-state antagonism must be treated as changeable and modifiable. Great powers may be diffident about early-stage small-power ethnic conflict and highly mobilized later on, or conversely be highly involved early in the conflict while subsequently playing a peripheral role after the difficulties of bringing their influence to bear upon the primary antagonists becomes apparent.[3]

But whatever the significance of great-power agreement, the decision to strive toward it will be subject to relationships between great-power countries that have little to do in practice with the character of the small-state antagonism. Those relationships are ordinarily more important for major-state interests than are great-power relationships with small states, yet they have been neglected as an independent element of the PD problem.

The Neglect of Great-Power Insulation

Rather than focussing upon relations between great powers, analysts have stressed the requirements of repairing problematic political, economic, and humanitarian conditions in small states, and the need for sustaining alternative frameworks between regime and ethnic challenger in those states over the long term. These requirements are often spelled out as normative guidelines for the major states, it being commonly understood that only the latter have the will and material assets to induce the local antagonists to satisfy those requirements. For example, Michael E. Brown notes how PD should be geared especially toward longer-term needs bearing upon intrastate conflict in order to prevent future violent outbreaks:

> Particular attention should be paid to political and economic development in troubled and potentially troubled parts of the world. In more concrete terms, this means working more aggressively to ensure that individuals and groups need not fear for their survival or security; overturn patterns of political, economic, and cultural discrimination; promote proportional representation in political and governmental affairs; establish and implement human rights safeguards; dampen the development of exclusionary national ideologies, whether they are based on ethnic or

> religious identifications; extend the benefits of economic prosperity and educational opportunities more equitably across societies; and work to develop civil societies by addressing the pernicious effects of distorted group histories and by promoting the values of compromise, conciliation, consensus, and tolerance.[4]

This analysis seems to presume that the likelihood of the major states rising to the occasion to intervene—especially on a proactive basis—depends heavily on an awareness of the broad elements of regime and peace building in fragile polities and societies. Judged in terms of intervention alone, the requirements are staggering, especially in countries in which the rudiments of stability are missing. That outside states need to address them is justified on moral grounds: great-power apathy in many cases would cause more intensified bloodshed (as for example recently in Rwanda). The requirements have also been addressed in terms of efficiency, distinguishing between early PD, in which violence between the local antagonists has not yet occurred and the great-power goal is to forestall it, from late PD, when violence has broken out and the great power goal is to prevent its escalation. As Brown has pointed out, "The longer international actors wait, the more intense conflicts become, and the more difficult conflict management becomes."[5]

While major-state policymakers should be proactive on interventionist PD, they also need proactive activity addressed to insulation of the local dispute as a great-power issue. Neglecting insulation, Brown's analysis assumes too easily that international actors can be brought to act in the most timely and promising manner—that is, early in the small-state conflict cycle—by a demonstration that proactive PD is much less traumatic and expensive for the major states than delayed intervention. To be sure, as Michael Lund has indicated, the yield of great power cooperation in interventionist PD may well be potentially greater when the local antagonists have not yet become polarized or employed violence against each other, because less international leverage would ordinarily be needed at that early stage to exert an impact on the primary antagonists.[6] But whether the outside states in practice wait, act proactively, endlessly debate, or procrastinate is a question that Brown's normative approach does not raise. The insulationist aspects of PD, in which the major states attempt to defuse specific small-power conflict as an issue among themselves, ordinarily take priority for them over how they act toward the local aspects of the conflict.

The normative approach is deficient not only in the omission of great power dynamics behind outside intervention in small-state internal disputes, but also in the reliability of its generalizations about great-power intervention. For example, after noting that early PD is likely to be more effective in dealing with small-state ethnic tensions than is action decided upon later on, Brown notes that the most useful early PD is the least likely to be forthcoming. "Unfortunately," he writes, "international motivations to take action are weakest in the early stages of internal conflicts, when levels of violence are low and windows of opportunity are open. Motivations to take action increase as levels of violence increase, but rising levels of violence also make conflict management efforts more difficult. In other words, international motivations to act are weakest when options are strongest, and motivations to act are strongest when options are weakest."[7]

That outside-state willingness to become involved in small-state internal disputes is initially low and grows over time is illustrated in a range of post-Soviet-American Cold War era cases in which tackling the small-state dispute has been of peripheral interest to the major states. A large number of such cases are analyzed in Brown's study. However, as already indicated, this tendency is not the only possibility: historically, PD has been vigorously applied in the early stage of small-state conflict to ensure that the great powers did not go to war over the dispute, a condition that required the major states to practice self-restraint.[8] That is, the likelihood that any one great power would abstain from intervention in the small-state dispute depended critically on all the others doing the same, a condition reflected in diplomatic practice. With respect to great power motivations for intervention, a great power perspective would suggest that motivations to intervene are likely to be weaker when, as at present, the number of unstable states has grown, the unequal character of political, and economic resources between states is clearly manifest, and the major states are not broadly competing among between themselves for worldwide influence. Great-power interest in intervening under these circumstances is likely to grow in response to outbreaks of intense violence produced by ethnic conflict, as in the cases of Bosnia-Herzegovina and Kosovo in recent years.

The main point, however, is that the propensity for great-power intervention is likely to depend on the scope and success of great-power insulation: if insulation is conditioned upon intervention, then intervention will occur at the early stage of conflict; if it is not conditioned upon intervention, then intervention is unlikely at that stage. Before satisfactory generalizations can be made about intervention, then, reference must be made to the dynamics of insulation, even if this leads in practice to outcomes different than those Brown generalizes about.

Brown is not wholly insensitive to the problem of insulation. His term "international motivations" suggests the existence of a consensus among consequential states on interventionist PD posture and indicates that when he discusses the shift of motivation of outside powers toward intervening in small-state conflict he has in mind collective PD. If so, however, the cost and consequences of the collective effort remain to be spelled out, and trade-offs between insulationist and interventionist priorities clarified. Costs are what states concede in action and in time to obtain an international consensus. A major state may refrain from particular action until conditions are more conducive to successful results. It may perceive, that is, that the value of hammering out agreed-upon goals or ensuring that some other great power abides by restraint outweighs the value of its own immediate unilateral intervention. The process of hammering out a collective great power position posture will often also delay interventionist initiatives. Finally, collective action will have consequences that are likely to interfere with optimum intervention, if the latter is defined as taking fullest advantage of the ample windows of opportunity present in the small state to manage the emerging local disputes.

A Typology of Insulationist PD

The distinctions just made—between insulation and intervention as PD objectives, between insulation based upon low individual major-state motivation to intervene and insulation that flows from a higher motivation to intervene, and between early and late stages of the local-conflict life cycle—can be integrated to define three types of PD insulation scenario. Each type of insulation scenario, it is argued here, offers a key to the potential of the major states to undertake interventionist PD, but each suggests a distinctive set of challenges for policymakers implementing PD programs. This section sets forth the essential features of the three types; the next presents a checklist of policymaking concerns raised by them.

The first two types of insulationist PD reflect the greatest differences in great-power motivation to intervene in small-state ethnic conflict. The first type (Type I) consists of cases in which individual great-power motivation to intervene in the small-power dispute is low in all stages of the local dispute. In the early stages, the low motivation reduces the need for insulation, and for small-power disputes of peripheral interest to the major states, insulation may not occur at all at that time. The importance of insulation in this type of case, however, is that even in the later stage of the local dispute—that is, when violence has broken out and may be quite intense—collective intervention will not occur until the major states have agreed upon a framework for defusing the small-state dispute as an issue among themselves. Even when such agreement has occurred, intervention may not happen if the major states decide among themselves to withhold support for intervention. The essential characteristic of this form of insulationist PD, then, is that because the great powers treat both insulation and intervention as of low urgency, collective intervention in the small-state dispute is likely to be weak over a long period of time, irrespective of developments in local small-state conflict.

The second form of insulationist PD (Type II) is characterized by high great-power motivation to intervene. Here the insulation dynamic is distinguished from that in Type I in three respects. First, because some major states are more inclined to intervene than are others,[9] and because the ability of one major power to gain unilateral and opportunistic advantage in the small-state dispute tends to be viewed by the others as impeding their interests, insulation becomes an urgent requirement for all major states. The less assertive major states use insulation to restrain the more assertive, but both the more assertive and the less assertive states value insulation of the question because of the perception that war between the major states is likely if insulation is not forthcoming. This urgency for the great powers in keeping the local conflict insulated as an issue among themselves will persist, whatever the course of conflict in the small state.

A second distinctive feature of the insulationist dynamic of Type II cases is that the insulation framework is likely to be severely strained if the local conflict worsens, because the major state most inclined to intervene will strongly wish to support its client in the local antagonism when the latter's fortunes are in doubt. This demand will in turn increase the suspicions of the other major states, impelling them to work harder to forestall unilateral involvement by the assertive major state. However, the price for succeeding in this goal is likely to be additional concessions from other major states to their more assertive partner; the former may be unwilling to provide them, and the assertive state is unlikely to be restrained merely by being threatened by the others with negative consequences. Under these conditions, insulation of the dispute may break down.

Finally, although as in Type I cases insulation here is a prerequisite to collective outside intervention in the small-state dispute, intervention in Type II cases is likely to be forthcoming in the early stage of the small-state dispute because the assertive, intervention-minded major state demands it. The latter uses its intent and capability to intervene on its own as leverage to obtain from the others a collective intervention program. Such a program is sometimes decided upon only after intense and prolonged bargaining, but under considerable time pressure.

Whereas the first two types of insulationist PD have consistent, persistent motivational features, the propensity of the major states to intervene shifts over time in the third type (Type III). Great power motivation to intervene early in the life cycle of the small-state local dispute is low in this type of case, but grows considerably later on. This shift can occur as a result of a change in major-state interests toward the small-state dispute. More commonly it is brought about by the perception of major-state leaders that the stakes of major-power involvement have become larger than they were previously determined to be. This change occurs, in turn, because of the onset of what are termed here "transition" developments, which include humanitarian emergencies, intervention of neighboring states into the small-state conflict, and provocations directed by the primary antagonists against internationally authorized forces.[10] The higher major-state motivation to intervene brings about energetic, often forceful intervention, but only in the later stage of the local conflict. The shift in major power-motivation to intervene later on, unplanned for in the early stages of the local dispute, places a major burden on great-power relationships.

Table 2.1 describes the distinguishing features of these three types of isolationist PD and the cases analyzed in this study that fit them.

TABLE 2.1
An Insulationist PD Typology

	Great-Power Motivation to Intervene		
	Early Stage	*Late Stage*	*Cases*
Type I	Low	Low	the Memel
Type II	High	High	Belgium Bosnia I the Congo Cyprus
Type III	Low	High	Greece Armenia Bosnia II

Policy Implications of the Case Types

A checklist of policymaking concerns that flow from this typology of insulationist PD is now provided. We analyze Type I and Type II cases separately from Type III cases, and for each of these categories we also distinguish the problem of case diagnosis from the need to make collective intervention effective.

Type I and Type II Cases

Case Diagnosis

Distinguishing Type I and Type II cases is situationally easy, because they are characterized by polar opposite forms of great-power motivation that remain constant throughout the life cycle of the small-state conflict. Type I cases reflect major-state disinterest in the dispute, while Type II cases reflect a high degree of concern for the local conflict. Type II cases feature the traditional tendency of the major powers to compete for influence; the perception that one great power's intervention into a local conflict will affect its relative strength relative to other major states will incline the others to resist that intervention. This competition for influence is missing in Type I cases.

The Impact of Insulation upon Intervention

Insulation is less of a constraint upon collective great-power intervention in Type I than in Type II cases. In the former, when insulation is not urgent, and when the major states may not even discuss insulation of the local dispute in its early stages, agreed-upon major-state intervention in the local dispute is likely to be modest and weak. Without a strong agreed-upon intervention program, major-state intervention is likely to be limited to conciliation, the application of coercive instruments being ruled out as too costly and risky to the major states. PD can make an impact in Type I cases only if persuasion is brought to bear upon the primary local antagonists, whether on a multilateral or a unilateral basis. At best, interventionist PD will be low key, supported by some insulationist framework, and with coercive instruments unavailable, directed at an early stage to the local dispute. It will not be sensitive to warning of the emergence of the local dispute because the major states will be less willing to act promptly on the basis of the information when their motivations are low.[11]

While the interventionist challenge in Type I cases is to accomplish more with fewer resources, the problem in Type II cases is that the major states are constrained much more by the requirements of insulating the local conflict as an issue between themselves. Here two problems may be distinguished. One is where insulation is extremely delicate, and subject to frequent reconsideration as the local conflict evolves. Without insulation, the danger of war between great powers as an outgrowth of the local conflict increases, and the effectiveness of outside intervention in the dispute is significantly reduced. The second problem is that the importance of insulation for the major states will overwhelm the priority given by the latter to intervention. Collective intervention, in other words, will largely serve the interests of major-state consensus and fall short of what is objectively required to defuse the small-state conflict.

Type III Cases

Case Diagnosis

Identifying Type III cases is more complex than identifying Type I and Type II cases because the indicators that define the former are not present in the early stage of the local small-state dispute as they are in the latter instances. For Type III cases the indicators that emerge from the perceived deterioration of local conflict can only be understood contextually. That is to say, policymakers can distinguish between apparent Type I and actual Type III cases only after political discussions among the primary antagonists have broken down and the use of force intensifies between them, with neither being able to obtain a clear-cut victory over the other. In the continuing test of strength in the local conflict, the behavior of the militarily stronger primary antagonist will constitute the most important basis for differentiating the two types of cases as the stronger antagonist violates international norms in an especially visible manner. The predilection of the stronger antagonist to violate these norms will become evident to the major states only in the later stages of the local dispute.

A Type III case emerges when major states shift their attitudes and behaviors toward the small-state dispute. Policy officials who in the early stage of the local dispute had no major concern for it and no inclination to broaden the scope of their involvement in it, become committed later to prevent the stronger primary antagonist from gaining a one-sided military victory and to force that faction to accept a compromise peace with its weaker opponent. *Such a shift is associated with both warning of the worsening of the dispute and a response to the warning.*[12] To be sure, as policymakers poorly inclined to become involved in the dispute will tend to emphasize the costs of doing so, bolder responses will ordinarily be slow in emerging. However, collective great-power action reduces the risks of failure in intervention efforts by encouraging coercion of the primary antagonists—in sharp contrast to the general unavailability of coercive instruments in Type I cases. In addition, collective action reflects the increasingly widespread great-power dissatisfaction over the flaunting of international values by one or more of the primary antagonists in aggravated local conflict.

Great-power governments can utilize two resources to prepare in advance for the shift in motivation toward small-power conflicts. First, intelligence staffs can be tasked with collecting information that warns in advance of the propensity of some local antagonists to act with impunity against their opponents and against great power desires. Such information can establish a strong case that the great powers should increase their will to act—that is, to ascertain that existing policy toward the small state dispute is failing, and to provide grounds for initiative among great power states to share the responsibilities and political risks of bolder intervention in the local dispute.

Second, major states can employ policy planning staffs to prepare on a contingency basis for a change in great-power motivation to become involved in specific local disputes. The three transition developments referred to earlier can and should be utilized as a basis for this planning. Planning, in other words, would be predicated upon hypothetical provocations to international forces, humanitarian emergencies caused by sharp escalation of governmental action against noncombatants of an ethnic group challenger, and the involvement of neighboring states, assuming these developments are conceded to have major political importance. For example, if international forces were introduced into or close to a small state to defuse its conflict, plans would anticipate provocations against those forces and prepare courses of action to prevent and to respond to them.[13]

The Impact of Insulation upon Intervention

When the local conflict is severely aggravated, major-state adoption of a bold collective posture will ordinarily be decisive for the effectiveness of interventionist PD. Indeed, from the viewpoint of great-power PD effectiveness, the earlier the shift is made, the more rapidly will PD succeed, for later-stage PD success depends upon the stronger primary antagonist

TABLE 2.2
PD Policy Implications: A Summary

Case Type	*Diagnosis*	*Insulation*	*Impact of Insulation on Intervention*	*Major Problems*
Type I	Easy	Unimportant	Small	Coercion unavailable
Type II	Easy	Important early	Large	Insulation hard to Sustain
Type III	Difficult	Introduced or modified late	Large	Credibility of coalition commitment to intervene in question

being persuaded that great-power calculations have changed, and can no longer afford (contrary to what it may have believed) to act as though the major states are unwilling to increase the scope of their collective intervention in the local dispute. Considerable disutility to the major states is associated with the misjudgement by the stronger primary antagonist of major state determination to intervene in Type III cases.[14] The longer the great powers delay in making this shift, the greater the difficulty they will encounter to persuade the stronger primary antagonist that the shift has been made.

Table 2.2 presents the highlights of the policy implications of each PD case type.

How Primary Antagonists Affect Great-Power PD

Preoccupied with intrastate ethnic conflict as an object of great-power activity, this analysis must take account of the ability of primary antagonists in such conflict to resist great-power intervention. Primary antagonist resistance can be substantial even when the willingness of the major states to become involved in local conflict is high. "Warring parties," Stephen John Stedman points out, "are unlikely to fear the consequences of continuing to fight if they feel that mediation is always available as a fallback option. The international community must therefore resist the urge to mediate whenever and wherever there is a war."[15] Even when primary antagonists reach agreements between themselves as a result of international pressure, "spoilers" have often undermined them later. "The biggest problem by far in implementing peace accords in civil wars," according to Stedman, "is getting parties who sign [them] to live up to their commitments."[16] Faced with local resistance, interventionist PD can indeed be highly difficult, whatever the great-power unity and motivation behind it.

Acknowledging this problem, this study must argue that it is not a decisive or an insuperable one. That is, the present study must demonstrate fruitful directions for overcoming the local resistance to great power action and for making PD worthwhile in spite of it. An important objective in investigating cases in this study is to empirically identify such directions and to clarify the circumstances in which a collective response is more likely to be forthcoming, as well as those in which a coalition program is likely to be more effective once instituted. No claim can be made that those directions are foolproof or risk-free, but awareness of their workability and their limitations can strengthen the hand of policymakers seeking to more effectively anticipate and respond to primary-state resistance to great-power intervention.

At this preliminary point, the concern with primary antagonist resistance is twofold. The first interest is to inquire whether great-power PD can generally be applied to overcome antagonist resistance and to capitalize upon the advantages of early intervention into local conflict prior to the onset of violence between the local antagonists.[17] A second concern is to connect the scope of primary antagonist resistance to the typology of great-power PD adopted in this chapter.

To these ends, three questions are directed to the primary antagonist resistance problem: (1) Can collective great-power PD employ coercive threats to overcome local impediments to peace when conciliatory PD methods are inadequate? (2) What policymaking guidelines support such intensified pressure? and (3) How does the difference between highly- and lowly-motivated great powers, as developed above, affect the potential of overcoming local impediments to PD? The first and second of these questions are discussed in this section; the third is addressed in the next.

First, Stedman points out that even major-state willingness to threaten using force will not suffice against unyielding primary antagonists if intervention efforts are dissipated by the politics of insulation. For example, contemporary threats of using force by a PD-minded international coalition in Namibia and in Bosnia-Herzegovina were defied by primary antagonists that determined they were not credible.[18] As Stedman puts it, "The need [for an international coalition] to act in a unified, strategic manner can conflict with the need to acquire leverage over warring parties."[19]

We have already stressed that the tension between insulation and intervention as PD objectives has important and possibly corrosive policy consequences for the great powers. To understand these consequences, it is helpful to focus more carefully on the timing of intervention over the life cycle of particular disputes. Initial obstacles and failures may well be a poor predictor of great-power effectiveness later on if—as is suggested in a number of cases studied here—the major state coalition can correct its mistakes. To be sure, more determined intervention later on, after violence has occurred between the primary antagonists, often seems to be more costly than is early mobilization for the same purpose; this higher cost is a disincentive to adopting a bolder posture. But the coalition may have stronger interests later on than it did earlier in relation to the primary antagonists in the local conflict, one being the perceived need to respond to primary antagonist provocations against the major states. The provocation factor, highlighted in some of the cases studied here, also cautions against attributing too much importance to the initial unwillingness of the major states to be drawn into the local conflict.

Moving now to the second question, Stedman's catalogue of PD intervention problems constitutes a prescription for general policymaking caution that suggests, as he puts it, that "[t]he international community must . . . resist the urge to mediate whenever and wherever there is war [and instead] must be willing to quit when the combatants are not sufficiently motivated to make peace."[20] While this advice will be favorably received by policymakers weakly motivated to initiate PD intervention, it too is insufficiently attuned to the distinction between earlier and later intervention in the local conflict.

On one hand, much of Stedman's analysis suggests that early intervention is futile, as when he notes that "parties in civil wars seek agreements, not out of a desire for reconciliation and peace, but *because military and political conditions compel them to stop fighting.*"[21] The same idea seems suggested by Stedman's point that "the mediator must establish ways for the parties to test their perceptions about their opponents and, if warranted, then change their perceptions."[22] Experiencing a deadlock can often be more instructive for the primary antagonists than anticipating it, since initial planning for intrastate war—as it is in interstate hostilities—is likely to be very one sided and inaccurate.[23] On the other hand, Stedman hypothesizes that early military intervention in civil war might have been useful. In Somalia and Bosnia-Herzegovina, he wrote, leaders in local conflict "decided on civil war because they thought they could prevail militarily and that the international community was powerless to help them," yet "if they had faced an early international willingness to use military force, then their calculations might have been different."[24]

Each of these views is consistent with Stedman's belief that "parties [to local conflict] usually do not begin to explore the possibility of a negotiated settlement until their military alternatives are in doubt."[25] But it remains unclear whether these doubts and correctives can set in prior to the actual test of military strength; if they cannot, then outside intervention is futile until later in the small-state dispute life cycle. The main question for interventionist PD is whether major-power planners and emissaries can substitute for the learning process that civil war experience brings about only in delayed fashion. If not, Stedman would counsel holding back interventionist PD until later; if it does, then he would apparently stress the importance of early intervention.

Linking Primary Antagonist Resistance to Great-Power Motivations

The thrust of the discussion presented here thus far of the problem of local-antagonist resistance to PD has been that great-power policymakers should not, and need not, confine their PD policy guidance to caution and to the virtues of commitment-avoidance.[26] When a series of cases are examined intensively, differentiating between them may point the way to policy guidance that increases the likelihood of proactive and effective great-power responses. The preoccupation with primary antagonist resistance must now be linked with the great-power orientation adopted here, and specifically with the distinction between highly and lowly motivated great-power states adopted in the typology presented earlier in this chapter.

Specifically, it will be argued that the significance of local impediments to PD will vary according to the ability of the major states to develop a collective PD posture to neutralize them. Local resistance can thus be an insuperable problem *only if other impediments associated with great-power collective action cannot also be overcome*. To develop this point, we return to the distinction between Type I PD cases, in which the low motivation of the major states reduces the likelihood and the consequence of great-power insulation of the local dispute, on one hand, and Type II and Type III cases, in which the major states are or become highly motivated to intervene in the local dispute, and insulation is highly significant for this purpose, on the other. Each of these types of PD is constrained primarily by a set of conditions outside the area of the local dispute, and, these, rather than the local resistances, deserve more study than they have received thus far.

In Type I cases, the primary constraint upon great-power action is domestic. Great-power interests are in such cases defined in a way that discourages great-power intervention in small-state disputes.[27] The interests can be linked to avoiding much-publicized local small-state resistance difficulties, but the calculation that defines the diffident great-power attitude is to be found in the domestic sphere of the great-power state. The low motivation to intervene in the small-state dispute is not subject to change. Consequently it can be confidently predicted that great-power capability to intervene in the local dispute is limited to conciliatory measures, and when those measures are resisted by the primary antagonists in the small-state conflict, the great power is unable to adapt constructively to the impediment. In sum, great-power intervention will be weak because potential major-state influence in the local dispute is relatively small. In other words, *the importance of the local resistance to outside PD is increased in cases in which the primary constraint to PD is internal to the great powers.* This condition characterizes the great-power posture at present in relation to most small-power intrastate disputes.

In Type II and III cases, by contrast, the primary impediment to great-power action is international. Insulation and intervention are in those instances partly competing goals, the competition between them presenting trade-offs in those cases in which the great powers become collectively engaged in a local small-state dispute. This can occur either in the early stage of the local dispute life cycle (Type II cases), or in the later stage (Type III cases). In Type III cases, we have seen, additional contextual problems are likely to impede great-power ability to translate a strengthening coalition into leverage over the primary antagonists. In this type of case, credibility problems of an international coalition PD program will be most severe.[28]

But if, as suggested here, the ability of the great powers to insulate a small-power intrastate dispute as an issue among themselves is a precondition to collective great-power intervention, then insulation is always worthwhile as a means to assembling a strong and effective interventionist PD program. Once insulation difficulties are overcome over time, the primary antagonists are unlikely to be able to resist a determined great-power coalition directed at defusing the local conflict.

PD Variability and Policy Interests

The framework for thinking about great-power PD that has been presented in this chapter is particularly informed by the needs of those making or advising on policy decisions on this subject. Policymakers must be attuned to variable interests and circumstances, affirming Bruce W. Jentleson's point that "there cannot be a standard preventive diplomacy strategy, one size fits all, any more than there could be a single strategy for any other area of foreign policy."[29] The framework presented here suggests that the variability extends not only to the utilization of conciliatory and coercive PD techniques, but also to policy motivation and to the link between PD as insulation and PD as intervention. The variability is a policy burden in that policymakers need to be attuned to a wider set of concepts and conditions than they might have assumed. Taking account of variability also enhances policy by assisting in planning and in ordering priorities, in clarifying issues, and in keeping a clearer idea of PD as an international political process.

In spelling out variability in great-power motivations and in the character of insulationist PD, the typology presented here specifies that insulation importantly constrains great-power interventionist PD activity when any one great-power state has interests inclining it to intervene unilaterally in a small-power intrastate conflict; collective great-power action is more likely to be forthcoming in those instances to forestall unilateral intervention. Insulation will be much less significant when no great power is likely to unilaterally intervene in the local conflict. Finally, insulation has considerable contextual importance when great-power motivations toward the local conflict shift, as the local antagonism begins to impinge upon great power assets and interests. The great powers must then make new decisions serving their emerging insulationist needs, and they must act to change the perception of the primary antagonists that the major states are uninterested in or unable to intervene in the local conflict. Each of these types of cases presents a different package of policymaking needs that comparative case analysis can clarify.

Taken as a whole, two features of the typology should be emphasized. The first is the relative importance of the ability of the great powers to insulate the local conflict as an issue among themselves as an element of PD, not only on its own but for its bearing on great-power intervention in local conflict. Especially significant in this regard is how insulation is a precondition to collective great-power interventionist PD. Indeed, the typology strongly suggests that insulation should be given as much attention as a PD concern as the much more commented-upon intervention objective.

A second general element of the typology, especially prominent in Type III cases but also present in the other PD types as well, is the contrast between great-power priorities and interests, on one hand, and those of the primary antagonists on the other. Some of the most interesting PD cases, in fact, highlight the opposition between major states and primary-antagonist interests when collective great-power intervention takes place. Oriented toward great-power interests and postures, the typology is primarily geared to investigating how, in light of such opposition, the major states are able to impose their views on the primary antagonists. The typology serves the primary interest of this study, which is to understand how the great powers exert causal effects upon local intrastate ethnic conflict.

Without neglecting the ability of the local antagonists to affect great-power behavior, this study asserts that for PD to succeed, the major states must exert dominant influence over the local antagonists, rather than the other way around. When the local antagonists are preeminent in relation to the major states, PD is stalled and ineffective.

Chapter 3

Forging Great-Power Consensus

To explain shifts in collective PD, this study traces collaboration and discord in great-power relations. Both elements shape great-power responses to small-state conflict, and major state influence over the small-state antagonists. But coping with small-state conflict is, as already noted, only one element in broader and more important great-power concerns for international stability and equilibrium. Adding to the complexity of great-power dynamics is that collaboration and discord are not in practice independent and separate from each other; to understand one dimension, it is necessary to comprehend the other.

This chapter presents a framework for understanding the process by which the major states initiate and sustain collective PD. The framework takes into account the degree of great-power consensus over local conflict and the great-power search for unilateral advantage in that conflict. It also takes into account linkages between cooperative and conflicting elements in great-power relations. For example, collaboration often brings conflict over the terms of cooperation, and sharp divisions over collective action often accentuate efforts to agree in order to prevent war between great powers. The framework distinguishes three patterns of great-power relationship in relation to small-state antagonism: Tight Concert, Loose Concert, and Prevailing Opposition. This threefold distinction guides the comparative analysis in this study of PD cases taking place in different time periods, the purpose of the analysis being to document PD commonalities applicable to the contemporary period.

Four conclusions about the process of creating great-power consensus are presented in this chapter. First, the major states frequently affect small-state internal politics collectively and multilaterally, containing their own rivalry and working to avoid crisis among themselves. But they also retain the option of acting unilaterally and opportunistically toward the local conflict, inflaming differences among themselves. Second, divisions within small states affect the degree of cooperation between the major states. How the great powers choose between acting collectively and acting unilaterally depends in part on local conflict developments. Discord between the major states over terms of PD cooperation, which often makes for turbulence, is commonly precipitated by the evolution of the local conflict. Third, the three patterns of great-power relationship distinguished here are better adapted for understanding the emergence of great-power consensus and collective action than is the commonly referred to distinction between multipolarity and bipolarity as international systems. And fourth, newer pressures upon states, from domestic elites, transnational groups, and international organizations, all increasingly salient following the end of Soviet-American Cold War, do not undermine the traditional power politics practiced by the major states.

Following a discussion of the general connection between great-power relations and local conflict, each of the three patterns of great-power relationship distinguished here is introduced in turn. The chapter argues that these three patterns better assist the comparison of PD cases in different time periods than do concepts of multipolarity and bipolarity. Finally, it rebuts the contention that newer nonstate developments in the international system undermine the conclusions reached above.

Great-Power Rivalry and Local Conflict

While remaining rivals, great-power adversaries often agree upon and operationalize enduring restraints upon their rivalry. At times they do so because they accept a condition of reciprocity to regulate their relations, irrespective of the level of their substantive agreement. The nineteenth-century great-power concert was based, as British prime minister Henry Palmerston saw it, upon "the usual state of reciprocal relations" between the major states.[1] Reciprocity, in the form of a tacit regime, also conditioned Soviet-American acceptance of principles of crisis management during the superpower Cold War.[2] At other times, great-power rivalry is contained by negotiations over issues of collective concern to the major states.[3] Paul Gordon Lauren has noted that crisis prevention, which he defines as "various kinds of rules, regulations, norms, agreements, undertakings, and procedures establish[ing] a sophisticated and highly differentiated array of regimes designed to prevent the outbreak of serious crisis,"[4] restrained major-state competitive behavior in the nineteenth century, when multipolarity reigned. And during the Soviet-American Cold War, the superpowers successfully worked out viable, mutually useful, negotiated arrangements on such security problems as the division of forces in Europe, competitive arms procurement, and the proliferation of nuclear weapons to other countries.

Some of the most interesting limitations on great power rivalry have been reflected in collective behavior toward problems between and within small states. As Marc Trachtenberg has pointed out, the major states since the nineteenth century regarded small powers—often understood as backward and less civilized—as legitimate targets for great-power intervention, even as the major states insisted on a general norm of nonintervention in relation to each other.[5] The record of such collective initiatives is particularly rich in the nineteenth century, during which the onset of crisis in small states commonly led the great powers to meet in ad hoc international conferences to seek ways of managing the problem.[6]

These initiatives, prompted by great-power fears of the disorder associated with the anarchical, each-state-against-the-other environment of the eighteenth century,[7] brought documented restraints on great-power involvement toward small states in such areas as mutual consultation and collective decisionmaking, localizing regional conflicts, delineating interests and areas of involvement, intervening by multilateral action, practicing the pacific settlement of disputes, and providing advance notification through consultation.[8]

In the latter half of the twentieth century, the documented record of agreed-upon great-power restraints toward small-state problems was more meager. One comprehensive account of Soviet-American cooperation on security issues notes that "the superpowers have . . . failed to make much progress in developing norms, rules, and institutionalized procedures for regulating their involvement in Third Areas. Apart from respecting (with some qualifications) each other's sphere of dominant interests, Moscow and Washington have not developed norms for limiting efforts to influence internal processes of political-economic change in Third World countries."[9] This is explained by the fact that Soviet-American Cold War rivalry focused most sharply on expanding influence in countries outside the respective superpower security blocs. Cold War great-power activity in the Third World was mainly restrained by the unwillingness of the superpowers to make war against each other, the fear of which, triggered by superpower confrontations over their Third World activity, facilitated restraint in that period.

Yet the great-power rivalry and discord prevailing in the nineteenth century were as important as in the late twentieth century in conditioning collective great-power behavior. Lengthy and contentious great-power debates have often taken place in both periods over whether and how the great powers should intervene in small-state disputes. The debates have been especially sharp when the major states considered intervening collectively in opposition to a small-state central regime through the threat or use of force. In such instances they have supported a challenger that could not defeat the regime on its own, while denying to the central regime the option of suppressing the challenger independently. Ad hoc great-power responses to cope with internal small-state problems have been so frequent because prior agreed-upon rules to govern such responses have usually been lacking. Even as the major states discussed collective action, individual great powers considered and implemented the search for unilateral gains in the local conflict, an option strengthened by the primary small-state antagonist search for outside allies. Conflicting great-power interests over local conflict were a source of great-power tensions in the nineteenth as well as the twentieth centuries.

In general, the need for crisis avoidance—especially where great-power conflict is significant—enhances the importance of preexisting great-power norms regulating rivalry over small-state questions. However, the frequency of the emergence of confrontation between great powers over local small-state questions shows the weakness of norms of behavior in these situations. At best, if the great powers desire a collective approach, then their ability to agree—often on an ad hoc basis, since rules for collective great-power action in particular cases are generally lacking—will determine the success of collective PD. But their desire for such an approach is weakened and at times undermined by their incentives to make gains on their own, incentives that can be strengthened by the primary local antagonists. These incentives are in turn checked by the tension-increasing consequences of unilateral great-power action in such cases.

The Tight Concert

In tracing collaborative as well as discordant elements of great-power relations, this study focuses on diplomatic statecraft as the primary instrument for forging collective great-power involvement in small-state problems. Gordon A. Craig and Alexander L. George, emphasizing the collaborative element of great-power relations, have defined a "viable international system" in terms of three requirements: great-power agreement on aims and objectives; the availability of a great-power structure to channel that agreement; and procedures, in the form of norms, rules, practices, and institutions to back up great-power agreement on aims and objectives.[10] Great-power consensus in such a framework reflects international system strength, and the consensus element can be studied as a reflection of international system requirements in specific issue areas such as PD. That is to say, at any particular time, great-power relations can be studied in terms of their approximation to an ideal linked to satisfaction of the system requirements posited by Craig and George. Although they have not studied the PD element of great-power relations, Craig and George employ this approach when analyzing the broad character of relations among the major states.[11]

The present study takes a different approach. Attaching special significance to weakness of international norms and to great-power relations associated with PD, as already indicated, it seeks to explicitly understand great-power agreement and discord as changeable and flexible elements in world politics. It uses the diplomatic record to register the strength of major-state willingness to agree and to collaborate, as well as the strength of inducements leading those states to divergent paths. In general, it understands the extent of great-power cooperation over a specific local antagonism in terms of (1) the degree of consensus between the major states over the local conflict; and (2) the propensity of specific major states to seek unilateral advantage relative to the others. These measures tend to move in opposite directions. That is, when consensus between the major states is high, opportunistic behavior and the unilateral search for advantage is smaller; conversely, when consensus is low, opportunism is more significant.

Different combinations of great-power consensus and opportunistic behavior yield three distinct patterns of great-power relations. First, when institutional cooperation between great powers is most developed, in what we term here the "Tight Concert," consensus is high and opportunism is low. A second pattern, the "Loose Concert," is an intermediate one characterized by considerable cooperation as well as divergence in great-power relations. And third, when cooperation is most limited and great-power divergence most intense, which we characterize as "Prevailing Opposition," consensus is low and opportunism is high. Figure 3.1 illustrates these patterns.

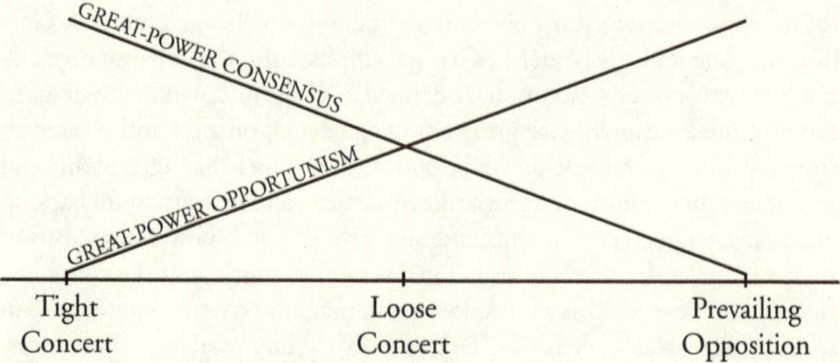

Figure 3.1 PATTERNS OF GREAT-POWER RELATIONSHIPS

Table 3.1 spells out the leading characteristics of each of these patterns, with special reference to (1) opportunistic great-power behavior; (2) insulationist PD; and (3) interventionist PD. The balance of this section explores the distinctive features of the Tight Concert, and the next two deal with the Loose Concert and Prevailing Opposition patterns, respectively.

The Tight Concert pattern, typically shaped by peace treaties concluding a major war, is one in which great-power cooperation is based upon a strong foundation of unity that guides collective great-power action on local issues. In this pattern, great powers set general principles and specific obligations to guide themselves and small states, and create an institution that can respond when new developments bring principles and specific obligations into question. They thus not only cooperatively shape the character of an international system but appoint themselves as executors of it, to act in concert to enhance its general stability and welfare. The pattern does not presume that all great powers participate in the collective enterprise, but only that most great powers cooperate at a given time, with the proviso that the cooperation is not aimed at the noncooperating major state or states. The great powers acted in this manner in the early stages of the Greek Revolution in the 1820s, and also in the dispute between German and Lithuanian factions in the Memel over the disposition of that city following the end of the First World War.

The major states participating in a Tight Concert depend highly on each other and are therefore vulnerable to the failure of other concert members to cooperate.[12] Each nevertheless accepts the vulnerability because collective action permits the major states to have a greater impact on world politics than they can have individually. This impact is manifested where collective great-power interests are strongly engaged, as defined by declarations and treaties.

TABLE 3.1
Leading Characteristics of the Three Patterns of Great-Power Relationships

Patterns	Characteristics
Tight Concert	*Opportunism*: low or nonexistent
	Insulationist PD: high great-power dependence upon major-state solidarity
	Interventionist PD: strong on central security issues; weak on peripheral issues
	PD flexibility: low
Loose Concert	*Opportunism*: significant; stimulates search for great-power agreement on insulation
	Insulationist PD: based on incentives to opportunistic-minded states; facilitated by great-power interest to avoid a breakdown in cooperation; frequently revisited, depending on great-power divergence and local conflict development
	Interventionist PD: depends heavily on insulation program
	PD flexibility: high
Prevailing Opposition	*Opportunism*: high; great-powers support opposing local-conflict antagonists
	Insulationist PD: impeded by conflicting great-power interests; its absence contributes to international crisis
	Interventionist PD: carried out by international surrogates, such as the UN secretary general
	PD flexibility: depends on how PD arrangements affect great-power interests

Great-power insulation of small-power conflict as a great-power issue, which as we have seen takes precedence over intervention, will not be problematic within those areas. PD intervention is facilitated because the great powers agree that affecting the local conflict and keeping small states in line serves their collective interests. The Tight Concert thus highlights the agenda and the relative influence of the great powers, as the small states are unable to act independently in the face of unified major state activity.

The Tight Concert's great strength is also its major limitation: it is valued by its participants primarily because of its activity on central rather than on peripheral issues. The Tight Concert reflects high consensus and high attentiveness on central issues, such as those associated with French boundaries and with the problem of nationalism in the area conquered by Napoleonic France, and those associated with the status of Germany after the First World War. Central questions are sharply distinguished by Tight Concert states from those on the periphery, such as areas unaffected by Napoleon's early conquests or territory taken from Germany and new states created from Austria-Hungary at the end of the First World War, in which great-power cooperation is more grudging and problematic.

In relation to peripheral matters regarded as unimportant by all the major states the Tight Concert will tend to drift. This occurred, for example, in relation to the conflict between Lithuanian and German-speaking sections of the population in the Memel following the First World War. And as peripheral questions are exacerbated relative to central issues, the Tight Concert will tend to become more divided, losing its essential character. For example, the Holy Alliance foundered by 1825 over the inability of the major states to agree on how to respond to the Greek revolt against Ottoman rule.

The Loose Concert

The Loose Concert pattern illustrates how limited consensus building between major states, sometimes in the form of ententes, can have far-reaching significance for those states whose discord outweighs collaborative interests.[13] In this pattern, the great powers most engaged in a local dispute cooperate in part while continuing to significantly disagree, being determined to act together in spite of pronounced differences.

Conflict stimulates agreement in this pattern in two ways. First, participating major states perceive a break or a downturn in relations to be mutually disadvantageous. For example, they may fear that their differences over local conflicts could lead to general war.[14] And second, major states may individually pursue agreement among themselves to facilitate striving for specific objectives that are disputed. One widespread motive for the major states acting in this manner—aiming at agreement and at self-interested objectives toward local conflict—has been to manage what Frank Hinsley has termed "interlocking jealousies and suspicions between all the Great Powers."[15]

The Loose Concert characterizes relations between great powers at the time of Anglo-French rivalry over the question of the creation of Belgium in the 1830s, Anglo-Russian rivalry over the creation of Greece in the mid- and late-1820s and 1830s, Austro-Russian rivalry over the status of Bosnia-Herzegovina in the 1870s, and Russian-American rivalry over Bosnia-Herzegovina in the 1990s. In these cases one or more major states desire to intervene militarily or politically in the local conflict, while others oppose it. In this pattern, intervention is addressed collectively by the major states and regulated by PD insulation of the local conflict.

Insulation, in turn, requires that those major states opposed to another's unilateral intervention provide the latter with incentives not to intervene. Differences remain over intervention and on the conditions stimulating them, and agreement in effect buys time for the participants to permit local developments to become more clearly defined and to gauge whatever collective great-power impact has been exerted. If the local situation remains unsatisfactory, the issue of unilateral intervention will subsequently be raised again. From the point of view of the most interventionist-minded major state, agreement thus avoids a break in great-power relations while avoiding the surrender of the right of unilateral action later. Agreement also offers to that state leverage in the form of a stronger diplomatic position if the local conflict deteriorates, or a cushion to defuse the partner's opposition if it later decides to intervene unilaterally.

In contrast to the Tight Concert, which is relatively inflexible toward local conflict and less effective in coping with local conflict on the periphery than in the central arena, the Loose Concert is quite adaptable to local conflicts on the periphery. The Loose Concert pattern was in effect, for example, when the great powers coped collectively with the revolution in Greece against Turkish rule in the 1820s and early 1830s, and with the civil strife in Bosnia-Herzegovina following that province's decision to separate from Yugoslavia in the early 1990s. And the Loose Concert was also in effect in central axis cases such as the separation of Belgium from the Netherlands in the 1830s and the revolution in Bosnia-Herzegovina against Turkish rule in the 1870s.

Whether the local conflict is central or peripheral for the major states, insulation of the conflict in this pattern is uncertain enough to require special diplomatic efforts and to raise questions of overall stability between the major states. This is for three reasons. First, since the limited agreement between great powers is stimulated by prevailing differences of viewpoint, the agreement needs to be frequently revisited as great-power divergence increases. The cooperative links are of no use unless they can be followed up later, whether or not the major states intend at the time they reach agreement to provide the follow-up. In a number of cases, including Belgium, Greece, and the Bosnia II case, the major states eventually come to be in almost continuous negotiation to hammer out an agreed-upon approach to intervene in the local conflict.

Second, the need for follow-up is increased by the evolution of the local conflict, in which at least one of the primary antagonists—most always the militarily weaker one—holds out for still better terms from the great powers, as in the Greek and the two Bosnia cases. At times these demands are bolstered by military activity in which one or more of the primary antagonists hopes to change the balance of local control, forcing the hand of the major states. Finally, the Loose Concert continually takes into account the likelihood of unilateral intervention by one or more great powers in the event of a failure in the concert's collective efforts. Since the major purpose of the Loose Concert is to discourage and prevent such unilateral efforts, the major states have a stronger will to defuse the local conflict in this pattern than in the Tight Concert. This translates over time into tougher intervention techniques: at times initially limited to persuasion and conciliation, the Loose Concert pattern often evolves into the use of deterrence and coercion later on.

These reasons, taken together, explain persistent efforts by the major states in this pattern to curb the local antagonists as well as each other. When the local antagonism is central for the major states, as in the Belgian and Bosnia I cases, one or more major states will have stronger incentive to capitalize on the local conflict for individual reasons, and international stability is widely presumed to prevent such unilateral behavior as well as to address conditions in local conflict that are otherwise conducive to it. And when the local antagonism is peripheral, as in the Greek and in the Bosnia II cases, the great powers will tend to be even more frustrated in their objectives, though the latter are less urgent. The consequence is that the collective great-power willingness to become involved in the local antagonism will tend to increase over time.

Prevailing Opposition

In the third pattern, Prevailing Opposition, the great powers are deadlocked and unable to agree on approaching the local conflict. They do not agree on even a limited framework to deal collectively with the conflict but promote the local rivalry, either by championing alternate sides in the local conflict or by appealing as rivals to the local ruling regime for support, as a means of pursuing rivalry among themselves.

Britain and Russia were appointed coprotectors of Armenian rights in Turkey in the 1878 Treaty of Berlin, but in practice the British only weakly defended Armenian interests while Russia defended the Ottoman regime's refusal to support Armenian rights. In Cyprus, the Americans sought to weaken and ultimately topple the regime of Archbishop Makarios, while the Soviet Union weakly defended it. And in the Congo, the Americans supported the overthrow of the regime of Patrice Lumumba, while the Soviets supported him. When the great powers compete for the attention and support of the central regime, as they did in the Armenian case, their effective power diminishes as the regime balances rival major states against each other, blocking initiatives from either one. Each of the rivals then supports the central regime in proportion to its fear of its opponent and its worry of the regime's collapse. In other cases, as in Cyprus and the Congo, great-power rivalry adds to domestic political instability, making it more difficult for a central regime to suppress a challenge to its authority. Those states, lacking strong statewide domestic institutions, define security threats from within rather than from outside. Using local conflict to weaken their great-power opponents, the major states are not well positioned to act collectively to defuse local conflict. This weakness is not problematic when local conflict is relatively benign—that is, when the political challenger does not employ force against the central regime. Then the major states are under no pressure to intervene collectively in the conflict, and the standoff between them can endure for a long time, as in the Armenian case. The major states are in effect able to insulate the local conflict as an issue among themselves by perpetuating their own standoff.

When local conflict worsens, on the other hand, the rival major states tend to suspend their competition because of their unwillingness to contemplate war against each other as a consequence of it. They practice crisis management to contain the effects of the deterioration by acting collectively to defuse the local conflict. For example, England and Russia intervened collectively with the Ottoman regime, along with other major states, to stop Turkish atrocities directed against Armenians during the mid-1890s, when failure to do so would have contributed to even greater calamities against the Armenian minority. On such occasions, the great powers suspend their rivalry for humanitarian reasons, but are again unable to agree after the crisis has passed. Not until 1912 did the major states act together to gain Ottoman acceptance of Armenian political rights, after Russia indicated it was prepared to intervene unilaterally in event of Armenian violence against the Ottoman regime.

In the Congo and initially in Cyprus, by contrast, conditions were persistently volatile. Congolese leaders confronted a secessionist regime, supported by outside military contingents, in Katanga province. And in Cyprus, a restive Turkish minority was vigorously supported by a Turkish government prepared to intervene militarily to safeguard interests of its ethnic compatriots on the island. Exacerbated tensions in the Congo and in Cyprus could have provoked Soviet-American hostilities. The superpowers therefore agreed to the introduction of UN peacekeeping forces and UN mediation in both of these local conflicts, using them as a screen to maintain their rivalry at what they perceived to be relatively less costly levels. They permitted the UN secretary general, strongly supported by middle-ranking members of the UN, to initiate interventionist PD to prevent the superpowers from deepening their engagement in support of one or another of the primary antagonists. At the same time, they attempted to capitalize on the unstable and volatile local situation to extend their influence at the expense of each other, serving their larger individual strategic interests.

The Typology and Polarity

The Tight Concert, Loose Concert, and Prevailing Opposition patterns are not linked to the commonly made distinction between bipolar systems of states, which have no more than two great powers, and multipolar systems, which contain at least five. It is argued here that the concepts of multipolarity and bipolarity fail to adequately capture the interplay between the major states and the local primary antagonists that shapes great-power attitudes toward the local conflict. This interplay is highly important for understanding the PD process. In addition, the multipolar-bipolar distinction cannot interpret features of PD process that overlap both types of international systems. Discussion here elaborates on these points, comparing features of multipolar and bipolar types of international systems with those of the Tight Concert, Loose Concert, and Prevailing Opposition patterns that have been outlined.

Table 3.2 lists cases investigated in this study, their patterns, and the multipolar or bipolar character of the international system in their time period. The table shows that two cases associated with a bipolar system are also characterized by the Prevailing Opposition pattern. The weakness of great-power cooperation in those cases (Cyprus and the Congo) has been ascribed here to a relationship of opposition between two major powers; alternately, the same condition could be attributed to the competitive position of great powers under bipolarity. Under this alternative explanation, the difficulties of forging collective PD would then be increased by the tendency of the major states under bipolarity to practice unilateral involvement in local disputes. Early collective PD, most efficient from the viewpoint of dealing with local conflicts before they become violent, is a likely casualty of such unilateral involvement.

However, the table shows that Prevailing Opposition does not only take place under bipolar conditions. In particular, the standoff between England and Russia over the Armenian question appears to have been as static and intense under multipolar conditions as that in Cyprus under bipolarity.[16] Moreover, the *primary* competitive position of the great powers under bipolarity does not mean that their strategic relationship stimulates competitiveness on every issue. As Alexander George has shown, the propensity of the superpowers to cooperate under bipolar conditions has depended in part on the centrality of the issue for their security concerns. "Generally speaking," he writes, "one would expect that the more central to fundamental security a particular issue is, the stronger the incentive to work out a cooperative arrangement to reduce vulnerability. Conversely, the less central the security importance of an issue, the weaker the incentive to seek a cooperative arrangement to reduce vulnerability."[17] Using this perspective, it can be argued that superpower cooperation was low in the Cyprus and Congo cases not because of the prevailing competitiveness of the United States and Soviet Union, but because the two issues were peripheral to the security concerns of both.

TABLE 3.2
Cases, Patterns, and the Character of the International System

Case	*Pattern*	*System Character*
1. Belgian Revolution	Loose Concert	multipolar
2. Greek Revolution	a. Tight Concert b. Loose Concert	a. multipolar b. multipolar
3. Bosnia I	Loose Concert	multipolar
4. Armenia	Prevailing Opposition	multipolar
5. The Memel	Tight Concert	multipolar
6. The Congo	Prevailing Opposition	bipolar
7. Cyprus	a. Prevailing Opposition b. Loose Concert	a. bipolar b. multipolar
8. Bosnia II	Loose Concert	multipolar

Many analysts argue that bipolarity, characterized by static alignments, is more predictable and stable than multipolarity, in which alignments are more changeable. They also believe strategic conflict is more manageable under bipolarity, when the number of major states is small, than under multipolarity.[18] A recent study of PD, agreeing with this outlook, has observed that "the variety of responses by the United States and other great powers in the post-Cold War reflects the extent to which, under multipolar arrangements, policymakers calibrate national strategic interests on a case-by-case basis." According to this same analysis, PD experience under these conditions reveals "the difficulties of overcoming inaction and competition among great powers in a multipolar international system."[19]

The bipolar cases examined here confirm a link between great-power standoff and static conflict over small-power ethnic conflict, but they do not reveal an association between bipolarity and *manageability* of the local conflict. Instead, the bipolar Cyprus and Congo cases were arguably *more difficult* to manage because of the tensions between the major states. This gap between case experience and alleged system tendencies may be explained, it is suggested here, by the focus of international system theory on the positional interests of the major states to the neglect of other countries. Such a focus is justified by the assumption that the great powers are primarily responsible for the degree of order in the international system and as such must be sharply distinguished from the weaker states. Yet the PD experience shows that under both multipolar and bipolar conditions, the character of the international system is shaped to a significant extent by developments outside the control of the major powers. In the Loose Concert pattern outlined here, developments in small states occasionally require the great powers to reconsider earlier collective decisions and to make new ones deepening their involvement in those developments; the new decisions are driven mainly not by the need to influence the primary antagonists but by the requirements of keeping the local dispute insulated as a major-power issue. And in the Prevailing Opposition pattern, we have seen that even when the great powers are antagonistic on the subject of the local conflict, they are more likely to act together if the local conflict is violent than if it is peaceful.

The effect of local conflict upon great-power calculations, and the possibility that great powers can neutralize each other's behavior under multipolar as well as bipolar conditions, weakens the assertion that great-power dynamics under bipolarity are more predictable than under multipolar conditions. However, when the Tight and Loose Concert patterns are also taken into account, great-power relations under multipolarity may indeed be less predictable than under bipolarity. That is, regularities may indeed be more difficult to pinpoint under multipolar conditions than under bipolar ones, because of multipolarity's higher degree of diversity in great-power dynamics. However, this does not mean that such regularities are missing, even if the great powers do make PD decisions in a multipolar context on a more ad hoc basis; this study searches for broader tendencies even under more diverse multipolar conditions.

On the other hand, *some* regularities under multipolar conditions may be similar to bipolar ones. Alexander George suggests that the incentive for Soviet-American cooperation during the Cold War depended upon the degree of dependence and vulnerability of each superpower to actions of its opponent, apart from the centrality of particular issues for the fundamental security interest of each side.[20] When dependence and centrality measures are treated as dichotomous variables, as in George's analysis, characteristics of great-power behavior under bipolar conditions appear to be similar to those manifested under multipolarity. For example, according to George, superpower dependence under bipolarity was tight in crisis periods, but more difficult security issues were raised for the superpowers when crises occurred in areas of central concern (such as Europe) than when they took place in Third World areas. A similar feature characterized the Tight Concert following the end of the First World War, as noted above. Under the Tight Concert, a high degree of dependence between great powers powerfully stimulated collective Anglo-French peacemaking with the former Triple Alliance powers. However, this stimulus for cooperation was much stronger on central issues, such as redrawing boundaries for the defeated Germany and Austria-Hungary, than in coping with the peripheral issue of the Memel territory in the Baltic area. In short, given tight dependence, the centrality-peripheral question has been a key element in explaining great-power incentives toward cooperation in multipolar as in bipolar eras.

In sum, it is argued here that the ability of the great powers to cooperate in relation to small-power intrastate antagonism can be better understood with reference to patterns of relationships between great powers than to multipolarity and bipolarity. This is not to argue that multipolarity and bipolarity are insignificant as causes of state behavior. On questions pertaining to the direct relations between great powers, the multipolar-bipolar distinction is likely to be more helpful. Moreover, the relatively small number of cases investigated here cannot yield a proof that the three patterns outlined are more fruitful to understand collective great-power PD than is the more commonly adopted conceptualization of multipolarity and bipolarity. But the three patterns permit capturing important, difficult, yet recurring international system issues. They help reveal why and how major-state world-order concerns bring about, under multipolarity and bipolarity, first, international consensus on small power disputes, and second, occasionally burdensome collaborative intervention to manage those disputes.

Newer International Developments

Thus far, the discussion has depicted the major powers as unconstrained by domestic and transnational forces, or by international organizations. However, developments such as (1) the growing prominence of nongovernmental elites in foreign policy debates; (2) the role of non-governmental organizations (NGOs) in transmitting and acting upon information about international developments; and (3) the prominence of interstate organizations dedicated to enhance peace and security have narrowed the ability of national leaders to calculate and implement state interests on their own.[21] Increasingly salient following the end of the Soviet-American Cold War, these developments are widely understood to have altered the character of the international system of states, and for this reason must be taken into account when generating even limited provisional generalizations about contemporary great-power behavior.

Accordingly, four more recent international developments are now considered for their impact upon collective great-power responses to local ethnic conflict: (1) on-the-spot media and NGO reporting dramatize local ethnic conflict and create new pressures for international intervention; (2) real-time NGO monitoring of large-scale political violence in small states, now possible for the first time, considerably assists national intelligence gathering; (3) the more highly organized character of the international state system ensures earlier and more productive international management of small-power ethnic conflict than in the past; and (4) the role of the United Nations has importantly affected great-power consensus-building.

This study concludes that these four developments do not fundamentally alter the role, outlook, and behavior of the major states from what they had been in the past. These newer trends affect states at the margins of the international agenda and significantly complicate the traditional pursuits of states, but they do not create fundamentally new bases for state behavior at odds with the prevailing practice of power politics.

They therefore do not impede this study's search for generalizations about that behavior.

Public Pressures from On-the-Spot Reporting

Televised and NGO reports of starvation and violence have increased pressures for great-power intervention to support the weaker challenger in localized ethnic conflict.[22] Two aspects of this development require consideration: (1) whether governments must be affected by these pressures; and (2) if they are, whether rapidly provided humanitarian assistance has transformed how the great powers have dealt with the underlying political differences between the primary antagonists. On the first issue, governments can and often do resist popular pressures. In the aftermath of the killing of eighteen servicemen stationed in Somalia as part of the American Operation Restore Hope, American policy guidelines then being drafted for supporting future humanitarian operations of this kind were considerably tightened.[23] These guidelines forestalled American participation in peacekeeping in Bosnia-Herzegovina from 1992 to 1995, in Rwanda in 1994, and in East Timor in 1999. Insofar as the guidelines prevented a more prompt response to ethnic violence (as in Rwanda and East Timor), and a stronger international presence to forestall the violence (as in Bosnia-Herzegovina), they have been questioned, but they nevertheless illustrate independent state action under crisis conditions. It may be argued that the guidelines illustrate how governments are nowadays more attuned than before to the domestic political climate of their countries, and less accepting of the costs of coping with small-state ethnic violence. In retrospect, however, the widespread assumption that the United States could have done more in these instances to protect international values—that is, that the United States missed opportunities in these instances to act in a more internationally responsible manner—indicates that the conduct of states, primarily, rather than their publics or NGOs, is being judged in this respect.[24]

The second issue generates attention to the *choice* of PD interventionist technique and to its *effectiveness*. With respect to the choice of PD technique, the impact of televised and NGO reports of ethnic conflict can heighten contrary pressures: on one hand, governments protecting the unwillingness of their citizens to take risks to pacify ethnic factions abroad are likely to promote conciliatory intervention; on the other hand, governments motivated to act by NGO assessments of humanitarian emergency in local ethnic violence are likely to act coercively. In practice, these sources of motivation are likely to neutralize each other.

On the question of PD effectiveness, there is no indication that humanitarian intervention itself improves major-state leverage on the primary antagonists. Far from removing differences between the great powers, which impede PD effectiveness, it may accentuate them. It also impedes PD effectiveness by postponing a hurting stalemate between the primary antagonists. And coercive intervention stimulated by humanitarian disaster can founder if, as sometimes happens, a mismatch sets in when the resources available to the major states are inadequate to implement their objectives.

Real-Time NGO Monitoring of Small-State Violence

Humanitarian NGOs, widely engaged in alleviating the effects of small-power ethnic violence, have become the most important collectors of information about ethnic violence in remote rural areas.[25] For this reason, they have become critical for early warning of ethnic confrontation, and the information they obtain and the conditions under which they share it can affect great-power interests, particularly where governmental intelligence agencies are not engaged in high-priority intelligence collection. However, before it can be argued that this new NGO role has had a major impact upon great-power behavior, the utility to governments of the NGO-generated information must be established. In practice, this utility is not as high as might first appear. First, at the earliest stage of local ethnic confrontation, the information generated by NGOs, which must negotiate with the primary antagonists for access to it, is quite limited and superficial.[26] The information of most use to governments, consisting of the causes of the local turmoil, the strategies of the primary antagonists, and the broader significance of the violence, takes the NGOs the most time to obtain and is often ignored by them because of their organizational interests. This information, the supplying of which may be incompatible with the interests of the primary antagonists, can be withheld from NGO representatives, who are at the mercy of local leaders.

Second, the role of NGOs as a substitute or complement to intelligence agencies is limited to localized ethnic conflicts of low intrinsic importance to the major states; because of the low importance of these conflicts, official intelligence priorities will usually be directed elsewhere. But it is precisely in low-priority cases that the information base for warning must be distinguished from the governmental response potential, the latter based on political considerations. Even if the information generated by NGOs in low-priority cases is of the highest quality, political incentives to intervene will nevertheless usually remain small.[27] The exception is where the localized conflict is extrinsically important because of the opportunity for intervention by another great power. In the latter instance, information becomes valuable primarily for making the argument for early insulation of the dispute and not for the needs of intervention.

The More Organized Character of the International System

Unprecedented linkages between states, especially in Europe, have encouraged early interventionist PD in small-power ethnic conflict since the end of the Cold War. Such linkages make it impossible for neighboring states to remain aloof when culture-based conflicts intensify in a region, and they also discourage opportunistic behavior in the conflict arena by those states. For example, the European Community (now the European Union) and the Conference on Security and Cooperation in Europe (now the Organization on Security and Cooperation in Europe) attempted to dampen rising internal ethnic tensions in the former Yugoslavia in the early 1990s, applying the "common regional home" theme suggested by rising linkages between European states; the intervention was apparently the most important brake upon Slovene and Croat secession from Yugoslavia.

But early intervention on the "common regional home" foundation and the accompanying threat of economic isolation can be inadequate to head off bloodshed and polarization in local conflict. Seeking to keep Yugoslavia whole, for example, the European Community strengthened the Serb leadership in Belgrade and undercut rebels in Slovenia, Croatia, and Bosnia-Herzegovina. (Because the Belgrade government stressed Serb nationalism, it was unable to benefit from this international recognition.) The interveners were not expert in PD or in peaceful change and did not coordinate their interventions well among themselves or with the UN, weaknesses that enabled the Serbs to make ample use of their initial military superiority in Bosnia-Herzegovina. Finally, the intervening institutions may have underestimated the depth of the internal conflict in Bosnia-Herzegovina, and thus PD requirements, given the long and close interaction of Muslims, Croats, and Serbs in that province. Even though confrontation between those groups was apparently predicted beforehand, its intensity was difficult or impossible to anticipate, as suggested by the rapid explosion of intergroup violence following Bosnia-Herzegovina's secession from Yugoslavia. In short, rising regional linkages among states do not undermine this study's basic finding that early interventionist PD is problematic.

The Impact of the United Nations

Creation of the UN has introduced new options and avenues for the great powers.[28] Of these, two broad alternatives for dealing with threats to peace and security can be distinguished. First, the organization was predicated on serving as a vehicle for great-power consensus-making to enable the major states to act collectively and responsibly. During the Cold War the UN rarely served this purpose, but following its end many anticipated that the organization could more effectively fulfill it. The second approach, shaped by UN Secretary General Dag Hammarskjöld during the Cold War, envisioned it as a great-power surrogate when the major states were deadlocked. For example, the UN worked to insulate local conflict in the Congo and in Cyprus from great-power rivalry. This second approach arguably constituted the UN's most important political innovation. But whether the major states would remain on the sidelines when no longer deadlocked, and whether the UN could then continue to act independently of great-power leadership, remained unclear.

Neither of these conceptions was fully established in the post-Cold War period. On one hand, the great powers did not collectively lead at the UN, adopting instead more circumscribed priorities. They have not been interested, for the most part, in intervening collectively in small-power intrastate disputes. On the other hand, they have resisted former UN Secretary General Boutros Boutros-Ghali's call for a more ambitious UN PD agenda, and have been less inclined than during the Cold War to support independent UN action in which they did not take the lead. While the major states continue to work to insulate local conflicts from becoming irritants in their relations, they have resisted UN action to define and apply the goal of insulation for them.

Whether deadlocked or in agreement, in fact, the great powers have remained key actors throughout the history of the UN. For example, when deadlocked the major states retained major capabilities indispensable for assisting UN operations. They retained a veto upon such operations, limiting UN independence as in the Congo case. We may conclude that neither during the Cold War nor in the present period has the UN fundamentally changed the major roles of the great powers, although it has sometimes masked them. Even before the Cold War ended, the major states collectively pursued PD while keeping the UN in the background, as with the UN Transition Assistance Group in Namibia and Angola.[29] Exercising special initiative at present, they may more often than in the past hammer out their own positions, using the UN to obtain wider legitimacy for their ideas but depending more on each other. But their circumscribed priorities, already referred to, are not likely to permit many special initiatives of this kind. Except in instances in which they have strong reasons to become involved unilaterally, the major states appear increasingly willing to give the primary antagonists in local ethnic conflict ample opportunity to resolve their conflict on their own, and intervene only when all else fails.[30] Under those circumstances, negative great-power attitudes will also dampen the likelihood of UN action.

Conclusions

Collective great-power action is often a prerequisite to successful PD and to peace. The Tight Concert, Loose Concert, and Prevailing Opposition patterns presented in this chapter spell out alternate sets of conditions for collective PD. Those conditions, highlighting diverse stimulants and hindrances to collective action, should comprise part of the information base for policy officials making contemporary decisions about PD.

The preoccupation with great-power behavior here has traditional and untraditional aspects. The traditional element is the preoccupation with statecraft—relating through plans and calculations the instrumentalities of the state to its interests—at a time when the centrality of the state for world politics has declined in many issue areas. The guiding assumption in this respect here is that the state remains as important for collective PD as it was in the nineteenth century. As in earlier eras, great-power states can now enhance collective major-state actions by working multilaterally to satisfy their national interests. Alternatively, those states can weaken collective action by acting on their own. However they behave, "[t]he particular international order that obtains at any time," as John Mearsheimer has written, "is mainly a by-product of the self-interested behavior of the system's great powers."[31] Whichever course is taken, local conflict developments pressure the great powers to choose and to act.

The untraditional element in this study is its interest in international history, long neglected as an element in contemporary decision making.[32] Basic to the present study is the belief that comparing great-power action in different eras is necessary and possible. These comparisons can be accomplished using the Tight Concert, Loose Concert, and Prevailing Opposition patterns developed in this chapter to compare nineteenth- and twentieth-century cases. Seeking to document regularities in great powers consensus and action on small-power intrastate conflict, this study in effect seeks to rehabilitate history as a source of policy-relevant insights.

Part II

The History

Source: Mauldin Collection, Library of Congress. Reprinted with permission.

Chapter 4

Eight Cases

The following profiles of eight cases form the building blocks for the analytical portion of this study. Each profile has been prepared to address the same seven questions listed in table 1.3, simplifying and abstracting from a variety of writings about the case to convey how specific local ethnic conflicts became international issues and how the great powers dealt collectively with them. Subsequent chapters examine these cases comparatively.

The Belgian Revolution (1830–1838)

The Belgians and Dutch were placed under a Dutch king by the great-power concert following the Napoleonic War primarily to contain French expansionist tendencies in Belgium. Although this union was opposed in the late 1820s by a movement demanding greater popular input into the political system, the outbreak of the Belgian revolution in late August 1830 was largely unexpected and occurred without warning. Insurrectionists in Belgium, emboldened by revolution earlier in Paris, postponed revolt, believing that the Dutch regime's popularity greatly reduced the chances of success. When revolt nevertheless took place (abetted by the staging in Brussels of an opera with revolution-inspiring images), the Dutch king first agreed to consider separating the Belgian provinces, but then sought to suppress the revolt by force, and when this failed, sought military intervention by the European concert to insure his rule.

Information problems left the great powers unprepared to respond to the revolt. The reaction of Great Britain, which originally argued that the revolt was a purely internal affair, "can be attributed, in part, to the lack of any skilled observers in [Brussels]. Sir Charles Bagot, the British ambassador, was in residence at The Hague. His reports depended upon the scanty information given him by royal government officials and the reports of travelers."[1] Fearing Bagot's assessment might be inaccurate, the British foreign minister sent three special agents to Belgium to consult with the revolutionists. Only on 12 September did the foreign minister learn about the deep cleavages between northern and southern provinces of Holland, and about the insurrectionists' aims. Since Prussia, Austria, and Russia followed British policy on the Belgian question, this delay had wider significance. By contrast, the French government was well informed from the beginning but determined to avoid even verbal assistance to the agitators; it closed its border with Belgium. The newly installed French king, Louis Philippe, wanted the best relations with the Dutch king, but not a Dutch request for military assistance.

No European great power had important strategic interests to intervene militarily in support of the Dutch king, but military intervention by any one major state was likely to be opposed militarily by another. The Prussians, whose king was related to the Dutch monarch by marriage, alone were capable of logistically effective intervention, but the French threatened to oppose it with forces of their own. Britain, mistrustful of the French, was determined to oppose unilateral military action by France. A key to managing the crisis was the French decision to use it as a means to gain recognition of the newly installed Louis Philippe by other European monarchs; France stressed the principle of nonintervention, and this was accepted by the other great powers. In effect, being unable to accept gain by other powers, each of the major states used the great-power concert to legitimate mutual self-denial. The French policy of giving advice to the Dutch king was the key to the revival of conference diplomacy, and the French request that Great Britain act jointly with France in Belgian affairs launched a thirty-five-year period of Anglo-French cooperation.[2]

The great powers obtained a Dutch-Belgian armistice by November 1830 and agreed to (1) the establishment of a free and possibly enlarged Belgian state; (2) the terms of Belgian separation from the Netherlands; and (3) the selection of the new Belgian king. However, the Dutch and Belgians failed to agree on terms of separation, and international as well as domestic instability persisted. While the French mostly upheld concert action, they attached greater importance to Belgian independence than did other major states. Independent French action twice brought confrontation when it threatened, or appeared to threaten, concert views.

After the London Conference agreed on 1 February 1831 that the future Belgian monarch could not come from any of the reigning houses of the great powers, the Belgian national congress two days later elected as king the Duc de Nemours, second son of Louis Philippe, provoking a war scare with the British. And in August 1831, French military intervention into Belgium to blunt a Dutch military campaign against the Belgians led to an international crisis when, after the Dutch troops departed, the French remained in the country. These crises were both dispelled by French retreat. They showed that concert PD was not solely predicated on agreement among the great powers, but was designed to withstand noncooperation from one key great power capable of intensifying conflict in Belgium. PD was thus enhanced by the use of compellence as leverage against the possibility of one key state's resistance. Such leverage in practice denied unilateral French benefit from the Belgian attraction to France. It also led the concert to hesitate risking war with Belgium over separation issues in May and June 1831, because war against Belgium could have led to war with France as well.

Not until 1838 did the Dutch formally agree to terms of separation in which Belgium gained a portion of Luxembourg and Limburg. An important incentive to this settlement was a technical arrangement worked out by British foreign secretary Henry Palmerston opening the Scheldt River to the commerce of Holland and Belgium. French differences with the other major states and informational problems had long been overcome by this time. French cooperation facilitated friendly representations by Prussia, Russia, and Austria-Hungary with the Dutch king to gain Dutch restraint. And the French successfully pushed concessions by the Belgians to the Dutch.[3]

The Greek Revolution (1821–1832)

The Greek revolution that began in May 1821 against Turkish rule, although not the first of its kind, occurred without warning, "almost without plan or system, in an accumulating series of random acts of violence."[4] Discouraged by Greek leaders in the Peloponnese, who feared Turkish retaliation, it was instigated by factions counting on and supported financially by Russian leaders hostile to the Ottoman Empire. The Russian government nevertheless condemned it, as did other European monarchical governments.

Information about the revolt at the disposal of European leaders initially little affected their response to it, when the Greeks, benefiting from

Turkish distraction by an internal struggle against the renegade Turkish resident Ali Pasha in Albania, defeated nearly all Turkish garrisons in the Peloponnese. In the long run, however, information available to those leaders about the war assisted the Greek cause when the Turks enjoyed military momentum. Information about the excessiveness and harshness of Turkish efforts to subdue the Greeks proved a decisive political liability, vindicating the Greek strategy of holding out as long as possible.

From the start, the revolutionists sought great-power support. In June 1825, they placed themselves under British "protection," and the following November they offered to submit to Russia in similar fashion. However, the major states were slow to respond. The British government supported the Greeks financially, and some of its liberally outspoken citizens fought on the Greek side; but it was also a long-standing ally of the Turks and was unwilling for strategic reasons to contribute to the unity of major European powers in any way. It was at first drawn in only to protect commerce and prevent piracy around its Ionian Island possessions off the Greek coast. Russia, having earlier patronized Greeks dedicated to weakening Turkish authority, cut off ties with them after the uprising began, even as it used the uprising as one of many issues to weaken the stature of the Ottoman Empire. The Holy Alliance, created to cope with democratically inspired revolution, called in 1825 for an end to the fighting short of Greek independence and offered mediation, proposals rejected by the Greeks and the Turks.

Differences between the great powers impaired their collective response to the revolution. Within the Holy Alliance, Russia alone supported coercing the Turks to accept Greek reforms, while her allies mainly wished to prevent Russo-Turkish war arising from the revolution. After the Holy Alliance foundered over this issue, Britain acted to bring about an Anglo-Russian entente to prevent the Greek question from leading to a Russo-Turkish war. According to the Anglo-Russian Protocol of April 1826, England and Russia would intervene "jointly or separately" if the Greeks and Turkey rejected great-power mediation. Separate intervention implied a threat of Russian use of force, and privately the two countries, aiming at a settlement short of full Greek independence but including the evacuation of Turkish forces from Greece, discussed a joint "pacific blockade." But this agreement masked a fundamental difference of approach: the British, and later the French who joined discussions begun in 1827 on collective enforcement action, used the entente to restrain the Russians and prevent war, while the Russians saw it as legitimating and facilitating military intervention, neutralizing great-power opposition if a peaceful solution was not reached.

Persisting great-power disagreement on peace terms made peaceful coercion of the Turkish Sultan impossible and Russo-Turkish war inevitable. A naval blockade of Greece by the three powers was put into place, leading to annihilation of a sizable portion of the Turkish fleet in Navarino Bay when the Turks challenged it in October 1827. But the Turks continued to resist a negotiated Greek settlement, and the Allies remained deadlocked on its terms. When Britain rejected an 1828 Russian proposal for joint Allied war against the Turks, Russia went to war against the Turks alone. Disagreement on peace terms thereupon hardened because of British suspicions of Russian intentions, the deadlock persisting until the end of the Russo-Turkish War in 1829.

Great-power differences were especially corrosive for the concert for two reasons. First, upon being reconstituted following the demise of the Holy Alliance, the concert consisted only of three countries, Prussia being indifferent and Austria supporting the Turkish Porte. Concert members could not coerce each other, and if any of the three had chosen to disaffiliate, no cushion was available. The differences were also corrosive because the concert had entered the enforcement stage without a clear plan of action. Having become engaged, the concert could not retreat from peace enforcement nor strengthen it, and consequently became vulnerable to new crises associated with Russia's military victory and resulting political gains over the Turks.

In the end, an Anglo-Russian crisis growing out of the Russo-Turkish war made possible a Greek settlement: after a Russian twelve-thousand-man force reached Adrianople, outside Constantinople, the British fleet in August 1829 anchored close to the Russian Mediterranean squadron in Besika Bay. Protecting Turkey from the Russian onslaught, the Western powers exacted Turkish concessions on Greece. In the meantime, the Greeks, capitalizing upon the concert deadlock, fought successfully against the Turks for more extensive borders.[5]

The Bosnian Revolution (Bosnia I) (1875–1878)

Orthodox Christians in Herzegovina revolted against Ottoman Turkish colonizers and the indigenous Moslem landowning class in July 1878, and the revolt spread to neighboring Bosnia the following month. Stimulated and assisted by fellow Slavs in Serbia, Austrian Dalmatia, Russia, and especially Montenegro, it was instigated by Herzegovinians who had fled to Montenegro the previous winter and who, after having been returned, rebelled against excessive taxes. It was preceded by vendettas between Christians and Moslems during a trip by the Austro-Hungarian Emperor through Dalmatia in April 1875. Warning of Christian-Muslim tensions in Bosnia-Herzegovina was thus provided prior to the outbreak of the revolt.

The great-power reactions to the revolt were inhibited because Bosnia-Herzegovina was of small intrinsic importance for them, and because their extrinsic interests counseled avoiding new decisions and commitments. England, allied with the Ottoman Empire against Russia, understood that weakening the Empire could contribute to Russian expansion. Austria and Russia each sought to contain the other in the Balkans, Russia capitalizing upon Pan-Slav attachments and Austria desiring to blunt those attachments. However, the major powers collectively addressed the revolt because it affected the balance of power between them, and because neither Bosnia-Herzegovina faction could fully dominate the other on its own. The rebels, who preferred absorption into an enlarged Slavic state, could not defeat the Turks even with volunteers, supplies, and sanctuary from their neighbors, while the Turks, with a weak presence backed by a few military garrisons, were unable initially to mount a major effort to suppress the revolt.

Urging restraint upon the rebels, and dissuading the Turks from attacking rebel sanctuaries in neighboring Slavic states, the great powers first formed a consular mission to Bosnia and Herzegovina to publicize rebel grievances after obtaining Turkish agreement not to use force. The consuls warned the rebels of their isolation and urged them to submit to Turkish authority, but the Turks attacked the rebels following a meeting with the consuls. Thereafter the great powers worked for an internal Ottoman reform program as an incentive to the rebels to lay down their arms. In the so-called Andrassy Note of December 1875, the Austro-Hungarian foreign minister Julius Andrassy proposed with the consent of all the great powers that the Ottoman rulers provide for complete religious freedom in Bosnia and Herzegovina, abolition of tax farming, and a mixed Christian-Moslem commission to supervise reform. The Turks accepted this program, but the rebels, influenced by neighboring Slav states, rejected it, seeking greater liberties.

In April 1876 the rebels made additional demands, and in the Berlin Memorandum the following month, Austria, Germany, and Russia conceded still more to them, proposing a two-month armistice, resettlement of the rebels, limitation of Turkish force movements, retention of arms by the rebels, and great-power supervision of Turkish reforms. If, after an armistice, discussions based on these proposals did not succeed, the three powers indicated in that memorandum that they were prepared to strengthen their action by "the sanction of an agreement, with a view to such efficacious measures as might appear to be demanded, in the interest of general peace, to check the evil and prevent its development."[6]

Major-power differences importantly affected intervention in the local conflict. Austria was less interested in satisfying the Bosnia-Herzegovina Christians than in ruling them herself if the Turks were unable to do so, her aim being to forestall restiveness from her Slav population. It rejected any autonomy for the Ottoman Christians because this would undermine Austria's ultimate aim of occupying the territory. Russia, using Pan-Slav ideology to enhance its influence, sought to weaken Turkey in relation to itself; it favored political autonomy for Bosnian and Herzegovinian Christians supervised by the great powers. Britain, at Turkish behest, undercut mediation by rejecting the Berlin Memorandum.

Still, Austria and Russia refused to permit strife in Bosnia-Herzegovina to cause war between themselves and persisted in seeking consensus. The Austrian approach rejecting Christian autonomy in Bosnia-Herzegovina had been accepted by the Turks, but continued insurgency led Austria to give priority to relations with Russia over those with Turkey. The two great powers anticipated by May 1876 military intervention by Serbia and Montenegro in Bosnia-Herzegovina and agreed to work together in that eventuality. When Serbia and Montenegro in fact entered the war in June 1876, Austria and Russia, backed by Germany, agreed to abandon mediation, defend the status quo ante in event of Turkish victory, and seek compensation for any territorial gains by Serbia and Montenegro resulting from a Serbian-Montenegrin victory.

The great powers ultimately imposed a settlement in Bosnia-Herzegovina, working against the local antagonists and against Serbia and Montenegro. The Turks defeated the Serbs, whereupon the Russians issued an ultimatum to the Turks to halt their advance; after the Turks stopped their offensive, Russia, fully supported by Austria, again threatened to go to war if the Turks failed to implement reforms in their Christian communities. Russo-Turkish war ensued after the great powers failed to persuade the Turks to reform, but the resulting Russian victory and Turkish territorial concessions lead the English to attempt to reverse the Russian gains made in the war. At the Berlin Conference in June and July 1878, the great powers in a general treaty authorized Austro-Hungarian occupation of Bosnia-Herzegovina while maintaining Turkish sovereignty there.[7]

Armenian Unrest in the Ottoman Empire (1878–1914)

While loyal to the Ottoman regime, Armenians protested despotic treatment by state officials and Kurdish peoples in Eastern Anatolia. As the regime did not respond, the great powers inserted into the 1878 Treaty of Berlin a requirement that the Ottoman regime implement improvements and reforms to alleviate the problem. The treaty did not specify details, and leverage to implement reform was lost when Russia, which occupied half of Turkish Armenia in the Russo-Turkish War of 1877–78, surrendered in the treaty settlement some non-Armenian districts it had also taken. However, in a memorandum of 30 May 1878, Russia agreed to give Britain joint power with it in intervening with the Ottoman regime on Armenian questions. In effect, the Armenians received two great-power protectors, both well aware by that time of local tensions in Eastern Anatolia.

The Armenians, favoring autonomy but prevailed upon by the major states to reduce their demands, rejected violence and pushed especially Britain and Russia to intervene with the Turks on their behalf—Britain, because as an ally of the Turks it was perhaps the most influential outside power in Constantinople, and Russia, because it had just militarily defeated the Turks. Both were well placed to monitor and pursue the Armenian question but inhibited from acting on it. The British, the strongest advocates of reform, were attracted by liberalism and ideals of good government, and understood that alleviating Armenian conditions in the Ottoman Empire would diminish the vulnerability of their ally to international criticism. A program they proposed in August 1878 for a gendarmerie in Eastern Anatolia commanded by Europeans, responsible tax collectors in each province, and a system of appellate courts, was stymied by Turkish resistance and delay, Britain being unwilling to threaten a break with Turkey over the issue. Russia by contrast used the Armenian question as a wedge to further weaken the Ottoman Empire and to facilitate its own expansion. A long-term tacit Russo-Turkish entente, based on mutual suspicions of Armenians, existed until 1910, when the new Russian foreign minister Serge Sazonov sought to pacify both Turkish and Russian Armenians.

Anglo-Russian inhibitions were importantly due to the two countries' suspicions of each other, which rarely allowed them to jointly approach the

Turks. Russian engagement as protector of Turkish Armenians in 1877–78 came during a period of confrontation with England, whereas England assumed the role of protector based upon mutual Anglo-Turkish suspicions of Russia. Russia assumed that British proposals for protecting the Armenians would exacerbate internal Ottoman instability, as had the introduction of rights in Balkan Turkish provinces, while England worried that Russian reform interests masked a desire to annex all of Turkish Armenia. Yet each understood that pushing reform on the Turks would strengthen the influence of its rival with the Turkish Court, a view reinforced by Turks, who played each side off against the other. The value of the Armenian protectorship was thereby reduced, and Armenian conditions worsened in spite of it.

The great-power concert nevertheless persisted in connection with the Armenian question, the great-power association—a longtime feature of Constantinople diplomacy—surviving the failure of PD while preempting other means of solving the Armenian problem. Prior to 1913, the concert actively responded to outbreaks of Armenian violence in the 1890s growing out of Armenian resistance to Kurdish tribute demands in the Eastern provinces and provocations against Armenians in Constantinople. Following harsh Turkish suppression of Armenian resistance in the Eastern provinces in 1894, which lead to massacres over a two-year period, and following massacres in Constantinople in 1896, the great powers collectively persuaded the Turks to stop the killing of Armenians. They could not, however, agree to impose a program of reform to prevent recurrent violence. In effect they accommodated Turkish resistance to reform to protect the presence at Constantinople they believed was indispensable to watch over each other. The Turks contributed to this attitude.

Only by 1912, when the Russians threatened to intervene into Turkish Armenia in the event of future Armenian massacres, and when the deteriorating Turkish position in the Balkans accentuated the perception of Turkish weakness and decline, was the great-power concert seriously able to consider a Turkish reform program. The major states gained Turkish acceptance in early 1914 of a watered-down scheme pushed hardest by Russia in which the Turkish government agreed to (1) ask the major powers to recommend two foreign inspectors-general for Eastern Anatolia, who would be permitted under contract to select higher political and judicial officials for nomination by the government, and to dismiss incompetent officials; (2) create an elective council in each of two regions, composed of Moslems and Christians in equal numbers; and (3) permit the great powers to supervise implementation of reforms through their ambassadors and consuls. Suspicion of Russian intentions spurred negotiations, as the other great powers sought to blunt an opportunity for Russian expansion, but implementation of the program was thwarted by outbreak of the First World War.[8]

German/Lithuanian Conflict in the Memel (1918–1939)

The Memel territory, consisting of the Baltic port of Memel and its hinterlands, first gained international attention when ceded by Germany to the victorious Allies in the Versailles Treaty of 1918. Only about 2,300 square kilometers in size, the territory contained a German ruling elite, a Lithuanian cultural grouping concentrated in the lower classes and in the smaller villages, and a hybrid "Memellander" group adhering to neither Germany nor Lithuania. It was tranquil prior to 1918, but subsequent rivalry between Germany and the newly created state of Lithuania for the control of the territory—each acting as defender and protector of its loyalists—introduced ethnic tensions. The Allies in June 1919 officially recognized the Lithuanian character of the Memel, but postponed deciding its permanent political status, installing on an interim basis early in 1920 a French civilian commissioner and a small French force, to be supervised by the four victorious Allied powers (England, France, Italy, and Japan). For the next three years, while this regime was in place, effective administration of the territory remained as before in the hands of the German community.

The Allies thereafter were inclined to avoid deciding the ultimate status of the Memel. They concentrated on much more important questions (such as the punitive peace with Germany) and lacked strong interests on the Memel. Their inclination was reinforced by the peaceful condition of the territory and by the general instability of the Baltic region, in which Lithuania was embroiled in disputes with Poland, another newly created state that sought trading rights in the city of Memel. The Allies linked a solution for the Memel to Lithuania's termination of claims to the city of Vilnius, occupied and claimed by Poland, but Lithuania rejected this linkage and demanded that the Memel territory be incorporated into Lithuania.

In exchange for Lithuania's acceptance of the internationalization of the Niemen River, the Allies in October 1922 appointed a committee to report on the final status of the Memel. However, when it was widely rumored that this committee would recommend establishment of a Free

State in the Memel under authority of the League of Nations, non-uniformed forces of Lithuanian origin invaded the territory in January 1923. The French, overwhelmed, withdrew after a short period of fighting, and the Allies agreed in February 1923 to attach the Memel as an autonomous territory to Lithuania; in exchange, Lithuania accepted the Memel Statute, a power-sharing arrangement to protect non-Lithuanians in the territory and its autonomous status. The statute contained rules about official languages, elections, the Memel Directorate, the status of the elected legislature, and the Port of Memel, and gave any member of the Council of the League of Nations the right to take alleged infractions of the statute to the Council.

The Council of Ambassadors, the great-power instrument responsible for implementing the Versailles Treaty, worked harmoniously on the Memel. The major states anticipated that, inasmuch as the issue of relative power within the Memel was left open by the Memel Statute, conflict over its implementation within the territory, and between Lithuania and its neighbors, would endure. Overall responsibility for the territory remained with the great powers, deadlocks under the statute being appealable to the League Council, where great power states enjoyed permanent membership. In practice, Council members preferred to have Memel disputes between Germans and Lithuanians settled locally, and until 1929 they mostly were, due to the determination of the German prime minister, Gustav Stresemann, to make the Memel Statute and its power-sharing arrangement succeed. Until 1929, while Stresemann remained in office, Germany and Lithuania agreed to enhance their economic linkages while working around their differences over the Memel, excluding Polish and Soviet involvement there. The great-power concert served during this period largely as a check against German-Lithuanian failure to reach solutions.

Following the advent of Hitler in 1932, Germany used the Memel Statute for divisive purposes, seeking the return of the territory to Germany. Beginning with the Polish-German alliance of 1934, the Germans took advantage of Polish-Lithuanian hostility to work for this objective. In March 1938, capitalizing on the Polish demand that Lithuania open its frontier and normalize relations with Poland, Germany threatened to invade Lithuania if it did not comply with Polish demands. A year later, by which time the Nazi party had gained full control of the Memel Parliament, Germany demanded and Lithuania conceded the reversion of the Memel to Germany in exchange for a guarantee of autonomy for the territory. In this period, the absence of active great-power concert involvement worked against the Memel Statute regime.[9]

Belgian Congo Conflict (1960–1964)

As colonizers, the Belgians prevented direct conflict in the Congo between Congolese tribes but did not break down tribal feeling. Following rioting in 1959 against the colonial regime in Leopoldville, Belgian and Congolese leaders agreed that the Congo would become independent on 30 June 1960 and that Belgium would be heavily involved in shaping institutions of the new country. Neither the anomaly between Belgian control of the Congolese army and the overall transition in the country to Congolese control, nor the decline in the morale of the army, excited much international attention. Prior to the independence date, riots aimed at Europeans by the rank and file of the holdover Congo army unexpectedly broke out, and Belgian officers in the army were removed. In response, the Belgian government authorized its army to intervene in the Congo wherever Belgian nationals were in danger, and in "all centers of importance" in Katanga, where in January 1960 nearly a third of the European population in the Congo lived. By 19 July 1960, 10,000 Belgian troops had intervened in twenty-three places in the Congo, engaging and disarming the Congolese army; the intervention spawned secessionist movements in Kasai and Katanga provinces.

Unable to pacify the country, the new Congolese government led by Patrice Lumumba requested outside assistance, first from the United States, and, when this request was rejected, from the United Nations. The UN authorized an international military force for the Congo to facilitate Belgian withdrawal and, still more importantly, to hold down Soviet-American Cold-War conflict in the country. The force numbered 8,300 by late July and 20,000 by the end of the year.

The United States and Soviet Union became involved in the Congo as part of their worldwide rivalry for influence, each using chaos in the country to weaken its opponent's position. Opportunity for the Soviets in the Congolese conflict was presented when Lumumba became increasingly impatient with the UN failure to immediately put down the Katanga revolt. Lumumba, who alone of the Congolese leaders had a wide following, strongly wished to unify the country under his authority. The Soviets offered to transport the Congolese army into Kasai, adjacent to Katanga, to prepare for an offensive against the Katanga regime. Once in Kasai, the army—unpaid and requisitioning food and supplies—was distracted by local tribal resistance and brutally suppressed it.

The United States, along with its European allies, cooled to Lumumba because of the excessive, uncontrolled behavior of the Congolese army and because of suspicions that Lumumba would ally with the Soviets. On 5 September 1960, Congolese president Joseph Kasavubu fired Lumumba, and nine days later Army Chief of Staff Joseph Mobutu seized power, canceling the invasion of Katanga. Late in November Lumumba fled from Leopoldville, where he had been protected by UN peacekeepers, and was eventually transported to Katanga and murdered.

While Lumumba enjoyed power, great-power consensus on the Congo was impossible, and the UN, opposed by major Congolese factions and by the superpowers, could not adequately keep law and order in the country, nor prevent outside states from capitalizing upon Congolese civil strife. After Lumumba was fired, UN Secretary-General Dag Hammarskjöld set out to conciliate Kasavubu and Lumumba, lessen the army's influence in civil affairs, and strengthen Congolese unity and territorial integrity. This conflicted with American refusal to deal with Lumumba and American support for Mobutu, and reinforced Soviet suspicions that the UN secretary-general was accumulating too much authority. When the head of the UN mission, Rajeshwar Dayal, attempted to reconstruct a Congo unity government including Lumumba, the Americans removed their support for Dayal and for the UN operation; the ensuing stalemate was broken only in May 1961 when Dayal and the anti-Lumumba British and American ambassadors in the Congo were removed from their posts.

Relations between the UN and the central Congolese government improved after Lumumba's death, the UN promising in February 1961 to give it full political and administrative assistance, including help in terminating the rebellion and ousting foreign mercenaries in Katanga. When the mercenaries, who had remained after Belgian troops departed in September 1960, refused to leave, they were compelled to do so militarily by the UN force in four military operations that ultimately suppressed the Katanga secession.

These operations were at odds with the UN peacekeepers' mandate, which excluded the use of force or interference in Congolese internal affairs, and UN consensus splintered. But the superpowers each tolerated UN use of force as an alternative to military intervention by their rival. The UN benefited from superpower inhibitions, as the superpowers employed the UN to screen their competition, sparing themselves the requirement of having to assume collective or unilateral responsibility for defusing conflict in the country. The United States gave major economic and logistical support for UN military operations, and facilitated reconstruction of the Congolese government in December 1961 when the leader of the Katanga secession was escorted in an American presidential jet to a meeting with the Congolese coalition government prime minister. By then, the United States gave priority to ending foreign interference in the Congo over strengthening Congo factions to weaken Soviet sympathizers in the country.

Following the end of the Katanga secession in January 1963, peace prevailed in the Congo for a short time, but new rebellion against the Leopoldville government in January 1964 caused the removal of the UN force six months later.[10]

Cyprus (1960 to present)

British rule in Cyprus was challenged during the 1950s by Greek-Cypriote guerrillas working for union, or *enosis,* between Cyprus and Greece, and by a Turkish-Cypriote resistance movement favoring partition of the island between Greeks and Turks. Rejecting *enosis* and partition, the British, supported by Greece and Turkey, implemented a power-sharing regime for the Greek and Turkish Cypriote communities. When the Republic of Cyprus became independent in August 1960, the regime included (1) a Treaty of Guarantee, making Britain, Greece, and Turkey protectors of Cypriote sovereignty, enabled to act jointly or separately to protect the status quo; (2) a Treaty of Alliance, permitting Greece and Turkey to deploy military personnel on the island; and (3) a Treaty of Establishment, granting Britain two military bases, defining power-sharing ratios between Greeks and Turks, and giving a Greek-Cypriote president and a Turkish-Cypriote vice president vetoes over legislation. The first Cypriote president, Archbishop Makarios, an advocate of *enosis*, set out to change the power-sharing rules, which had been necessitated by mistrust between the two Cypriote communities. The ensuing unrest, which erupted into intercommunal violence in December 1963, did not surprise the international community.

The British and their American allies were alerted in advance to the problem of Greek-Turkish Cypriote tensions by their awareness of Makarios's intentions and of how mistrust between Greek and Turkish Cypriotes, combined with power sharing, virtually paralyzed the Cypriote government. They were much less concerned about the welfare of Cypriotes and their government than about preserving unity in NATO's eastern flank. To ensure Greek-Turkish cooperation to contain the Soviet Union, the Americans in particular sought to reduce tensions between Greek and Turkish Cypriotes by working as closely as possible with their Greek and Turkish allies. This placed the United States at odds with Makarios, who resisted the NATO framework. In 1964, an American plan for *enosis* plus partition of the island, supported by Greece and Turkey while undermining Makarios, failed when Greek-Cypriote violence against Turkish towns provoked Turkish bombing. When the Greeks succeeded in overthrowing Makarios in 1974, his successor was recognized by the United States, which only weakly resisted the Turkish invasion in response to it.

Makarios resisted the Anglo-American Cold War approach. Following the outbreak of the 1964 violence, with Greek and Turkish Cypriote leaders being unable to maintain a cease-fire, and Greek and Turkish commanders refusing to join three-nation truce patrols, Makarios unilaterally terminated the Treaty of Guarantee, and later he denounced the Treaty of Alliance. He also requested aid from the Soviets in 1964 to deal with the Turkish invasion threat, and a Soviet-Cypriote alliance was formed, intensifying great-power rivalry on the island and further complicating efforts to reconcile Greek and Turkish Cypriote communities. He agreed to unilateral British military intervention to forestall a threatened Turkish invasion, but rejected a broader-based NATO force proposed by the British. When the British rejected peacekeeping alone beyond three months, a peacekeeping force was urgently formed mostly from NATO-member contributions under UN auspices, becoming operational in March 1964 and totaling 6,500 two months later.

The UN, also clashing with the Anglo-American approach, supported the principle of Cypriote integrity, permitting Cypriote independence from NATO and peaceful change among Cypriotes. The UN Security Council specified upon approving the Cyprus peacekeeping force that the latter should "contribute to . . . a return to normal conditions,"[11] and it provided a mediator for this purpose. The second UN mediator proposed in 1965 Cypriote renunciation of *enosis*, prohibition of partition, and a guarantee of Turkish-Cypriote rights by the UN; mediation efforts on this basis continue at present, as does deployment of the UN force in a neutral zone between Greek and Turkish areas.

The UN force was at times inadequate to manage intercommunal violence and Greek and Turkish links to it. When fighting persisted in 1964, a Turkish decision to invade in June was revoked only by strong American opposition; two months later, Greek-Cypriote attacks against Turkish villages led to Turkish bombing of Greek-Cypriote towns. New Cypriote violence in 1967 brought a Greco-Turkish crisis that was defused by American mediation and Greek agreement to reduce its much augmented military presence on the island. And when a Greek military regime attempted to overthrow Makarios in 1974, the Turks invaded and partitioned the island politically and demographically.

Differences between the United States and the Soviet Union during the Cold War period prevented collective great-power effort to improve and stabilize Greek-Turkish Cypriote relations. However, superpower rivalry dissipated when crisis on the island threatened the outbreak of Greco-Turkish war, into which the superpowers could be drawn. In the 1964 crisis, for example, the United States and the Soviets indicated they would not support a Turkish invasion, and a cease-fire was arranged through the UN. In 1974, also, the superpowers both worked for a cease-fire after the Turks invaded.

Since 1974, and extending into the post–Cold War period, reconciliation of Greek and Turkish Cypriotes has been impeded by the territorial division between them. As before, great-power involvement has been mostly limited to defusing confrontations between the two communities. Periodic efforts by UN mediators to reconcile Greek and Turkish Cypriote leaders have failed. Turkish Cypriotes insist on a loose confederation that provides some sovereignty to the third of the island they control, while Greek Cypriotes want a close-knit federation within a single state. At issue also is the resettlement of Greek and Turkish Cypriotes who lost their homes as a result of the 1974 Turkish invasion, and the restructuring of a unified state. A stumbling block to negotiating success has been the volatile and often strained relations between Greece and Turkey.[12]

The Cyprus conflict is in an endgame stage as a result of intense negotiations spurred by UN Secretary-General Kofi Annan early in 2004. The negotiations produced what Annan called a final plan for the reunification of Cyprus, to take effect before Cyprus joined the European Union in May of that year. Requiring separate approval by referendum ballot by Greek and Turkish Cypriotes, the plan failed when it was approved by Turkish Cypriotes but rejected by the Greek community in April 2004.

Croat/Muslim/Serb Conflict in Bosnia Herzegovina (Bosnia II) (1992–1995)

Following the death of the Yugoslav dictator Josef Broz Tito in 1988, and the subsequent emergence of Serb nationalist leadership in Belgrade, the provinces of Slovenia and Croatia rebelled and separated from Yugoslavia. Outside states attempted to prevent these developments, which provided warning of later violence in neighboring Bosnia-Herzegovina, but were unable to do so. Bosnia-Herzegovina decided on separation by referendum on February 29 and March 1, 1992, whereupon it was confronted by two invasions, each associated with widespread atrocities against its mostly Muslim civilian population. One of these, by the Serb-dominated Yugoslav army moving from the north and east, besieged the Bosnian capitol of Sarajevo and supported poorly disciplined Serb irregulars, who assaulted Serb towns and ultimately gained control of 70 percent of Bosnian territory. The army withdrew shortly afterward, turning over its weapons stocks and administrative centers to Serb rebels. Second, newly independent Croatia attacked to the south and west, protecting Bosnian Croat enclaves against Muslim refugees fleeing the Serb attacks and besieging the city of Mostar. The fledgling and largely unarmed Bosnian government requested UN assistance to contain the ensuing humanitarian disaster and the threat to its own authority from these onslaughts.

Warned about instability in the former Yugoslavia and informed about the effects of Bosnian violence, the major states were politically constrained in their response. The United States and the Soviet Union, once rivals for influence in Yugoslavia, no longer were prepared after the end of the Cold War to intervene strongly in its internal affairs. The Soviet Union had itself fragmented by 1992, and the United States, freed from the pressures of a worldwide competitor, sharply reduced the scope of its Balkan interests and deferred to the most important Western European states, including Britain, France, and Germany, on Bosnian questions. Those countries, energized by the prospect that European countries could now take more responsibility than before for managing conflict in their region, focused on the immediate emergency associated with the ethnic cleansing of the Muslim population by Bosnian Serbs and on supplying food to cities cut off by the violence.

International humanitarian support for the Bosnian government was unequivocal. A UN mission headquarters was put in place by April 1992, and a peacekeeping force with a nucleus of British and French forces was first deployed between Muslims and Serbs the following July in the Sarajevo area and numbered 9,000 by November 1992. UN peacekeepers were also stationed between Muslims and Croats following a February 1994 truce in Mostar, and an informal power-sharing agreement was established for that city with a European Union-appointed mayor. The UN also began to airlift supplies and provide overland supply routes through Serb towns to Sarajevo. Its presence, later extended to six additional Muslim "safe areas," was intended to stop the fighting, permit negotiations on a settlement, and protect civilians, but without taking sides in the civil war. UN and EU mediators devised a peace proposal (the Vance-Owen Plan), according to which a single demilitarized Bosnian state would be divided into ten provinces, each with a multiethnic government. However, truces in the fighting were regularly broken, especially by the Bosnian Serbs, as each side exploited the UN presence. The Serbs occasionally used UN soldiers as military shields and took them hostage, the Muslim-dominated Bosnian regime was enabled to concentrate solely on fighting the Serbs, and each primary antagonist employed UN-negotiated truces to strengthen its forces. The antagonists deadlocked on the Vance-Owen Plan.

Efforts to stop the violence and to negotiate a settlement were hindered also by major-state differences. The British and French emphasized conciliatory rather than coercive intervention, anxious that the Serbs might react to coercive measures by targeting UN peacekeepers. The United States, strongly opposed to the Bosnian Serb use of force for territorial gain and to the use of American ground forces to oppose the Bosnian Serbs, proposed in the spring of 1993 lifting an earlier-enacted UN weapons embargo for Bosnia-Herzegovina, and implementing air strikes against Bosnian Serb emplacements. Britain and France vigorously resisted those proposals. Subsequently, the Americans covertly armed the Bosnian Muslims and arranged a Muslim-Croat confederation to shift the balance of power against the Serbs. Russia supported the Serbs because of traditional Slavic ties, resisting any use of force against them. A "Contact Group" of five major states (the United States, Russia, Britain, France, and Germany), established in the spring of 1994 to reconcile these differences, was deeply divided on the conditions for removing UN punitive sanctions placed against the Serbs for their use of force, on the use of force against the Serbs, and on the practicality of forcing the Serbs to retreat from areas in Bosnia under their control. In light of this deadlock, UN involvement in Bosnia-Herzegovina discouraged more flagrant unilateral involvement by outside states, which could have widened the fighting. But it also undercut the chances of punitive action for truce violations, despite the futility of conciliatory intervention between the parties, and it permitted the primary antagonists to persist in aiming at a one-sided solution.

The deadlock was broken in the summer of 1995, as joint Muslim-Croat military action made gains at the expense of the Serbs, and as the Serbs, by shelling Muslim safe zones in eastern Bosnia, provoked a more energetic opposition within the Contact Group. NATO rather than the UN took the lead in employing force coercively against Serb targets in September 1995, and the Serbs accepted a cease-fire on the basis of a Contact Group proposal giving them control over 49 percent of the country, with the remainder being controlled by a Muslim-Croat federation. The three sides accepted this plan, designed to keep Bosnia-Herzegovina intact, at a November 1995 conference at Dayton, Ohio. The plan's implementation has been very slow, as cooperation between the primary antagonists has been grudging and limited.[13]

Part III

Case Analysis

Chapter 5

Local Ethnic Conflict as an International Problem

The interplay between localized ethnic antagonists and the international political environment is evident in the earliest stages of the cases presented in chapter 4. This chapter studies the emergence of local ethnic conflicts and the impact of the great powers upon them. It discusses the background of the local conflicts, the conditions that intensified them, and the local consequences of collective great-power activity. Analysis here is limited to the calculations that brought the local antagonists to seek great-power intervention, and how that intervention, when it eventually occurred, affected the relationship between the local antagonists. Why and how the major states intervene collectively in localized ethnic conflict, and how the ethnic antagonists react to it, will be extensively discussed later.

In general, the primary antagonists seek to use the great powers to legitimate local positions, compensate for weaknesses in those positions, and prevail locally in spite of these weaknesses. Desiring great-power support on their own terms, they value that support as it serves as a "power multiplier" favorable to their local interests. The multiplier effect is larger and more significant when the balance of forces in the local conflict is one-sided.

The local conflicts are exacerbated by four specific causes, each of which is discussed in this chapter. Local causes include a problematic relationship between the central government and its ethnic challenger and the challenger's political and economic grievances. Other causes of such conflict are demonstrated effects of conflict outside the local arena and outside actors' involvement in the local arena. Of these sources of localized ethnic tensions, economic and political grievances directed at the ruling government constitute the most important. Nationalism—unified identity on the part of the ethnic antagonists—is unexpectedly weak or missing at the outset of each of these cases.

The absence of nationalism in these conflicts has two major consequences. First, it weakens the insurgents relative to the regime governing them, increasing for those insurgents the importance of sympathetic outside states to remedy their weakness. This dependence renders them vulnerable to manipulation by those supporters. Second, the absence of nationalism contributes to internationalizing the local conflict, as weaker primary antagonists seek major-power intervention to gain greater accommodation from the opposing antagonist. The possibility that great-power influence can be brought to bear in this way upon the stronger local antagonist importantly affects whether or not the weaker side intensifies the local conflict. The stronger ethnic rival is also required to formulate and pursue policies to shape the positions of the major states, and to reconcile these policies with its behavior toward its opponent.

This chapter also deals with important differences in political outlook between the primary antagonists in local ethnic conflict, on one hand, and the great powers on the other. While some great-power activity is indeed shaped by the local antagonists, the major states tend to be more concerned about each other than about the primary ethnic antagonists, and unlike the latter, are required to defend broadly defined international positions. They therefore tend to view local ethnic conflict in terms of their broader interests. Any particular great power's response to local conflict is likely to be conditioned more by the propensity of other states, and especially other major states, to intervene on their own in that conflict than by the specific attributes and attitudes of the ethnic antagonists. When disinclined to intervene, the major states may even be relatively disinterested, especially at first, in the local conflict.

Contributors to Local Ethnic Tension

Intrastate ethnic tensions are brought about by (1) the central government's relationship with its ethnic challenger; (2) the challenger's political and economic grievances; (3) demonstration effects outside the arena of ethnic tension; and (4) the involvement of outside actors in the local arena. These will be discussed in turn.

The Primary-Antagonist Relationship

Each of the eight cases reflects a relationship between a central government, or core political entity, and a cultural group or groups resisting the central government's authority in some specific area possibly quite distant from the center. The types of rule employed by the central government determine whether the subject peoples enjoy cultural or political autonomy in relation to core institutions—that is, whether they are allowed to protect their cultural traditions and their freedom to petition to gain redress of grievances. The strength of rule by core institutions is defined here in terms of the degree of autonomy provided to subjects of different ethnic persuasions. Weak rule is said to prevail if the ruling government permits cultural autonomy to the peripheral subject group, or, in the absence of such autonomy, if it creates a decentralized political system allowing that group to share power (Belgium, Greece, Bosnia I, Armenia, Cyprus, and Bosnia II). By contrast, strong rule in the area of resistance allows for no cultural or political autonomy for ethnic groups living in that area (the Memel, the Congo). Table 5.1 describes this distinction.

In the weak-rule instances, cultural and political autonomy are not produced by demand of the subject peoples but by the convenience of the dominant power, which prefers more detached rule to more forceful or direct administration. This choice is logical in light of the geography of occupation: each of the contested areas in question is of peripheral rather than central importance for the dominant power. For example, Belgium, ruled for several centuries from Madrid, Vienna, Paris, or The Hague, is said to have been prior to its independence "always an unintegrated periphery of

TABLE 5.1
Weak and Strong Types of Peripheral Rule

Weak rule	Belgium Greece Bosnia I Armenia Cyprus Bosnia II
Strong rule	the Memel the Congo

some distant dynasty."[1] Greece was at the periphery of the Ottoman Empire; inasmuch as Turkish rule was relatively weak and the Greeks were free to amass economic fortunes, the Ottoman system, in which rights for Christians were bought through economic payoffs, allowed some Greeks to benefit enormously relative to their fellows.[2] Such a condition helps explain why Greek revolutionary leaders were such intense rivals during their war for independence that their armies fought each other on several occasions when they were not fighting the Turks.

Bosnia-Herzegovina was the most distant from Constantinople of any province in the Ottoman Empire in the 1870s. The frontier between Bosnia-Herzegovina and Montenegro was then poorly controlled by the Turks and heavily trafficked by bandits, and the frustration of Christian Slavs in the region was mainly directed at Moslem landowners, who were substantially independent of Turkish rule. The Armenian homeland in Eastern Anatolia was also on the periphery of the Ottoman Empire, being substantially remote from both Turks and Armenians in Constantinople. By the late nineteenth century, Ottoman rulers in that area were only weakly policed from Constantinople, a condition that helps explain why the Sultan's repeated approval of reforms for the Armenians were, even if sincere, invariably ignored. In 1954 the British offered Cypriotes limited self-government under British sovereignty, and self-government was also provided to all inhabitants of Bosnia-Herzegovina within the federal system of Yugoslavia.

The Memel and the Congo, in which no autonomy was given to a peripheral area, illustrate strong rule from the center and no desire for localized separation from it. In the Memel at the time of the outbreak of the First World War, "there was little to set it apart from the rest of North-eastern Germany. During the four years from 1914 to 1918 its population did not waver once in their loyalty to Germany, but thought of themselves always as Germans."[3] The ethnic problem in the Memel was precipitated when the territory was severed from Germany in peace arrangements concluding the First World War.

The Belgians exerted strong authority in the Congo, administering it as a sound business venture and neglecting the needs of the African population. When rioting occurred in the colony in January 1958, the Belgians were totally unprepared to cope with the resulting instability. The Belgian government could not even attempt to control the colony by force, the Belgian constitution specifying that only volunteer military service was allowed in the Congo, and the rioting shattered the Belgian myth that all was well in the territory. By 1960, when Belgium first announced a willingness to permit self-government there, "the breakdown of security in the Congo," according to Catherine Hoskyns, "made an agreement of some kind more vital to Belgium than to the Congolese. In the event of a deadlock the Congolese leaders could return to the Congo and organize a campaign of civil disobedience all over the country. Such a campaign would further discredit the administration, yet short of using the army Belgium would have no means of controlling it."[4]

Irrespective of whether rule from the center is strong or weak, nationalism, defined as mass loyalty to an ethnic group,[5] is initially weak or absent within the cultural groupings investigated here.[6] This is not because of political rulers' suppression of the cultural identity of their subjects; in none of these cases, in fact, did the rulers suppress the essential elements of their subjects' cultural identity. (Far more sensitive and disputed was the subject group's demand for local self-government.) The weak national identity of the subject cultures can be attributed to premodern cultures in which there was little or no intermingling with the ruling culture (Bosnia I, Armenia, and the Congo) or, alternatively, to the intermingling of cultures associated with economic modernity (Belgium, Greece, Cyprus, the Memel, and Bosnia II). Table 5.2 displays this distinction.

The premodern cases are all instances of institutionalized political discrimination directed at the subject culture in which the inequality could be expected to discourage social and economic intermingling. Although the Dutch king granted the Belgians a liberal constitution, with equal Belgian representation in one house of the Dutch parliament, Belgian complaints occurred about taxation, about the predominant Dutch public administration in Belgium, and about Dutch control of banks and schools. The Greeks, despite having economic autonomy from the Turks,

TABLE 5.2
Prenational Cultures

Premodern	Belgium Greece Bosnia I Armenia the Congo
Economic modernity	Cyprus the Memel Bosnia II

were discriminated against in land ownership. In Bosnia I, the Turks depended on Muslim converts to rule over their Christian subjects, and the Christians were kept politically and economically subservient. In Armenia, by the late nineteenth century the Turks relied heavily upon the Kurds to control their Armenian subjects, and Kurdish demands and the absence of protection against those demands in the Turkish system constituted the major Armenian grievances. And in the Congo, the Belgian settlers and missionaries, supported by Belgian administrators, enjoyed a dominant political and economic position.

Political frustrations of the subject cultures are not in these cases associated with well-developed cultural consciousness, because such a consciousness had not yet been created; for the same reason, cultural characteristics of the subject peoples did not directly inspire collective political action. In some cases political frustrations did not increase cultural identity because the rulers depended on leaders of the subject peoples for their overall authority in those areas. Chiefs of the subject group, as in Greece, Belgium, and Armenia, while giving nominal allegiance to the empire, amassed enormous power of their own relative to their countrymen. An Armenian economic elite in Constantinople came to be most responsible for trading and financial affairs in the Ottoman Empire; but this elite was psychologically distant from the more provincial and much less well-off Armenians in Eastern Anatolia, who were subjected to arbitrary mistreatment at the hands of the Kurds and systematically denied political equality in relation to the Muslim population. At the outset of the Greek revolution, more modernized Greeks on the offshore islands depended for their livelihoods on peaceful ocean-going trade with their neighbors and were less sympathetic to war against the Turks than were Greeks on the mainland.[7]

By contrast, in the modern cases, in which ruling and subject populations were considerably intermingled, cultural consciousness was retarded by economic interdependence. It has been argued that "economic development—increased social mobilization and communication—appear to have increased ethnic tensions and to be conducive to separatist demands."[8] The idea is that nationalism presupposes awareness of ethnic differences with other groupings, a condition that necessitates economic interaction with those groups. But where there is considerable intermingling of populations, as occurred for example in the Memel, in Cyprus, and in twentieth-century Bosnia-Herzegovina, the modernized multiethnic character of an area inspires peaceful interaction rather than separatism. Perhaps the classic instance in which modernity contributed to pacific relations between ethnic groups was in the Memel, where lengthy peaceful pursuits across ethnic lines in a relatively provincial area resulted in the creation of a hybrid ethnic group—the Memellander—that became the largest ethnic grouping in the territory.[9] In Cyprus, where Greeks comprised 80 percent of the population and Turks 20 percent, the island prior to independence was characterized as "an ethnographical fruit-cake in which the Greek and Turkish currants were mixed up in every town and village and often in every street,"[10] making ethnic separation extraordinarily difficult. A similar condition appears to have characterized Bosnia-Herzegovina up to the early 1990s.

To be sure, violence between government and ethnic challenger accentuates cultural associations and thereby promoted the challenging group's determination to separate from the alien state, as in the Greek, Cyprus, and two Bosnia-Herzegovina cases. However, in such cases ethnic unity founders over the longer term, either because of rivalries between the challenger's factions or because of the challenger's dissatisfaction with the behavior of an ethnically allied state, whose assistance is depended upon. In the Greek case, intense rivalry existed between revolutionary factions; civil war among Greeks broke out in the fourth year of the ten-year Greek insurrection against the Turks.[11] Slavic unity in the 1875 revolution against Muslim landowners allied with the Ottoman Empire diminished following Turkish defeat of Serbia and Montenegro in 1876, when Russian-Serb relations were strained. Serb ethnic unity increased in Bosnia II during four years of war, yet the subsequent sharp strains between the Serb-dominated Belgrade government and the Bosnian Serbs over the scope of negotiated Serb concessions in Bosnia-Herzegovina illustrated the tendency of such unity to deteriorate with the onset of military stalemate and political setbacks. The split between the Greek military government and Greek Cypriote leader Archbishop Makarios in the 1960s caused by the American-pushed double *enosis* project was another example of deteriorating ethnic unity.[12]

Grievances of the Ethnic Challenger

While ethnic self-awareness in these cases tends to be low, economic and political grievances are frequently important causes of ethnic conflict. Two types of economic and political grievances are reflected in the cases. Economic grievances are directed to (1) arbitrary restrictions directed by the central government toward the ethnic challenger, which relegate it to secondary status (Greece, Bosnia I, and Armenia); or to (2) general economic adversity affecting all sectors of the population which, in the context of broader dissatisfaction, lessened the challenging group's acceptance of the central government (Belgium, Bosnia II). Political grievances are directed to (1) inequities in treatment by political institutions, including the difficulty of bringing court suits; or (2) the failure of the police to prevent impositions against the ethnic group carried out by other members of society, which stimulate efforts by the group in question to gain redress (Belgium, Armenia, Bosnia I, Cyprus, and the Congo). In the latter instance, when the ruling government does not redress these grievances, the ethnic challenger can upgrade its demands, shifting from petitioner to demander of equal treatment (Belgium, Bosnia I, the Congo, and Cyprus), or it can remain a petitioner (Armenia).[13] Each of these four types of grievance, displayed in table 5.3, will now be elaborated upon in reference to our cases.

In Greece, Greeks enjoyed considerable economic and social autonomy from the Turks, and Turkish political rule was relatively mild. There, arbitrary economic restrictions were a major Greek irritant.[14] The extremely difficult conditions for Serbs in Bosnia-Herzegovina relative to Muslim landowners, and for Armenians relative to the Kurds, promoted demands by the repressed peoples for economic reforms. In the Belgian and Bosnia II cases, economic adversity stimulated dissatisfaction with the ruling regime. In Belgium deteriorating economic conditions led to demands for greater political influence for the non-Dutch population. In contemporary Bosnia-Herzegovina, where the federal government had an important social welfare role in the political system, the lessening of that role in the post-Communist era created uncertainties for the poorer sectors, providing incentives for ethnic communities to provide substitute social-welfare benefits.[15]

TABLE 5.3
Economic and Political Grievances

Arbitrary Economic Restrictions	*Economic Adversity*	*Arbitrary Government*	*Upgraded Political Demands*
Greece	Belgium	Belgium	Belgium
Bosnia I	Bosnia II	Bosnia I	Bosnia I
Armenia		Armenia	the Congo
		the Congo	Cyprus
		Cyprus	

Political grievances challenge the basis for central-government authority, and in some cases directly affect the expansion of the challenging group's political aims. Here the point is that the challenger ordinarily does not reject the central government's authority at the outset of the local conflict. In Belgium, for example, opposition to the Dutch by 1828 was based on a program demanding freedom of the press, instruction, and worship, and for allocation of ministerial responsibility to Belgians.[16] Even after the start of the Belgian revolution in 1830, its leaders at first sought Belgian autonomy under Dutch rule. The Slav revolution in Bosnia-Herzegovina is said to have been "in essence a rising against agrarian conditions, grinding taxation, and brutality,"[17] and in the Armenian case, political action was taken to ease Kurdish and Circassian impositions upon Armenians and arbitrary Turkish taxation of them. In the Congo and Cyprus cases, those who sought to ease colonial rule initially had in mind the retention, following independence, of considerable power in local affairs by the former colonizing state. In the Congo, for example, the revolutionaries at first sought continued Belgian control of the Congolese army so as to more effectively stamp out localized opposition to the new regime; after Cypriote independence, Great Britain retained considerable involvement in the new state through the Cypriote power-sharing framework and through continued British use of air bases in the country.

The passage from a petitioner phase to what I. William Zartman has termed a "consolidation" phase of challenging and resisting the central regime varies in these cases.[18] In Belgium, Cyprus, and the Congo, the passage from one phase to the next was accomplished very quickly. The rapid sequence in the latter instances is attributable either to the high level of grievances (Cyprus, the Congo) or to the absence of any traditional accommodation with the particular rulers (Belgium). For the Christian Slavs, on the other hand, the shift from the first phase to the second was delayed, and affected by efforts by Austrian, Russian, and Serb pan-Slav societies and by Serbia and Montenegro to direct the Slavic revolution in Bosnia-Herzegovina for their own purposes. Those supporters of the Slavic revolution appeared to stimulate the revolutionists to steadily increase their political demands upon the Ottoman colonizer.[19] In Cyprus, the new phase appeared to coincide with Makarios's 1963 decision, strongly supported by Greece, to torpedo the power-sharing agreement in favor of *enosis* for Cyprus. And for the Armenians, who delayed formal resistance even after their petitions were repeatedly rejected, the subsequent phase apparently never arrived.

Demonstration Effects

Demonstration effects occur when the ethnic challenger's resistance to the central regime is spurred by awareness of prior rebellion elsewhere (Belgium, Bosnia I and II, Cyprus, and the Congo). Wider ethnic unrest was provoked by the French Revolution, which contributed to insurrection by the Belgians and the Greeks, and by European decolonization, which stimulated revolt in Cyprus and in the Congo. More specifically, revolution in Belgium in 1830 was preceded one month earlier by insurrection in Paris. Serbs in Bosnia and Herzegovina in the 1870s were stimulated by repeated revolutionary uprisings against the Turks in Montenegro, by a prior Herzegovina insurrection in 1863 which ended with political gains for the Serbs, and by violence between Muslim and Christian Slavs in neighboring Austria-Hungary in the months preceding the Bosnia-Herzegovina revolt. And a substantial part of Bosnia (except for much of the Serb population) was encouraged in 1992 to separate from Belgrade by prior insurrections in Slovenia and Croatia.

According to Walker Connor, the catalytic effect of outside events upon localized ethnic assertion has been increased by modernization and advances in communication.[20] Among the cases studied here, ethnic demonstration—that is, the impact of outside unrest carried out by culturally similar peoples—is visible only in the Bosnia cases, in which cultural groupings were both large and did not coincide with state boundaries. In the Bosnia I case, premodern Slavic peoples in Bosnia-Herzegovina revolted more than a decade after initial restiveness by neighboring Slavs in the Ottoman Empire, while in the Bosnia II case, Serbs inside the newly created state of Bosnia-Herzegovina imitated their Serb brothers in neighboring Croatia, who had successfully defied the new state of Croatia only a few months earlier. By contrast, political demonstration brought about by ethnically unrelated peoples is more linked to broadly significant international developments. "Since the advent of the Age of Nationalism," Connor has written, "contacts between groups, each of whom possesses even a dim sense of a separate ethnic heritage, have tended to cement and reinforce the sense of uniqueness."[21] For example, revolution in Belgium was linked to prior unrest in Paris because of the historical connection between late-seventeenth-century revolutionary activity in Belgium against Austro-Hungarian authority there, on one hand, and the immediate aftermath of the French Revolution of 1789, on the other. For prenationalist cases, such as that of the Congo, contacts between cultural elites implant the sense of uniqueness that spreads later on. For example, Lumumba's attendance at the December 1958 All-African Peoples Conference in Accra, Ghana, only two months after the forming in Leopoldville of his MNC party aimed at creating a national consciousness for his country, is said to have been decisive for his personal development and the development of his party. In Accra he was first exposed to the broader effects of European decolonization of African self-determination.[22]

The Involvement of Outside Actors

Finally, the ethnic challenger's rebellion is precipitated by outside actors in six of the eight cases: Russia stimulated revolution in Greece; Serbia and Montenegro stimulated revolution in Bosnia in 1875; the British and Russians compelled the Turks to accept Article 61 of the 1878 Treaty of Berlin, which required the Ottoman Porte to introduce reforms as demanded by Armenian local residents and to ameliorate their living conditions; Greece sought to be united with Cyprus; and Serbia and Croatia stimulated revolution against the newly created state of Bosnia-Herzegovina. Finally, separation of the Memel from Germany was first sought by Lithuanians living in the United States in 1914 and then, following the end of the First World War, by a Lithuanian delegation to the Versailles peace conference seeking recognition for Lithuania as a state.[23]

In these cases, the tie between sympathetic outside powers and local loyalists among the primary antagonists provides a kind of national incubation, in which an ethnic community poorly conscious of itself is guided into political expression. The outside actor is always *initially* the active agent and the primary antagonist passive, but under revolutionary conditions the relationship can be transformed. Thus, selected members of the Greek elite initially acted as agents of the Russian government in stirring revolution against the Turks. When the Russian government subsequently rejected the consequences of its own support of revolution—because of its suspicions of nationalism that had grown out of the French Revolution—the Greeks, whose social ties to the Russian government were limited to the Christian Orthodox religion, turned to other European states for assistance, most notably England. In Cyprus also, the already assertive Greek-Cypriote government became by the mid-1960s still more activist, following the emergence of right-wing Greek governments dedicated to the double *enosis* objective; Makarios used the United Nations and the Soviet Union to counterbalance pressures against him exerted by Greece and the United States.

Outside instigation of ethnic revolt, as in the Greece, Cyprus, and Bosnia cases, is made possible by the largely fictitious character of state frontiers. Under such conditions, cultural ties across state lines can as in the two Bosnia cases be manipulated by an outside government to compete with and prevail over the disaffected group's nominal government for that group's attachment. In the Cyprus case, on the other hand, the competition was not based on ethnic attachment but on more common political rivalry as a Greek right-wing military regime sought to topple the Makarios government in Cyprus by covert means. And where outside attachments of any kind were less strong, insurrectionist leaders can maintain ties with a number of governments, the connections with which can ultimately be decisive but only slowly mature. In the Greek case, in which linkages with European states ultimately proved crucial for the Greek cause, a hundred foreign officers serving in private capacity, whose cadres included at least five different nationalities, were by 1822 formed into a single combatant unit under a Greek commander.[24]

Instigation of ethnic revolt by outside powers makes forecasting ethnic insurgency more difficult. When instigation is common knowledge, the instigator would wish to time the revolt or its own involvement so as to enhance the chances of its success, choosing a time when other outside interested parties are distracted or otherwise unable to respond. That is to say, it would wish to interfere with other interested parties' ability to forecast the event. This is illustrated by the Lithuanian invasion of the Memel in 1923, which occurred shortly after French military intervention in the German Ruhr. By contrast, Russian instigation of revolt in Greece and the Slavic countries' involvement in the first Bosnian revolt were secretive. In the latter two cases, instigation was designed to expose the weaknesses of the occupying Ottoman occupier and to pressure the great powers to intervene diplomatically to compel the Empire to retreat from its forward position. However, insofar as the revolutionary activity would probably not have occurred in the absence of the hidden linkage, the instigating countries' determination to hide their link to the insurrections would have impeded the ability of outside states to forecast them.

The Impact of Collective Great-Power Activity

Collective great-power PD has a major impact on the local ethnic conflict. We may distinguish collective major-state interventionist PD in the early stage of the local conflict, on one hand, from PD later on when the local antagonists are ready for accommodation. In both instances, major-power interests affect the timing and mode of collective intervention, but differences are evident between them in the purposes for the intervention and in the interplay between local antagonists and the major states. Initial collective PD aims at preventing the local conflict from intensifying and deteriorating, while later PD establishes a framework to regulate relations between the local antagonists.

The balance of influence between ethnic antagonists and the great powers shifts, moreover, over the life of the local conflicts. In the initial stage of the conflict, one local antagonist typically contributes to great-power involvement, defining a problematic issue that the major states come to address. The importance of this contribution must be understood in light of the resistance of the opposing antagonist, typically the local central regime, to this involvement.[25] By contrast, local antagonist influence on the great powers is more curtailed in the endgame stage of the local conflict. Prior to the endgame, the resistance to great-power involvement and the gap between the antagonists' positions ensures the failure of great-power interventionist PD. To succeed, interventionist PD requires independent action that leads each local antagonist to accept a compromise agreement.

Initial Collective Great-Power Intervention

The major states are stimulated to collectively intervene in small-state ethnic conflict by two considerations stemming from the local conflict: (1) they are commonly asked to do so by the weaker of the primary antagonists; and (2) they are led to do so following prior intervention into those conflicts by neighboring states. The first consideration highlights how the major states work to level primary-antagonist capabilities in the local conflict (Belgium, Greece, Bosnia I and II, Armenia, the Congo, and Cyprus). The second plays up how, in the wake of outside state provocations of local hostilities, PD sometimes take the form of great-power crisis management (Belgium, Bosnia I and II, the Memel, the Congo, and Cyprus; table 5.4).

Initial collective interventionist PD commonly aims at compensating the weaker ethnic faction for the superior strength of the stronger. In this regard, PD becomes more difficult in proportion to the military inequality of the primary antagonists; the more clearly superior militarily the stronger side perceives itself to be, the more likely it is to discourage outside intervention

TABLE 5.4
Local Precipitants of Initial Great-Power Intervention

Primary Antagonist Request	*Local Crisis Management*
Belgium	Belgium
Greece	Bosnia I
Bosnia I	the Memel
Armenia	the Congo
the Congo	Cyprus
Cyprus	Bosnia II
Bosnia II	

and concentrate on applying its own military strength. In the Greek, Slav, and Armenian cases, the Ottoman Empire was militarily stronger. Its problem was in the widely perceived excesses of its attempts to subdue its ethnic opponents by force. Its occasional brutal suppression of its opponents stimulated great-power intervention in those cases—the Greek Revolution and Armenian agitation—in which the great powers had not yet intervened forcefully; in the Greek case the consequence was a steadily deepening great-power intervention, and in the Armenian case the excesses led to occasional great-power steps to halt the violence.

In Bosnia I, the major states sought to discourage Turkish military suppression of the revolt in order to enhance the chances of successful mediation. In this instance, the Turkish military presence was limited to only a few fortified garrisons; other than to relieve garrisons besieged by the rebels, the Turks observed military restraint as long as the neighboring Serbs and Montenegrins practiced it—that is, until the latter intervened in Bosnia-Herzegovina in June 1876, about a year after the revolt broke out. In the Congo case (with respect to the military intervention by Belgium and the Katanga secession) and in contemporary Bosnia, preponderant strength was on the side of the insurgents. In the latter instance, the Bosnian Serb political problem was similar to the one facing the militarily formidable Ottoman Empire earlier. In general, great-power PD is situationally easier when the primary antagonists are more relatively balanced, as in Belgium, the Memel, and Cyprus. The more one-sided the relationship between the primary antagonists, the more difficult becomes the great-power challenge of coercing the stronger side to approve a settlement acceptable to both sides.

As a leveller of primary antagonist capabilities, the major states succeed even before the problem-solving stage in preventing the stronger primary antagonist from pursuing and possibly imposing a military solution in each of the cases examined here. Thus they prevented the Dutch government from using force to respond to the Belgian revolt; they prevented the Ottoman government from forcibly putting down opposition in Greece, in the Bosnian insurrection of 1875, and in Armenia; they prevented war between the new Congo government and military forces in Katanga; they defused conflict between Greek and Turkish Cypriotes; and they acted as an antidote to Croat and especially Serb military action to partition Bosnia in the 1990s.

A second local reason for collective great-power intervention is the prior publicized involvement of outside states sympathetic to one of the primary antagonists, as in French support for Belgian independence from the Dutch; Serb and Montenegrin volunteer participation in the Slav revolt against Muslim landowners and the Turks in 1875; Belgian support for European interests in the Congo, and in the Katanga secession in particular; Greek and Turkish support of the rival Greek and Turkish factions in Cyprus; Belgrade's support for Serb irregular action against the new Bosnia-Herzegovina government; and Lithuania's military support of the Lithuanian uprising in the Memel.[26] Except for Yugoslavia's support for Serbs in Bosnia-Herzegovina, the outside sympathizers desired collective great-power intervention to compel the central regime to retreat and thereby avoid wider hostilities. However, the major powers do not intervene primarily to satisfy the prior intervenors or to compel the central regime to concede to the rebels. They become involved to counter outside-state legitimation of local resistance to central authority, and to forestall potential dangers associated with outside-state involvement in the local conflict.

These dangers are partly local: involvement of sympathetic outside states promotes hostility and often violence between the local factions, and often increases the central regime's determination to suppress the resistors. But the dangers are also broader, as sympathetic outside-state involvement raises the danger of war between outside sympathizers and the embattled central regime.[27] The latter problem is exacerbated by hard-to-control developments that heighten problematic interstate aspects of the local conflict—either because they provide incentives for unilateral involvement by major states (as in the possibility of French intervention in Belgium or Russian intervention in the Slavic revolution) or, if the central government is to be overwhelmed by the resistance, they encourage neighboring countries—including great powers—to fight over the spoils (as was threatened in the Congo, in the Memel, and in the joint Croatian-Serb effort to partition Bosnia-Herzegovina). As the level of perceived international danger from the local confrontation increased, the major states practice PD as crisis management.

But while PD under these circumstances is perceived as more urgent, the outlook for success is more problematic. This is because the central regime is here more inclined to be suspicious of outside efforts to assist the ethnic rebels, to act to suppress them on its own, and to defend its political prerogatives. The exacerbation of local hostilities thus contributes to the launching of PD but also to its deadlock.

Great-Power Problem Solving

Political problem solving in these cases is linked to great-power rejection of a categorical military settlement. Three types of political solutions may be distinguished (table 5.5): (1) power separation, in which the rebellious ethnic group is allowed to form its own distinct state (Belgium, Greece, Bosnia I, and the Congo); (2) power sharing, in which the antagonists are provided with incentives and protections to remain in the same state (Armenia and the Memel);[28] and (3) a combination solution, in which the antagonists remain in a common state but the state is divided into zones in which one or another group is ascendant (Bosnia II) (table 5). In power-separation agreements, ethnic rebels are aided in ending their subordination to the central regime despite the lingering interests of the latter to retain authority over them. These agreements do not regulate political relations among factions of the newly independent states.

Power-sharing agreements regulate relations between diverse ethnic groups in a particular state but do not extend to neighboring states, which continue to be actively interested in the outcome. In the Memel, Nazi

TABLE 5.5
Great-Power Problem Solving

Power Separation	*Power Sharing*	*Combination Solution*
Belgium	Armenia	Bosnia II
Greece	the Memel	
Bosnia I		
the Congo		

Germany ultimately torpedoed the power-sharing agreement by aggressively attempting to politically attach the power-sharing area to itself. In the case of Armenia, Turkey's decision upon the outbreak of the First World War to invade Armenian Russia promised to undermine the Armenian power-sharing arrangement in any event: had the Turks prevailed in the war, they would only with great difficulty have been able to treat Russian Armenians differently from Armenians residing within the prewar Armenian homeland, and Turkish defeat in the actual case emboldened Russian Armenians to defend their Ottoman counterparts. Finally, in the combination solution of Bosnia II, power sharing could function only as long as the Croat, Muslim, and Serb military contingents were separated. The new Bosnian central government has been unable to enforce its authority in Serb-controlled areas, although it has desired to do so, and therefore is exceptionally weak in the confederal structure created for it.[29]

The great powers have the greatest impact upon ethnic conflicts when they worked to separate the revolutionary group from the alien state governing it. Under power sharing, the conflict inspiring the tension that led to power-sharing arrangements persists and can easily be manipulated for partisan purposes. The Memel case and the power-sharing agreement worked out in 1959 by Great Britain, Greece, and Turkey as guarantors of Cypriote independence show that an outside power can have such a large incentive to capitalize on this tension that the great powers would be unable to deter it from doing so. Moreover, as in the Cyprus case, an opportunistic state working to undermine a power-sharing agreement can be assisted in this object when also serving as a nominal guarantor of that agreement. The Dayton Agreement in Bosnia II provided for just this type of guarantor arrangement by Croatia and Serbia over both power sharing and power separation in Bosnia. The weaker the Bosnian state, the more delicate has become the role of Croatia and Serbia as guarantors of it.

In none of these cases is national self-determination implemented through great-power intervention. The new Belgian state required Flems and Walloons to coexist and share power. The same problem, much magnified, affected the fate of the Congo Republic in the 1960s after the great powers ensured its creation. The head of the new Greek state chosen by the great powers was Prince Otto of Bavaria, as the great-power governments rejected the national principle for the newly independent Greek state. The 1875 insurrection in Bosnia-Herzegovina led to Austro-Hungarian occupation of that territory in 1878, and to Austro-Hungarian annexation of it thirty years later. Armenia remained under Ottoman authority when political reforms were finally approved in 1914. Power sharing was imposed on the Memel, in Cyprus, and in Bosnia II as an obstacle to neighboring countries' demands for a national solution in the territories.

Two reasons may be cited for great-power rejection of the national self-determination principle. First, the stronger the national consciousness of one ethnic contender, the less chance it can coexist with other ethnic groups. A solution in these cases that serves the ideal territorial needs of one antagonist would only inflame its local opponents and pose continuing problems for the great powers no longer wishing to be burdened with them. This helps explain the great-power attraction for power-sharing arrangements *in those instances in which the primary antagonists were not to be separated.*

Second, the search for separation by the indigenous group can become a delicate issue for the great powers not only because one or another of them might seek preponderant influence over the group, but because a newly independent nationalist state would be more easily tempted to defy their demands. Thus the Russians, who had initially promoted the Greek cause in relation to the Ottoman Empire, disdained Greek nationalism;[30] the Austro-Hungarians squelched Slavic unity in Bosnia-Herzegovina in 1878 by occupying the territory; and the Americans, pursuing an even-handed policy, sought double *enosis* in Cyprus and the blunting of both Croat and Serb nationalism in Bosnia.

In short, where the great powers help create a new state, they fudge the question of nationality and deliberately reject new nation-states. And where they impose power-sharing arrangements, they not only fudge the national question but muddy the issue of political authority in the state. The most important reasons for these tendencies are to be found in great-power motivations, the subject of the following chapters.

Conclusions

Local antagonists' political and economic grievances are the most important cause of local ethnic conflict. By contrast, the degree of unity in ethnic antagonist groups to cultural ideals and attachments is relatively weak, and these ideals and attachments are generally insignificant for the emergence of ethnic conflict.

These tendencies are an important source of opportunity for collective great-power interventionist PD, for the lack of ethnic antagonist unity and national identity makes local antagonists more dependent upon outside assistance and support. As the great powers satisfy local antagonist needs, they become more consequential for the evolution of the local conflict. In particular, they can employ the local antagonists' dependence on them as leverage to help collectively manage that conflict. When they do so, they do not act to accentuate national differences but instead deflect them. Power separation and power sharing are much more important than are culture-based ideas for managing such conflict.

Providing opportunity for interventionist PD, the local antagonists' lack of unity and national identity also increases the difficulty of making intervention effective. Because of their weakness, ethnic antagonists can depend upon unilaterally minded outside actors, including great powers, bent on extending their own influence in the conflict area. Such outside states are frequently more willing than is an international coalition to satisfy antagonists' needs for assistance and support. When they support ethnic challengers against their central regime, or when they set in motion international rivalry for influence in the conflict area, these outside actors may precipitate confrontations that threaten wider war. Apart from preventing such a war, a collectively interventionist-minded coalition of major states must under such conditions seek to defuse or deter interventionist propensities by opportunistic states, and to prevail upon the local antagonists to depend on the coalition rather than on unilaterally acting states for support. The scale of this formidable assignment, its acceptance by internationally minded major states, its fate, and its pitfalls are detailed in the chapters that follow.

Chapter 6

Great-Power Objectives and Agenda Making

Moving beyond the local aspects of great-power PD initiatives, this study now addresses the timing and scope of PD in terms of great-power relationships. The interest here is in how relations between the major states affect their willingness and ability to practice insulationist and interventionist PD. It is argued that the timing and scope of collective great-power PD depend on (1) an agreed-upon great-power framework facilitating collective action toward the local conflict; (2) unilateral steps taken by some major states in the local conflict; and (3) primary antagonist initiatives designed to draw in the great powers into the local standoff. This chapter will discuss each of these.

PD initiatives are examined here by distinguishing four specific PD objectives present in all of our cases: (1) mutual consultation and collective decision making; (2) preventing great-power relationships from being perturbed by local conflict; (3) working toward the pacific settlement of local conflict disputes; and (4) persuading and coercing the local antagonists to accept collective great-power PD proposals. The first two of these objectives are linked to insulationist PD and the last two to interventionist PD. A fifth PD objective, limiting the supply of military capabilities to the primary antagonists, is present in three of the eight cases and is discussed in chapter 7, where it is treated as a force-dampening initiative.[1]

The first part of this chapter discusses insulationist goals, and the second part interventionist objectives. The process by which the great powers attempt on their own to forge consensus on both types of objectives is traced. One major conclusion is that insulationist goals are almost always easier for the major states to agree upon and collectively pursue than interventionist ones because of their perceived importance: they determine whether major-power relations are peaceful or warlike.

A second conclusion is that agreement on insulationist PD is necessary but not sufficient to realize interventionist PD. Concerned especially about insulationist PD, the major powers are repeatedly able in the case studies presented here to cope peacefully with disputes among themselves about the local conflict. Moreover, having succeeded in insulating the local conflict, they shift their collective attention to intervention questions. However, insulationist PD can be strong, while interventionist PD is weak or nonexistent.

Local-conflict developments leading the major states toward greater cooperation or division, and the collective ability of the great powers to influence the primary antagonists, are discussed in chapters 7, 8, and 9 of this study.

Insulationist PD and Norms of Cooperation

Norms of great-power cooperation, present in each of our cases on the emergence of local ethnic conflict, assist the insulationist objectives of consultation and of removing the local conflict as a factor in great-power relations.[2] In some instances, the norms reflect major-state action on the same issue in the past, and the great powers merely revisit the issue later on.[3] When the British and French governments decided in 1830 to call for a European Congress on Belgium, and were supported by the other three major European states, they were revisiting a question that preoccupied the major states in 1815. That year, the major states decided, in the Treaty of Paris concluding the Napoleonic War, to unify the former Austrian Netherlands with the newly restored Kingdom of Holland. As in 1815, the major states that had fought against Napoleon were determined to prevent, as efficiently as possible, French expansion into Belgium. Collective PD in the Bosnia I and Armenian cases was legitimated by a provision in the peace treaty concluding the Crimean War, in which the Ottoman Empire accepted the involvement of the major European states in protecting Christians in the Ottoman Empire. Austro-Russian entente on the Balkans and Anglo-Russian concerns about the Armenians followed frustrated major-state attempts to pursue these subjects and reflected the widely perceived deterioration in the ability of Ottoman political administration to safeguard Christian interests. Major-power responsibility for the Memel issue was grounded in the decision at the Versailles Conference to separate the Memel territory from Germany in the peace treaty concluding the First World War.

Prior action toward these local conflicts facilitates insulationist PD when those conflicts reappear, as the major states collectively build on the record they established earlier to legitimate mutual consultation and collective decision making and to insulate their relationship from developments in a particular region. The insulationist PD problem for the major states, pursuing these objectives, is to address in greater detail what they agreed upon in the past. In effect, a key agenda-setting contributor in these cases is widespread major-power determination to *implement*—under new and often difficult conditions—older priorities from a previously created collective framework.

In the Belgian case, consultation by British and French officials (notably between Charles Tallyrand, the French ambassador, and British leaders in London) and collective decision making (as in the joint Anglo-French decision to propose the holding of a European Congress to discuss the Belgian question) helped defuse the Belgian revolution as a problem for their relationship. In Bosnia I, extensive discussions took place between Austria, Russia, and Germany—spurred on by the German chancellor Otto von Bismarck, anxious to forestall Austro-Russian war over Balkan questions—over the terms of Austrian mediation between the primary antagonists in Bosnia-Herzegovina. Anglo-Russian consultations were more intermittent on the Armenian question, as England and Russia became rivals for influence with the Porte in Constantinople. England and Russia could then agree only that their rivalry in the region should not lead to war, and that the Turks should be required to conform to minimal humanitarian considerations in dealing with the Armenians. Finally, in the Memel, great-power consultations and localizing efforts were limited by the fact that the Memel was in practice a peripheral issue for the major states.

Great-power action toward the other four cases of ethnic conflict does not constitute revisiting of older decisions, the major states not having acted upon them earlier. In those cases, great-power norms of cooperation are more general and diffuse. Prompt, energetic major-state PD was forthcoming among these cases only in Bosnia II, a case emerging after the end of the Soviet-American Cold War. With the United States and the Soviet Union then much less engaged in Eastern Europe than they had been during the Cold War, four European interstate associations—the European

Community, the Conference on Security and Cooperation in Europe (CSCE), NATO, and the Western European Union—attempted to localize and dampen the revolution in Bosnia-Herzegovina. The guiding assumption of these organizations was that defusing internal disorder in any European state was a collective responsibility of European states, based on the "common European home" concept.

Regarding the other three cases for which international norms are general and diffuse, collective PD does not come about until some time after the local conflicts emerged, the major states being unable to insulate the conflicts as issues among themselves until they worsen considerably. Prior to the outbreak of the Greek revolution in 1821, the major powers of the European continent had created the so-called Holy Alliance to help suppress nationalist uprisings in Europe. However, this interest was limited to Christian Europe, and the Greek revolution against the Ottoman Empire was not discussed when the Congress of great powers met at Verona in 1822.[4] At the time of the Cyprus and Congo cases, norms for great-power cooperation consisted of collective Soviet-American responsibilities to deal with threats to international peace, as defined by the United Nations Charter, and of the need for superpower crisis management to avoid nuclear war.[5] Norms from the UN Charter were undercut by prevailing Soviet-American rivalry, but this development paradoxically underscored the need to successfully manage regional confrontations such as those in Cyprus and the Congo. In the Cyprus case, Soviet-American consultation and common action were limited to Greco-Turkish crises, as in 1974, and superpower agreement to localize the Congo and Cyprus from great-power rivalry existed only on the most informal level, as reflected in superpower approval—subsequently hedged and conditional—to permit the United Nations to broker relations between the primary antagonists in those countries.

In general, insulationist PD toward local conflict tends to be prompt when a prior history exists of collective great-power action toward that conflict or, when such prior action is absent (as in Bosnia II), the norms counseling insulation have especially strong efficacy. Specifically, agreement on the need for mutual consultation and collective decision making and on localizing and restricting a region from great-power rivalry anchors great-power relations despite chaotic or changing conditions in the local conflict. Insulationist PD tends to be delayed when local conflict arises in a geographic area excluded by prevailing norms (as in Greece) or where major-state rivalry is especially strong.

Insulationist PD and Great-Power Opportunistic Behavior

Unilateral great-power opportunistic activity and other major states' fear of it also contribute to insulationist PD objectives, but only by increasing tensions between the major states, most of whom resist specific actions by another major country acting alone. To spur consultation and to prevent the local conflict from affecting great-power relations, resistors of unilateral action must communicate and insist upon limits in unilateral behavior to any great power contemplating such action. That is, they must inform a great power that would act alone of the consequences of both unilateral and collective behavior, and persuade or coerce it to decide in favor of cooperative collective action.

In all but the Memel, in which the major states were generally unified, unilateral action in these cases is important for the interests of one or more great powers, and resisted by the others. When in the Belgian case the French offered to place a son of French king Louis Philippe as ruler of Belgium, and when the French later on intervened militarily to defend the Belgians against Dutch war making, the British resisted, and a diplomatic crisis resulted. Russian war making against the Ottoman regime in 1828, the outgrowth of the Greek revolution, interrupted British-French-Russian cooperation designed to force a settlement of the Greek issue. In Bosnia I, Turkish resistance to Russia in the late 1870s was facilitated by the appointment of a British admiral to head the Turkish navy, engagement of British engineers to serve on Turkish naval vessels, and appointment of a British military official to serve with a Turkish military contingent in Bulgaria.[6] These steps reflected broader British interests in containing Russian influence. On the Russian side, Slavonic Benevolent Committees directed the insurgents in Bosnia-Herzegovina and collected contributions to aid them.[7]

The Austrians, for their part, subsidized Prince Nicholas, the Montenegrin ruler, and permitted Montenegrin purchases of rifles from the Austrian war department to weaken Russian influence and to divide Montenegro from Serbia.[8] The Austrians had in fact prepared earlier for annexation of Bosnia-Herzegovina if the Turks lost control there.[9] The major Austrian motive behind this preparation was defensive: triumph of the Slavs in Bosnia-Herzegovina, or even the granting of autonomy to them by the Turks, would accelerate similar restiveness of Slavs within Austria-Hungary, threatening its disintegration. (A similar motive was behind later

Russian determination to annex Turkish Armenia if the Turks lost control over that area.) In the Armenia case, by the 1880s the Ottoman Sultan increasingly turned to the Russian government for support to resist British initiatives made on behalf of the Armenians, the Russians attempting to weaken the British influence in Constantinople. In the Congo, the Soviets supported Patrice Lumumba, the Congolese Prime Minister, while the United States worked against him. The United States worked against the regime of Archbishop Makarios in Cyprus, while Markarios turned to the Soviet Union for support. And in Bosnia II, the United States provided political and military support to the fledging Bosnian regime, while Russia assisted the Serb-dominated Belgrade government that aided the Bosnia Serbs fighting the Bosnian regime.

This experience points up not only the compatibility of rivalry between great powers with insulationist PD, but also the larger need for insulation created by such rivalry. In none of these cases do the major states enter into hostilities over opportunistic behavior in local conflict. Tensions, which at times bring the major states close to a rupture in relations, reflect to be sure the greater importance for some great powers of opportunistic relative advantage compared to the mutual benefits collective action provide, and insulationist PD is thus frequently very delicate. The affirmation of collective action is thus a risky endeavor for the major states bent on underscoring norms of cooperation. Tensions and crises between great powers occur when norms are strained through unanticipated developments in small states and through unilateral actions—or the potential for them—by the major states capitalizing on shifting small-state conditions. The tensions and crises serve as a warning of the danger of mutually undesired great-power war and, by accentuating the fears of such war, strengthen the norms and principles that by general assent serve as the most reliable war preventive. Such crises thereby become an important agenda-setting mechanism for PD.[10]

When norms of cooperation are stronger, as in loose-concert pattern cases in which a prior history of collective great-power action on the local conflict area exists, the major states can closely probe each other's broader positions and pose clear-cut choices between unilateral and collective behavior. Belgium was the best example in this study in which unilateral great-power activity reinforced insulationist PD when the consequences of unilateral and collective action were underscored.[11] In that case, the consequences of French unilateral action were defined by the other major states, and principally Great Britain, as being incompatible with insulationist PD. Britain in particular posed a clear-cut choice to the French: if the French persisted in efforts to determine the Belgian leadership—by choosing and dictating the identity of the Belgian king or by launching military intervention into Belgium without agreement from the other major states—France would be confronted by a united front in opposition and would risk war. On the other hand, if France cooperated with the other major states over Belgium, it would be assured of the termination of Dutch authority over the Belgians and of ample peaceful opportunity for the Belgians to interact with France. Blunting French opportunistic action in Belgium, the British practiced "containment by engagement," in which incentives for collective action were in practice employed as leverage in influencing a unilaterally minded great power.

A similar strategy was practiced by Great Britain in Bosnia I, after civil strife in Bosnia-Herzegovina widened to include neighboring Serbia and Montenegro and, once the Turks were victorious over the Serbs and Montenegrins, after Russia embarked upon military hostilities against the Turks to defend her defeated Slav allies. When Russian victories in 1877 forced the Turks to retreat to the vicinity of Constantinople, the British, allied with the Turks, threatened war against Russia if the latter did not end its military advance and agree to surrender some Turkish territory it took in military action. The Russians agreed to do so, and the Congress of Berlin subsequently reaffirmed the strength of the great-power concert, so that containment here also was promoted by engagement. The great-power concert also capitalized in the Greek and Bosnia II cases on the incentives to unilaterally minded great powers (France in the Greek case, and the United States and Russia in Bosnia II) to take part in a collective solution for an international problem rather than to remain outside it.[12]

Containment by engagement cannot be practiced in the prevailing-opposition cases because unilateral activity is then more vigorous and important for the great-power undertaking it than under the loose-concert pattern. In the Armenian case, Anglo-Russian rivalry for influence in the Turkish administration was acute; the British and Russians could act together only in instances in which Turkish brutality toward the Armenians was openly manifest, as in the 1896 Constantinople Bank incident. In Cyprus, insulationist PD could only be practiced during periods of crisis, such as in the Cypriote civil war of 1967 and the Turkish military intervention on the island in 1974. In the Congo, Hammarskjöld was the primary means of insulationist PD, his intent being to keep Soviet-American competition out of the internal Congolese problem.

In short, in loose-opposition and prevailing-opposition cases unilateral great-power opportunism increases international tensions but also creates a perceived need to operationalize restraint. The more important the great-power jockeying for relative advantage, the more important also appears to be the operationalization of restraint. As a measure of such restraint, insulationist PD often requires crisis management. Such PD can therefore also be crisis preventive when it legitimates behavior that other major states do not find objectionable.

Primary Antagonists' Struggle for Great-Power Support

The final contributor to agenda setting in PD, the petitions and influence of the primary antagonists, is strongly connected with the just-discussed unilateral great-power search for advantage. We saw in the last chapter that the great powers are much less willing to be drawn into the ethnic conflict than the primary antagonists desire. But to the extent that unilateral interests inform their behavior, the great powers, endeavoring to enhance their own influence in the local conflict, will then primarily serve the interests of the primary parties struggling for support and for supremacy over each other.

Collective action, and especially insulationist PD, is an important way of dampening major-state rivalry so that the great powers can exert influence upon the local actors and resist serving as their agents. However, insulationist PD, shaped by unilateral great-power search for relative advantage in the local conflict, is often limited and delicate. Particularly in the prevailing opposition cases, the leverage of some great-power states on other unilaterally minded ones tends to be small, and insulationist PD formal or otherwise weak, limited to local crises or dependent upon another international actor such as the United Nations. In such instances, the major states are handicapped in pushing the local antagonists to accept collective mediation and to reject their most extreme demands.[13] On the other hand, one-sided assistance to a specific local antagonist by one or more great powers can be sustained as long as other major states do not challenge it.

But even when norms of great-power cooperation are stronger, and the foundation for insulationist PD not merely formal, major-state divisions enhance primary antagonist leverage in assisting their respective causes. In Greece and in Bosnia II collective interventionist PD was spurred not by containment needs but by the dynamics of primary-antagonist conflicts. The beleaguered and weaker primary antagonist used ongoing intensive local hostilities to affect the great-power agenda by dramatizing its plight and the illegitimacy of its opponents' cause. Great-power intervention occurred as a result of the humanitarian crises widely associated with combatants' or noncombatants' victimization: in the Greek case Turkish military excesses led to the intervention, and in Bosnia II Serbian military excesses brought it about. (The Armenian case is another in which the weaker faction publicized its case by capitalizing on the violence of its opponent, as in the Constantinople Bank incident. Here, however, the great powers only temporarily became engaged to end the violence and did not deal with the root causes of the violence.) Thus, where the great powers are slow to act forcefully on their own in relation to the local conflict, weaker primary antagonists, capitalizing on violence, can take most advantage of major-power divisions to find an influential great-power advocate.

The influence of the primary antagonists on great-power behavior depends, then, on the strength of collective great-power interests. Whether those interests are strong or weak depends in turn on major-state relations, not on the relative power of the major states and the primary antagonists. Insulationist PD can modify the priorities of an opportunistically minded major state, but it can also help rationalize those priorities when the major states accept continuing rivalry among themselves in the arena of the local conflict.

Great-Power Relations and Interventionist PD

The major states do not merely insulate the local conflict as an element of their relations, but intervene in it to pursue two specific objectives: (1) facilitate the pacific settlement of local disputes; and (2) provide incentives to persuade or to coerce reluctant local antagonists to accept settlement proposals. While local antagonists often stubbornly resist these proposals, the major states themselves are also frequently impediments to successful interventionist PD. Specifically, the great powers can constrain interventionist PD in two ways. First, one or more great powers can work against ongoing intervention in local conflict launched collectively by other major states. Second, major-state divisions impede the initiation of interventionist PD. Each of these is discussed in turn.

When ongoing great-power intervention, in the form of mediation of disputes and influence tactics, is opposed by other great powers, sometimes the opposition can be quickly overcome; more often, considerable time is required before it can be neutralized.

In one case (Belgium), opposition by one major state to interventionist PD was overcome relatively quickly. Timely, broadly supported interventionist PD then came from a rare combination of circumstances. First, the Dutch requested great-power intervention to help suppress the Belgian revolt, having concluded that they were not strong enough to accomplish that objective alone. Second, independence of the Netherlands and Dutch occupation of Belgium were agreed to fifteen years earlier by the great powers following the end of the Napoleonic Wars. The responsibilities of the great powers in this region, linked to a long and troubling war, were thus dramatized by recent experience. Third, the major powers that had earlier defeated Napoleon understood the connection between the condition of Belgium and the strength of France. They had vital interests to contain the French, and in particular to prevent extension of French influence over a newly independent Belgium. Finally, had the great powers not acted collectively in relation to the Dutch-Belgian conflict, the French would have been likely to intervene on their own. To head off unilateral French intervention, British prime minister Henry Viscount Palmerston secured French cooperation with collective great-power intervention in which the French participated.

Major-state agreement to insulate the local ethnic conflict thus not only permitted collective intervention and brokering in Belgium, but depended upon it. Palmerston made it clear that Great Britain intended to press for containment of French influence in Belgium with or without the cooperation of France. While the French could choose not to cooperate, the British provided incentives to them to do so. Belgium was to be detached from the Netherlands, as France desired, and the French were given a voice in determining the terms of the separation. In exchange, the French were asked to accept the principle of mutual denial to govern great-power intentions toward Belgium. The likelihood of French acceptance of these terms was undoubtedly enhanced by (1) the French desire to avoid isolation in the post-Napoleonic period, an objective strengthened by the recurrence of revolutionary activity in Paris shortly before the outbreak of the Belgian insurrection; (2) the deference shown by other major states to French views; and (3) the prominence of France in making the intervention work, including the great-power-authorized use of French force against the Dutch in August 1831 and December 1832. Each of these contributed to the successful use of the already-noted technique of containment by engagement, as a result of which the French adhered to the prevailing consensus view that major powers should not be permitted to expand opportunistically at the expense of small states without the permission of the other major states.

In four other cases (Bosnia I and II, Cyprus, and the Congo), great-power opposition to an interventionist PD program was overcome only after considerable delay. In Bosnia I, England, which had been cooperative but peripheral to early collective PD to reconcile Turks and Slav insurgents in Bosnia-Herzegovina, sought, beginning with its rejection of the so-called Berlin Memorandum of May 1876, to block mediation proposals that it believed were too one-sided against the Turks.[14] Subsequently, after the Turks defeated Serbia and Montenegro and Russia thereupon mobilized forces to compel the Turks to accept an armistice with Serbia and Montenegro, the British attitude hardened further. The British opposed Russian use of force to coerce the Turks, and successfully undertook to strengthen Turkish resistance to Russian demands. This resistance led to Russian war-making against Turkey in April 1877. The British were brought back to collective PD only by means of the Congress and Treaty of Berlin in July 1878.

In the Congo, Hammarskjöld, whose program had been initiated to overcome great-power deadlock, attached much more importance to insulating the country from superpower Cold War than on reconciling the diverse factions. He shifted his priorities in September 1960 to work to reconcile President Joseph Kasavubu and Prime Minister Patrice Lumumba, only to be opposed by the United States. The Americans refused to accept Lumumba, believing him sympathetic to Soviet aims, and therefore worked to undermine the Hammarskjöld program insofar as it was predicated on dealing with Lumumba. And the Russians, also contrary to Hammarskjöld's objectives, sought to assist Lumumba's effort to subdue the Kantanga insurrection by force. Even after Lumumba's death, American views sharply conflicted with those of Hammarskjöld and his deputy, Reshawar Dayal, over the issue of working with the de facto Mobutu regime. But the United States in particular came to support UN efforts after Dayal withdrew as Hammarskjöld's Congo representative, and the United States took the lead in reconciling the successor regime of Cyril Adoula with the secessionist leader Tshombe.

In Cyprus, the United States also for a time worked against the UN-centered program for reconciling the Cypriote regime with the Turkish-Cypriote minority. It sought in particular to bring about double *enosis*, which amounted to partition of the island between Greece and Turkey.[15]

Even after the death of Makarios, with whom the United States was unreconciled, the Americans were not prepared to press their Greek and Turkish allies to compromise and to promote reconciliation between the Cypriote regime and its Turkish opponents. UN mediation efforts have remained deadlocked over differences between the two Cypriote communities and between their two secondary-state sponsors.

Finally, in Bosnia II, the Americans supported the early EC and UN efforts to keep Yugoslavia whole, but once this proved impossible—with the secession of Slovenia and Croatia—the Americans sharply divided from European and UN mediators on the priority to be given to defending the Moslem-dominated regime against the Serb military onslaught. It repeatedly worked against UN proposals for a Bosnian settlement on the ground that they gave up too much territory to the Serbs and thus rewarded Serb ethnic cleansing in the region.[16] And it worked against the UN arms embargo to the region by promoting the supply of arms to the Sarajevo regime to enable it to resist the Serbs. In the spring of 1994 the United States constructed an entente with Russia in which both countries worked against the UN-EU-proposed Vance-Owen plan, and shortly afterward it succeeded, with UN-EU support, to establish the so-called Contact Group of five major powers that was the vehicle for the American-sponsored Dayton settlement of November 1995. Differences over the Vance-Owen peace plan and the American proposal for "strike and lift" were resolved by rejecting both proposals and coalescing mediation efforts behind the American-sponsored 51-49 percent territorial proposal for Bosnia-Herzegovina.

These four cases show how a recalcitrant great power, attaching high priority to the local conflict, leads the interventionist coalition to take account of its complaints and to accommodate it by revising the coalition's consensus toward that conflict. The challenger, on the sidelines in earlier developments shaping interventionist PD, comes to demand further debate over the appropriate framework for settling the ethnic conflict, while older participants strongly prefer to avoid such a debate. The challenger belatedly prevails by forcing reconsideration of older PD, vetoing it, and pushing its own proposal when invited to do so.

A different problem characterizes those cases in which the major powers are unable to agree on any intervention program. Interventionist PD then has to wait until the great powers can reach a consensus. In the Greek case, Russia opposed both independence for the Greeks and military suppression of the revolt, and the Holy Alliance could not agree on a mediation plan, being divided between encouraging the primary antagonists to invite mediation and coercing the Turks to accept Greek autonomy in the Ottoman Empire.[17] The English, whose position in the Ionian islands was heavily affected by the insurrection, likewise refused to act unilaterally.[18] Great-power intervention and initiative to bridge Greek-Turkish differences depended upon constructing a concert *de novo*, starting from British efforts to use an entente with Russia to prevent a Russo-Turkish war over Greece, and progressing to French participation in the joint naval blockade of the Peloponnese.

Weakness of the major powers is reflected in the Armenian case, where despite Turkish and great-power legitimizing of England and Russia as co-protectors of the Armenians, the two major states mistrusted each other and were unable to agree on a reform program until 1914. Even when in that year an agreement to protect Armenian political rights was at last hammered out with the assistance of a number of European governments, the Russians and English were still suspicious of each other's intentions on the subject of Turkish reform.[19] With respect to the Memel, the great powers delayed a decision about its ultimate status, treating it as an international zone and tolerating the local status quo for some years. Finally, a committee appointed by the Council of Ambassadors to make recommendations on the final status of the territory concluded by January 1923 that it should be made into an autonomous territory. Before this recommendation was made public, Lithuania invaded the Memel in January 1923, whereupon the great powers negotiated a power-sharing agreement to protect the German population. The decision about sovereignty in the Memel was effectively forced by military intervention of an interested secondary power.

These cases reflect the low priority attached by major states toward interventionist PD in local ethnic conflict. The low priority was strikingly at odds with the perceived high importance repeatedly attached by the major states to insulation of these ethnic conflicts as an element in their relations.

In short, resistance by some major-states to great-power interventionist PD, and the absence of strong great-power coalition support for such PD, significantly constrain the ability of the major states to provide good offices and mediation in instances of local ethnic conflict, and to exert leverage upon the local antagonists on behalf of collective great-power objectives. Collective interventionist PD is subject to this constraint irrespective of whether insulationist PD is practiced, and irrespective of the character of local antagonist resistance to great-power intervention. The constraint in effect enlarges the importance of local antagonist resistance to great-power intervention and provides local antagonists with opportunity to employ divisions between the major states to push substitute pacific settlement proposals of their own.[20] However, the impediments are not equally problematic for the major states. Objections from major states to collective interventionist PD can be surmounted by enlarging the coalition; this includes the technique of containment by engagement. More difficult are those cases in which interventionist PD lacked coalition support at all.

Conclusions

Forging great-power consensus on insulationist and interventionist PD has often been arduous, subject to confrontation between the major states, and associated with significant lingering differences in major-state interests. When the major states lacked consensus, opportunities have been opened for the primary antagonists to affect major-state support for their cause. However, as rivalry between great powers becomes more acute, the perceived need for operationalizing restraint has grown, to ensure that differences over the local conflict do not lead to hostilities between the major states. Great-power relations are usually flexible enough to forestall such hostilities. The particular importance of insulationist PD in our cases is reflected in the absence of war between major states despite the confrontations between them.

Insulationist PD is shaped by great-power norms of cooperation, unilateral search by some major states for relative advantage, and by the local antagonists capitalizing on major-state differences. Interventionist PD has at times been weak or nonexistent even when insulationist PD was practiced. Particular great powers at odds with the prevailing collective interventionist PD approach of the major states have repeatedly gained a revision of that approach, illustrating the priority attached by the major states to insulationist PD relative to intervention.

Chapter 7

Conciliating the Antagonists

Having discussed the background to collective PD, giving special attention to great-power attitudes and relationships, this study now turns to the effect collective diplomacy has on the primary antagonists. Interventionist PD includes conciliatory and voluntaristic aspects, as well as coerced and imposed elements. We deal in this chapter with its conciliatory form; coercive PD is addressed in the next chapter.

Conciliatory PD is voluntaristic in two ways: it aims at *eventual* voluntary bridging of differences between the primary antagonists, and it presumes local as well as international acceptance of the *process* of mediation and dispute settlement. Two broad purposes for conciliatory PD diplomacy can be distinguished: (1) reconciling the antagonists through suggestive proposals and persuasion, and (2) forestalling confrontations that would interfere with reconciliation efforts. The first of these is served by the promotion, from outside the ethnic conflict area, of mediation, direct negotiation between the parties, and normalization of the primary antagonists' relationship. Actions associated with the second objective include introducing military forces to discourage unauthorized use of force by the antagonists; large demonstrations of force; forestalling military intervention by secondary states into the conflict; limiting the supply of armaments to the antagonists; and providing international assistance to facilitate public law and order in the conflict arena. Reconciliation efforts appeared in all eight cases studied here, and voluntary pacification steps—or, as they will be termed here, "force-dampening"—in seven of the eight.

International reconciliation and force-dampening efforts are usually constrained by highly problematic ethnic conflict conditions. In all but the

Memel (in which relations between the antagonists were tranquil and normal), ethnic conflict in our cases featured civil hostilities between the antagonists—in steadily recurring or continual fashion in Greece and in Bosnia I and II, and more sporadically in Belgium, Armenia, the Congo, and Cyprus. Where war was not general, major outbreak was often threatened by unstable political conditions—either by nonexistent political institutions (the Congo) or by their breakdown (Belgium, Cyprus, and Armenia). To this domestic instability was added the common propensity of outside states to intervene to assist one of the primary antagonists in a way that—whether deliberately or not—exacerbated that instability. In *every* case studied here, outside military intervention complicated maintenance of internal stability by overwhelming the central regime in the conflict arena (table 7.1).[1]

This chapter inquires about the adequacy of great-power conciliatory interventionist PD in local ethnic conflict. Problematic small-power ethnic

TABLE 7.1
Problematic Background to Collective Great-Power Conciliation Efforts

Cases	*Character of Primary Antagonist Hostilities*	*Unilateral Outside Military Involvement*	*Unilateral Military Involvement Directed Inside or Outside Arena of Ethnic Confrontation?*
Belgium	Short-lived, sporadic warfare	Yes	Inside
Greece	Seasonally intense war between Greeks and Turks; war between Greek factions in several other periods	Yes	Outside
Bosnia I	Recurring warfare, periodic armistices	Yes	Inside and Outside
Armenia	Local resistance, state suppression, some local insurgency	No	N/A
The Memel	None	Yes	Inside
The Congo	Virtual civil war	Yes	Inside
Cyprus	Virtual civil war	Yes	Inside
Bosnia II	Recurring warfare, periodic armistices	Yes	Inside

conflict often stimulates force-dampening initiatives, but it also often limits the effect of conciliation efforts and—ironically in light of great-power crisis prevention objectives—causes them to be crisis driven. The chapter also notes inhibitions of the major states toward using threats to back up pacification steps. These inhibitions reduce the influence the great powers exert upon the primary antagonists, for two reasons. First, the major states hold back in this phase threats that otherwise would underscore the difference between their power and that of the primary antagonists. And second, they introduce a gap between their unwillingness to use coercion in relation to the primary antagonists and the willingness of the latter to do so between themselves. These great-power inhibitions work at cross-purposes with the dependence of the primary antagonists on the great powers to cope with exacerbated local conflict. The former weakens interventionist PD, and the latter strengthens it.

Reconciliation of the Antagonists

Timely intervention does not enhance the chances of successful bridging of differences between the primary antagonists for three reasons. First, host government motivations for inviting mediation are often not served by the outcome of the mission. Second, mediation is a convenient screen for weaker host governments or challengers to play for time and to obtain military strength from other sources. And third, mediation is initially brought to bear when the disputes with which they deal are not ripe for settlement, a settlement framework having not yet been agreed upon by the primary antagonists.

Timely international mediation is facilitated, as in Belgium, the two Bosnia cases, the Congo, and Cyprus, by the central regime's receptivity to it. In each of these cases, the central government accepted great-power or surrogate mediation in the belief that mediation would support its claims to rule its subject peoples and enable it to do so peacefully. For example, the Dutch believed themselves incapable of putting down the revolt directed against them by the Belgians. The Congolese leader, Lumumba, also acting from weakness, invited the United Nations to send military forces primarily to expel the Belgians, who had entered to protect Europeans from the undisciplined *force publique* and from the general breakdown of law and order, and who appeared allied to the Katanga secession. By contrast, Ottoman officials, convinced of their military superiority over Slav rebels in

Bosnia-Herzegovina, were persuaded by Austro-Hungarian foreign minister Andrassy to hold back militarily in favor of peaceful measures while the great powers held the province intact for the Turkish administration.

In these cases, timely mediation temporarily deflected and suppressed efforts by the central government to militarily suppress the revolt. In Cyprus and Bosnia II, the central governments were in a different position, having to fight for their very existence without the military capabilities to do so. In Cyprus, the Makarios government sought to escape from the NATO-imposed framework that required power sharing between Greek and Turkish Cypriotes, and even more from implementation of the American Acheson Plan. The Muslim-led Bosnian regime, in even a weaker position, needed international recognition and immediate protection against the Serb and Croat onslaughts.

From the viewpoint of the central regime in these cases, mediation was attractive on the condition that it would be one-sided, but success was not obtainable on those terms, and timely mediation foundered. Dutch and Ottoman leaders were disillusioned by the great-power intervention, for instead of satisfying Dutch and Ottoman political aims, the concert worked to detach Belgium from the Dutch and to weaken the Ottoman hold upon Bosnia-Herzegovina. Instead of assisting Lumumba in the goal of removing the Belgians, the UN at first concentrated on restoring law and order, returning the *force publique* to its quarters, and assisting local authorities in building political institutions; this led Lumumba to fear that the UN was actually allied with the Belgians. And in Bosnia II, the Vance-Owen plan would have weakened the hold of the central regime by dividing Bosnia into a tripartite cantonal system, giving the Serbs 43 percent of the territory of the new state, a significant portion of which was gained by force. While the UN deployed peacekeeping forces to protect Sarajevo (and later five other so-called safe zones), these were hardly adequate to deal with Bosnia's neighbors, who because of their greater military strength benefitted in relative terms from the 1991 UN arms embargo on Yugoslavia.

With the exception of the Makarios government, which remained too weak and constrained to contemplate military action on its own, disillusioned central regimes in these cases turned to war to accomplish their aims, as in the Ten Days War launched by the Dutch, the Turkish effort to relieve the besieged Niksich fortress in Herzegovina, and Lumumba's determination to confront the Katanga forces with his own troops. The United States intervened to protect the Bosnian government and urged rejection of the Vance-Owen plan until changes were made in it. While evading acceptance, the Bosnian regime sought and received sizeable American weapons stocks enabling it to struggle on the battlefield.

For the ethnic challenger, mediation can compensate for weakness in relation to the central regime, or, if the challenger is stronger, can be evaded. In the Memel case, great-power mediation seemed to the Lithuanians the next logical step after the Memel was detached from Germany in 1919; Lithuanians in the Memel were not on their own able to dislodge the German elite from power after their territory was severed from Germany, and thus they depended on great-power mediation. The Greeks on the Greek mainland and in the Peloponnese, the Slavs in Bosnia-Herzegovina, and the Armenians in eastern Turkey were likewise unable to dislodge the Turks from their superior position. They hoped mediation would provide treatment of them as equals, but the great powers in the latter two cases were unwilling to propose such treatment, and in the Greek case did so only many years after the revolution began.

In Bosnia I, relative weakness of the Slav insurgents in Bosnia-Herzegovina was compensated by heavy involvement in that case of Slav advocate states Serbia and Montenegro. The great-power approach to mediation in that instance was at odds with Serb and Montenegrin determination to end Turkish sovereignty over the Slavs in Bosnia-Herzegovina. Thus, Prince Nicholas of Montenegro seemed to have controlled the political agenda of the Slav insurgents, and saw to it that the latter would demand more than the Turks would accept.[2] In short, mediation between Christian Slavs and the Ottoman regime failed principally because of international Slav solidarity, which the Russian government also encouraged. Where the challenger was stronger than the central regime, international solidarities even more strongly contributed to evasion and undoing of mediation efforts. In Cyprus, the lure of double *enosis* undermined the initial UN mediation up to 1974, as both Greece and Turkey challenged the authority of the Cypriote government at that time. And in Bosnia II the Serb regime in Belgrade, while receptive to EU-UN mediation in Bosnia-Herzegovina, continually attempted to abort it.[3]

The problem of timely intervention and mediation can also be linked to the literature on the ripening of international disputes. The ripening process, I. William Zartman argues, permits the antagonists to test alternative settlement frameworks, so as to eventually reach a mutually agreeable one.[4] Two key framework questions are at issue in small-power ethnic conflict: the balance of power between the antagonists—that is to say, the equality or inequality of their relationship, and the degree of interrelationship between them—and whether they are to be separated or integrated. The point is that at the beginning of their confrontation, the primary antagonists will not agree on the appropriate framework, and the great powers are limited—*from a conciliation standpoint*—in legitimizing one or another of them.

Given the lack of legitimacy of the framework, and the character of opposition between the ethnic antagonists, the latter have strong incentive to use war and violence as tools of the ripening process. Further, since negotiation is necessary for the ripening of issues, the fact that the primary antagonists lack channels to negotiate also biases the antagonists toward this result.[5] Without negotiation, hostile steps that intensify conflict between the primary antagonists may be necessary to obtain a new agreed-upon framework. "There are two ways," Zartman has written, "in which the ripening [of issues] can be perceived: one as an "unripening" or exacerbation of conflict away from an initial regime, and the other as the evolution of the conflict toward a new (but not necessarily final or resolving) formula. The latter is more helpful, because it fits into a broader interpretation and provides insights into the evolution and resolution of conflict and crisis."[6]

Mediation forthcoming later is less likely to disillusion, or be evaded by, the central regime than if it is initiated early. It is also more likely to be launched when the primary antagonists share ideas about a negotiating framework. But applying mediation later on did not assure success in these cases. Mediation brought to bear later in the conflict cycle was affected by the increased polarization between the primary antagonists, and the costs of the antagonists' confrontation led them to increase their demands and become more inflexible.[7]

Force-Dampening Activity

Noncoercive actions designed to calm tensions, contribute to normal interaction between the antagonists, and facilitate negotiations to resolve conflict appear in all of our cases except the Belgian revolution. Controlled by diplomatic rather than military needs, these actions do not prevent the most serious kinds of confrontations and are not designed to cope with them. They are useful where the primary antagonists wished to avoid confrontations but where their relationship is nevertheless conducive to them. They are inspired by dangers in absence of a political settlement between the primary antagonists. The analysis here deals with the impact of force-dampening on civil strife in these cases, and with the effect of tense primary-antagonist relationships on force-dampening.

TABLE 7.2
Types of Force-Dampening Activity

Type of Activity	*Cases*
Peacekeeping	the Memel the Congo Cyprus Bosnia II
Pacific blockade	Greece
Discouraging military intervention by outside secondary states	Bosnia I Cyprus Bosnia II
Arms control	the Congo Cyprus Bosnia II
Supply of officials to facilitate governmental operations	Bosnia II the Congo Armenia

Five kinds of force-dampening activity can be distinguished: (1) peacekeeping with international military contingents; (2) "pacific blockade" introduced as a form of military escalation; (3) diplomacy to discourage military intervention by interested secondary states; (4) limiting or preventing the flow of armaments from outside states to the primary antagonists; and (5) export of competent administrative, judicial, and police officers to oversee political institutions in a tense region. Each of these force-dampening modes is useful and significant within a limited, and sometimes narrow, range of conditions. Table 2 lists each type and the cases studied here that illustrate them.

Peacekeeping and International Policing

Peacekeeping as a mode of international policing is seen in the Memel, in the Congo, in Cyprus, and Bosnia II. In the Memel, the Conference of Ambassadors provided a French force garrison to supplement a French administrator charged with overseeing conditions there. Conditions were outwardly tranquil in the Memel but politically abnormal because sovereignty over the territory was left in abeyance, and the great powers did not decide this question or announce how it would be decided. After the Second World War, by contrast, peacekeeping and policing were almost entirely directed to areas where trouble was actually occurring and not where conditions were tranquil, the idea being to capitalize on widely understood international dangers to gain confidence in international institutions.[8] First seen in the UN efforts to cope with the Sinai war of 1956, in which the dangers were between states, it was subsequently used mostly in cases of domestic instability. In the Congo, peacekeeping forces were to substitute for the undisciplined Congolese army, which was widely believed to be a threat to domestic peace rather than an aid to it. In Cyprus, the forces—recruited from NATO members—were interposed between rival Cypriote military contingents, dampening incidents between Greek and Turkish Cypriotes and thereby lessening Greek and Turkish propensities to intervene militarily. And in Bosnia II, following the outbreak of civil war in 1992, peacekeepers were to police cease-fire arrangements between Moslem and Serb contingents and protect civilians targeted by Serb warfare.

In three cases, peacekeepers were overwhelmed by invasion fomented from abroad—the Lithuanian invasion of the Memel in 1923, the 1967 Greek decision to implement double *enosis*; the 1974 Turkish invasion of Cyprus, and the Serb military pressure against Sarajevo and other Moslem safe havens from 1993 to 1995. These military actions, on a scale for which the peacekeepers were not prepared, created crises for PD and posed a threefold choice for authorizing agencies and peacekeeping force commanders. Should the international framework be formally revised to accommodate the military action? Should peacekeepers accommodate informally to the unilateral military action? Or should the old framework be defended by force? In Cyprus, the peacekeepers in 1967 were unable to cope with the deliberate challenge from the Greek force on the island led by George Grivas, but the Greeks were persuaded to desist by Turkish invasion threats. In 1974, the peacekeepers mostly accommodated informally by abandoning positions in the North of Cyprus, though sometimes (as near Nicosia) standing their ground and blunting the Turkish onslaught. In Bosnia II, UN peacekeepers at first accommodated the Serbs to prevent war with them despite earlier threatening to retaliate against Serb war-making; later, UN representatives allowed NATO to implement strong punitive air attacks, which helped induce the Serbs to negotiate an agreement in Dayton on a revised framework for Bosnia. And in the Memel, a new and mutually satisfactory framework was constructed, bringing peacekeeping to an end.

The fourth case—the Congo—illustrates a very different response to a local military security problem. UN peacekeeper commanders in the Congo decided, after being authorized by the Security Council in February 1961 to deport foreign military personnel and mercenaries, to implement this objective energetically.[9] Proceeding against foreign military personnel and mercenaries in Katanga, UN forces became the target of hostile action by the mercenaries in April 1961 and, after initiating their own military action later in the year, successfully achieved their objective by December 1961.

Taken together, these cases highlight the difficulty of working toward law and order without penalizing the chief instigators of civil strife. Those instigators risk disturbing the local balance of political power, preservation of which is essential for the even-handed approach required in conciliation. On the other hand, representatives of international bodies can also affect the local political balance, even if unintentionally. For example, action taken by UN representatives in the Congo to close airports and the radio station and to pay Mobutu's troops, while helping to calm tensions, placed Lumumba at a disadvantage in the internal power struggle. One careful analysis of the Congo case concluded that the UN needed to maintain "at least the principle of non-intervention [that is, impartiality] if member states are to call upon it in the future" in similar situations.[10] But virtual civil wars such as that in the Congo placed a particular burden on restoring law and order precisely because the existing balance of political power was so fragile.[11]

Civil instability can also make local law and order more difficult to realize from an international point of view, the international aspects of civil war—Hammarskjöld's highest priority in the Congo—being thereby harder to separate from the domestic issues.[12] Thus, even if international representatives are sensitive to the fragility of the domestic power balance, that sensitivity can handicap them in dealing with interested outside states poised to intervene. Finally, taking strong action to maintain law and order irrespective of the effect on the power structure—as did Congo and Bosnia II peacekeeper commanders—leads directly to force use that is difficult to distinguish from peace enforcement. Military action is understandable when the peacekeepers are challenged and humiliated by the primary antagonists, but the commanders in those instances—those most prepared for and capable of the necessary military action—were not inclined to pursue diplomatic conciliation; they had coercive goals in mind. The peacekeepers could prevail in such instances, it appears, only by placing conciliation itself at risk.[13]

The Pacific Blockade

In the Greek case, a pacific blockade was discussed between England and Russia beginning in 1825, after the Greek civil war had been underway for four years. It was later implemented by the two states acting together with France as an intermediary step between the offer of mediation to the parties and the possibility of a guarantee by the great powers of a new, more progressive tribute status for Greece within the Ottoman Empire.[14] The general purpose of the blockade, begun after the Turks (but not the Greeks) rejected the mediation offer, was to prevent neutral and Turkish vessels from bringing supplies to the Turkish forces in the Peloponnese. Launched at first by the British, whose naval forces were joined later by those of the other two states, the blockade especially sought to prevent an Egyptian flotilla, known to have been recently sent under Turkish authorization to assist war-making against the Greeks, from providing aid to the Turkish forces. Despite the blockade the Egyptian fleet, joined with a Turkish fleet off Asia Minor, reached the southern Greek peninsula. When its naval captains persisted in ravaging the Greek countryside and refused Allied-power demands to return to Egypt, the fleet was destroyed by the combined three-state squadron at Navarino Bay in October 1827.

The pacific blockade is of interest as conciliatory force dampening first because it demonstrates an evident will to act. It was a police action aimed at protecting the military status quo in Greece, and it warned that a Turkish force buildup would bring action that upset Turkish interests.[15] Steps of this kind require military superiority, but are not coercive.[16] Second, the demonstration is part of a larger program. "Preventive measures will carry far more weight," Brian Urquhart has written, "if they are part of a systematic course of international action, a progression of measures."[17] While peacekeeping forces can be part of such a program, they are designed to calm tensions and are not introduced on the assumption that they would be deliberately challenged. A program of action becomes practical, as in Greece and Bosnia II, only after prolonged great-power inactivity or frustration brings sustained collective attention to a persisting problem. It has been argued that agreement on such a program is difficult to reach in the earliest stages of confrontation because bargaining then tends to focus on more conventional political questions, the use of force being then regarded as an "ultimate but somewhat unreal sanction."[18]

The pacific blockade also faces obstacles in the field. First, deterrence and warning were more difficult to effectuate in the Greek case because the blockade was launched late in the conflict cycle, the Turks as superior military antagonist being especially committed to war-making and less likely to be affected by a naval demonstration.[19] Second, as in the case of Congo peacekeepers moving against foreign mercenaries and military personnel, the pacific blockade was implemented by commanders poorly in touch with their political leaders at home. Greek leaders cooperated with the blockade, apparently because they understood that the geographic scope of the blockade decided upon in London fit the territorial demarcation of Greece that the great powers were prepared to accept. They accepted an armistice in the civil war proposed by the naval commander, while the Turks rejected the armistice. The British naval commander was pro-Greek and quickly tired of Turkish noncompliance with the blockading force. In the end, the blockade was applied to suit the needs of the blockading fleets to avoid an expensive prolonged stalemate, while the overall interests of their governments were much more divergent than the solidarity of their fleets suggested. According to C. W. Crawley, "[T]he position of the triple alliance was certainly curious, as ironically described by Metternich: one mediating Power (Russia) at open war with the Porte, with one half of its squadron engaged in a hostile blockade of the Dardanelles and the other half in a 'pacific blockade' of the Greek coast; a second Power (France) engaged in 'amicable hostilities' by land with a nominal vassal of the Sultan, but neutral at sea; the third Power neutral but 'ally and accomplice' of the other two."[20] In this sense the interests shared among the great powers (referred to in the last chapter) were here very inefficiently implemented in relation to the primary antagonists.

Discouraging Intervention by Secondary States to Alter the Political Status Quo

Successful PD requires keeping interested secondary powers from intervening among primary antagonists on behalf of their ethnic associates. The cases studied here included the following examples of such efforts: (1) discouraging Serbian and Montenegrin participation in the 1875 Slav revolution; (2) discouraging Greece and Turkey from making war in Cyprus; and (3) dampening the ardor of Croatia to ally with Serbia in the 1990s at the expense of Bosnia-Herzegovina. Overall, the results are not impressive. In Bosnia I, Serbia and Montenegro became formally engaged about a year after the uprising in Bosnia-Herzegovina began. The Turks used force against Cyprus in 1964, 1967, and 1974 in response to activity by Greece on behalf of the Greek Cypriotes, including an effort to attach all of Cyprus to Greece (1964), and actual and attempted coups d'état (1964 and 1967). In Bosnia II, Croatia and Serbia intervened immediately upon the Sarajevo declaration of independence from Yugoslavia, the Serbs fighting a sustained war with the new government and Croatia acquiescing in a very uneasy peace that was occasionally interrupted by intense violence.

The question of intervention by secondary states is not determined through a test of strength between those states and the major powers. Instead, the stronger states tolerate informal intervention by the lesser ones. In Bosnia I, Serbia and Montenegro intervened with weapons and volunteer military personnel from the very beginning of the Slavic revolution. Again, the 1960 Treaty of Guarantee agreed to by Britain, Greece, and Turkey when Cyprus became independent provided for unilateral action by any one of them, when concerted action was not possible, to forestall alterations to the treaty framework. And in Bosnia II the Yugoslav military establishment maintained bases and weapons depots within Bosnia-Herzegovina. Quarantining the immediate arena of conflict from outside-state influence was thus impossible in these cases legally, politically, and militarily, and the influence on the ground of the secondary states was an important wedge for even larger influence—if those states wished to become still more involved.

Nor are the major powers generally in a quarantining mood. On the contrary, major states play a double game, officially supporting mediation between the primary antagonists but privately working for the advantage of one of them. Russia was tied to Serbia in Bosnia I by ethnic association, and did not attach high priority to pacifying the Serbs in relation to the Turks; Austria-Hungary worked harder at Montenegrin abstention from war, but apparently did not oppose her decision to go to war in July 1876, given Serbia's decision to enter and also the lack of substantive agreement between the primary antagonists and between Austria and Russia over how to handle the Slav revolution. Austrian and Russian involvement helped to defuse the consequences of informal Serb and Montenegrin participation in the rebellion against Turkey; Austria in particular dissuaded Turkey from initiating war against Serbia and Montenegro to punish those countries for that participation. In addition, by making it clear that an expansion of Turkish war-making against the neighboring Slav states would lead to stronger Austrian and Russian support of Serbia and Montenegro, Austrian diplomacy permitted Serbia and Montenegro to wage war at a time of their own choosing. (This advantage did not, however, prevent those countries from being militarily defeated by the Turks after they elected to formally intervene.) Once Serbia and Montenegro formally decided to participate in the war against Turkey, Austria and Russia agreed (in Reichstadt) to assist their allies if they were defeated and to deny their allies political gains if they were victorious.

In Cyprus, Greece and Turkey were assisted by the United States in working toward double *enosis*, and the Americans also approved toward this end the actions of the Greek military junta in overthrowing Makarios.[21] Finally, Russia supported its Serb ally in Bosnia II, weakening the effect of UN and NATO threats against Serbia for violating UN-sponsored cease-fires in Bosnia.

Significant great-power pacification efforts occur in all three cases: in Bosnia I, when Austria as the leading mediator weathered war scares associated with the supposed imminence of Turkish war-widening, in the Cyprus case when the Americans brokered a resolution to the 1967 crisis; and in Bosnia II when the Americans initiated formation of a Croat-Bosnian federation to prevent war between Muslims and Croats and to better contain Serb military pressures. At the brink, when force-of-events developments threaten war-widening that interfere with their objectives, the major states are able to work intensively and successfully to resolve the crises. Indeed, they *need* to work hard on such occasions, because their *private* agendas embroil them in ways that add to their vulnerability at the hands of the secondary states. Those private agendas can dampen their ardor to prevent war-widening—as when the Austrians and Russians agreed in Reichstadt to compensate themselves for gains made by Serbia and Montenegro in war against Turkey, and when American attraction to double *enosis* led to only a feeble effort to forestall Turkish invasion of Cyprus in 1974. Private agendas at times weaken major-power commitment to curb the aggressiveness of the secondary states. They also diminish major-power leverage for pursuing such curbs when the major states elect to take a firm stand.

Arms Control

Restricting all or part of the supply of foreign military contingents and weapons was important in the Congo, Cyprus, and in Bosnia II. In the Congo, the assassination of Lumumba helped shift UN opinion away from emphasizing reform of the Congolese army and toward withdrawal of all foreign military personnel in order to control the civil war in the country. A February 1961 UN Security Council resolution called for immediate withdrawal of all Belgian and foreign military personnel and political advisors not under UN command, and of mercenaries, and an April 1961 UN General Assembly resolution called for complete withdrawal and evacuation of such personnel within twenty-one days, failing which it specified that action should be taken in accord with the UN Charter.[22] In Cyprus, Greece and Turkey had been allowed in the 1960 Treaty of Alliance to station 950 and 650 military personnel, respectively, to train the Cypriot army, and the British also were permitted sizable forces and base rights there.[23] However, the number of Greek advisors swelled in the estrangement between the Greek government and Makarios after the 1964 Cyprus crisis, reaching perhaps 10,000 by November 1967 and fueling Turkish fears that they constituted a spearhead for *enosis*. Turkey demanded removal of this force during the 1967 confrontation on the island.

Finally, in Bosnia II, the UN Security Council approved an arms embargo in September 1991 for all of Yugoslavia. Subsequently, the United States argued for lifting the embargo to protect the embattled Sarajevo regime, which was unable on its own to combat Bosnian Serb forces aided by Yugoslav bases and weapons stockpiles in Bosnia. The Americans aimed at the most expeditious containment of the Serb military offensive, but were opposed by other states, including their European allies, who argued for restraining military supplies to retard warfare and for observing evenhandedness between the primary antagonists. Furthermore, even before pressures to lift the embargo became significant, Western European governments and the United States tolerated and indeed in some cases condoned illicit Croatian arms supply efforts from abroad early in the conflict. These covert shipments ultimately became the most important means employed by the United States to strengthen the Sarajevo government, whose arms were delivered through Croatia. The Croats thereby built up their forces without limit and controlled the level and quality of arms reaching Bosnia-Herzegovina.[24]

Foreign military assistance, not surprisingly, is strongly sought by protagonists in civil war. The humanitarian motive for supplying arms, remedying a mismatch in the balance of forces, can be distinguished from the strategic motive, which uses arms as a wedge to exercise dominant influence over the primary antagonists.[25] The two motives have different effects in our cases. Humanitarianism motivating the Belgians and their outside allies in the Congo, and also the Americans in Bosnia, depended upon publicizing a particular cause as a matter of principle. The Belgians and the Americans in these cases shared a sense of outrage over the excesses of the Congolese army and of the Bosnian Serbs, respectively. Both desired to protect the underdog, which in turn was able to take advantage of these moral scruples.[26] On the other hand, where armaments serve as a wedge for influence, as in the Greek buildup on Cyprus, they reflect concrete interests difficult to deflect or to bargain away. The imposition of barriers to the realization of these interests commonly leads to demands for compensation or to consideration of war as redress. Such interests usually reflect some close-by or regional concerns rather than interests projected at considerable distance. Because the military supplier is in this instance usually situated close to the arena of ethnic conflict, war in that arena can spill over into it.

Crisis is a mainstay in the demand for weapons as well as in the demand for weapons control. The demand for weapons, we have seen, emanates from the confrontation between ethnic groups; the demand for weapons control emanates from the ease with which armed contingents and weaponry can be supplied across fictitious borders, and from the way in which outside military assistance overwhelms international force-dampening efforts. Thus the role of foreign military personnel and mercenaries in sustaining the Katanga secession was increasingly recognized internationally, constraining the ability of UN peacekeepers to contribute to law and order in the Congo. The surge in the Greek National Guard impaired the ability of the UN Cyprus peacekeepers to maintain law and order when Greek forces acted to overthrow the UN-maintained framework on the island. And in Bosnia-Herzegovina, violations of the Yugoslav arms embargo led to more war on the battlefield and to a diminished propensity on the part of the primary antagonists to accept and abide by cease-fires and peace arrangements. These developments severely strained the capabilities of UN mediators and peacekeepers. Thus, military assistance from outside ultimately threatens to undermine PD altogether.

Outside toleration for military assistance varies in these cases. In the Congo, toleration was low because the UN commander was unwilling to accept violent actions against his troops committed by the Katanga mercenaries, and because the growing UN consensus was that troops and mercenaries in Katanga were critically important in sustaining the Katanga secession. In Cyprus, tolerance was still lower in 1967, not because of UN opinion, but because of Turkish sensitivities toward Greek intentions. When the Turks demanded that the Greeks reduce this force, the Greeks, unwilling to fight and subject to American pressure, decided to acquiesce. Later, when the Turks—whose estimates of the size of the Greek National Guard were apparently higher than the actual figure—objected that the withdrawals were moving too slowly, subsequent Greco-Turkish negotiations led to agreement that withdrawals would be verified by the UN peacekeeping force for Cyprus, and in some cases specifically by the force commander.[27]

Finally, in Bosnia II, the milder, evenhanded approach of UN commanders tolerated military rebuffs and embarrassments, and also outside military assistance, far more than Congo peacekeeper commanders. Such aid, benefitting all three primary antagonists, was regarded by the chief UN mediator for Bosnia as "just about tolerable, provided governments did not *overtly* break the arms embargo, for then we would have members of the Security Council supplying different sides in the war and risk a collapse in Security Council cooperation."[28]

Administrative, Judicial, and Police Assistance

Where indigenous governmental officials are corrupt or ineffective, emplacement, supervision, or training of international police contingents can narrow domestic controversy over the maintenance of public order. Such assistance, neglected in the literature on international force-dampening efforts,[29] graphically underscores the erosion of the distinction between "domestic" and "international," and is therefore especially sensitive for central governments. Because even weak states tend to be jealous of their independent prerogatives, central regimes that could objectively utilize international contingents are often unwilling to do so or, having done so, hinder their effect.

We may distinguish assistance ancillary to peacekeeping operations from assistance provided on its own. The latter was extensively discussed as a key reform element in Turkish Armenia, to cope with Armenian complaints about unequal treatment at the hands of the Ottoman authority and to provide protection from Kurdish depredations, especially against Armenians but also against Moslems.[30] Because the Kurds were a formidable presence in all of Turkish Armenia, there appears to have been an international consensus that "a police force of military character" organized by European officers was required there, as was the participation of such officers in its implementation.[31] Such a force was never provided because of the opposition of the Ottoman regime. The British—at first the most vigorous advocates of good government reforms in Armenia—had rejected coercing the Ottoman government, and by 1880 were reduced to pressing for limited and mostly symbolic changes, including Ottoman appointment of a British general as commandant of the Ottoman gendarmerie in Kurdistan, Ottoman appointment of financial inspectors nominated by European embassies in Constantinople, and English officer accompaniment of two reform commissions appointed by the Ottoman government in that year for the Armenian districts.[32] Prior to agreement on political reform for Turkish Armenia in 1914, the Ottoman government rejected appointment of any European officer who was to be placed in a position of responsibility superior to his Turkish counterpart, the Ottoman view being that acquiescence in any European political interference would bring still larger intervention later.[33] Only after lengthy negotiations did the Turks agree in 1914 to a reform plan for the Armenian districts stipulating that the European powers would recommend to the Turkish government two inspectors-general who would be given significant judicial powers.

Where assistance in basic governmental functions has been supplied as an ancillary tool the results have been less contentious and more encouraging, apparently because the preconditions for local cooperation are more favorable. In Bosnia-Herzegovina, for example, the UN International Police Task Force was given authority to monitor, train, and advise local police on organizational, administrative, and human rights questions. Lacking traditional police functions of its own, this group assists in the implementation of the Dayton accords for Bosnia-Herzegovina by training local police and advising police cadres on law enforcement standards. Police assistance also has been provided as an ancillary tool in other contemporary cases, including the UN Congo operation.[34]

It has been argued that police assistance in particular is vital for international peace operations in cases where the criminal justice system has collapsed or where it requires reform.[35] Where a peace operation is in progress, successful international police intervention will depend on the overall political objectives of the operation, which either sidesteps or diminishes the role of the central government (as in northern Iraq during the regime of Saddam Hussein) or enhances it (as in Bosnia II). If these objectives succeed, the international body then must provide incentives to local leaders to support international police personnel. Much less attention has apparently been given to governmental reform or rebuilding assistance in the absence of some larger military operation, when the goal is instead to work directly at diminishing local grievances. Then the formal supremacy of the local central regime needs to be acknowledged by all parties, and the aggrieved ethnic group given internationally guaranteed protections. In such a situation it is more difficult to give the central regime incentives to cooperate with the international presence, because the regime—which has been declared *formally* superior—can be expected to cooperate only on the assumption that doing so will *enhance* its own authority, a goal that is at odds with the purpose of the international guarantees.[36]

Opportunities for Conciliatory PD

The forgoing suggests that the usefulness of collective conciliation directed to small-power ethnic conflict is severely limited. The outlook for reconciliation proposals seems especially clouded because of the difficulty faced by the major states in providing incentives to each primary antagonist in the ethnic conflict to work to bridge differences in the local arena. If the great powers reject coercing the primary antagonists, the attractiveness of their proposals for conciliation will depend heavily on these incentives. For both challengers and the central regime, confidence in the conciliation process depends on the distribution of incentives by the great powers, because each is often subject to a security dilemma in relation to the other, being unable to avoid associating every gain provided to the opposing group with enhancement of the latter's aggressive intent.[37] For the ethnic challenger in particular, these incentives must be larger than previously offered by the central regime, whose authority it questioned. The longer the negotiations proceed, the more delicate each primary antagonist's confidence in the process of conciliation is likely to be, as in the Belgian and Bosnian cases. Great-power planning for conciliatory PD should therefore take into account the possibility that the conflict between the primary antagonists is not negotiable in this conciliation stage. In Bosnia I, the great powers were unable to give the Slav insurrectionists sufficient incentives to make a peaceful solution possible, in spite of adding considerably to those incentives.

Three other considerations complicate the distribution of negotiating incentives. First, decisions on a formula to support an agreement are primarily in the hands of the great powers and not the primary antagonists. For example, for reasons understandable to the major states but not to the primary antagonists, the former favored Belgian independence, but also the retention of sovereignty of the Ottoman Empire over Greek and Slav subject peoples. But while critical great-power interests were behind these concepts, the concepts themselves and their supporting details needed to be shaped to suit the interests of the primary antagonists, whose assets and aspirations did not adapt well to the overlay of collective great-power concerns. If the conflict arena is to be kept intact for the central regime, then the latter's interests will be strongly reinforced at the expense of the ethnic challenger; if the arena is to be politically divided for the benefit of the ethnic challenger, the central regime—faced in that eventuality with grave losses in its authority and control—can do much to resist that result.

Highly important in affecting the impact of conciliation efforts, we have seen, is the presence of neighboring states culturally associated with one or another of the primary antagonists, which are prepared to intervene in support of their ally. For example, incentives offered by Andrassy in 1875 and 1876 to the Slav insurrectionists in Bosnia-Herzegovina were far more likely to be found inadequate because of the involvement of Serbia and Montenegro in the cause of the insurrectionists. Serbia and Croatia were in a comparable position in relation to their Bosnian allies in Bosnia II. The propensities of Greek and Turkish Cypriotes to coexist in a common framework were highly affected by the dispositions of Greece and Turkey. These secondary states automatically become involved (whether recognized as such or not) whenever incentives to agree are being discussed by the primary antagonists. They have a veto on agreements between those antagonists, and negotiating incentives need to be shaped with *their* interests also in mind. They also have powerful unilateral options to undermine the negotiations in favor of a result primarily benefitting them. The Akritas Plan and Turkish planning for invasion of Cyprus both reflected long-term policies geared to taking advantage of situational incentives quite incompatible with a negotiated solution.

In short, great-power conciliation cannot affect the will of primary antagonists—and their secondary and major-power allies—where contrary intentions prevail, and it will likely be constrained so much by the requirements of keeping the confidence of the antagonists that it cannot pile sufficient incentives upon the parties to *change* their will. Rather, taking opportunism of the primary parties as a given, conciliation can at most affect conditions on the ground, adding to disincentives to the search for unilateral solutions by the primary antagonists, and making those disincentives understood in advance. Here is found the major argument for force-dampening initiatives that support international reconciliation efforts. The cases studied here show that while force-dampening initiatives can be overwhelmed by the contrary will of the primary antagonists, they can at particular times and places add significantly to local stability. They also show that in the absence of successful conciliation, problems on the ground may already be considerable. Those problems need not, however, interfere with conciliation efforts; to the contrary, much of the force-dampening initiatives and the collective conciliatory approaches to ethnic conflict discussed here are born in crisis.

The finding that severe problems on the ground afford opportunities for conciliatory great-power diplomacy is paradoxical and unexpected. We recall, for example, that the objectives for PD held by great powers have typically been linked to crisis prevention rather than crisis management.[38] The finding that such diplomacy is actually enhanced by confrontation suggests that agreed-upon great-power programs are vulnerable to disruptions in the immediate ethnic conflict arena. Having agreed on concerted common action, the great powers must evidently anticipate such local disruptions, for *the crisis prevention interests of the great powers will not ordinarily be duplicated by the primary antagonists.*

The issue is therefore whether great powers can sustain conciliatory PD when *localized* confrontation develops between the primary antagonists that could affect relations between the great powers as well. Conciliatory PD can and should capitalize—as did Canadian foreign minister Lester Pearson in the mid-1950s—on widely understood international dangers for its legitimacy.[39] If conciliation is applied as local crisis management, then more and not less controversy becomes useful where the primary antagonists are far apart and lack incentives to agree. (This presumes that the immediate antagonists can still envisage their own mutual restraint. The great powers can then keep order where they can make the disincentives of greater disorder more apparent to the primary antagonists.) Such diplomacy is then especially associated with an inherent risk of failure. Indeed, if the dangers are linked to confidence in the process of diplomacy and its ancillary activities, manipulating the risks of failure is apparently central to success. Furthermore, success may be short-lived, lasting until the next local confrontation.

Conciliatory PD is not always associated with crisis and danger; routine rather than danger can also support such diplomacy. It is necessary to distinguish cases in which local war or the likelihood of spillover was considerable from those (the Memel and much of the Armenian case) where it was not. Where crisis is prevented, the primary antagonists can adapt to the situation to create a semblance of normality between themselves.

Force-dampening through peacekeepers and supply of governmental officials can be a method of working toward normalization even in the absence of reconciliation. But it is precisely the absence of reconciliation that often contributes most to widespread desire for it, and to local acceptance of international methods of conciliating the opponents. If all the elements enumerated above that *interfere* with reconciliation are recalled, and considered as the sources of danger and crisis, then awareness of those elements and their dangers, as emphasized by the great powers, paradoxically seems to do most to keep conciliatory PD high on the agenda of the primary antagonists.

CONCLUSIONS

Most of this chapter has considered collective conciliatory interventionist PD from the viewpoint of the primary antagonists, whose receptivity to it is mixed. PD designed to reconcile the antagonists tends to be ineffective because of the suspicions the primary antagonists have for each other, and because of great-power unwillingness to support reconciliation proposals coercively.[40]

Force-dampening PD initiatives are more useful, local antagonists being unable to cope with the consequences of their mutual hostility on their own. The harsher and more destructive are those consequences, the more important is this great-power role. Since destructive consequences of conflict is a feature of hurting local stalemate,[41] the great powers have much to say about that stalemate. The stalemate would become more acute in the absence of collective great-power PD, but the willingness of the great powers to defuse the intensified local conflict undercuts the imperative of local conflict resolution.

From a great-power perspective, the chapter highlights how the major states repeatedly address small-state hurting stalemates that do not produce conflict resolution. They adapt for the goal of tension-reducing PD an impressive variety of measures to win the support of the primary antagonists, reflecting their flexibility in particular circumstances. But the success of these efforts is hardly assured. And the persistent need for such efforts is created by primary antagonist rejection of great-power initiatives to promote local conflict resolution. Frustration of that PD can accentuate divergence between great powers, threatening the foundation of collective interventionist PD. Great-power willingness to persevere with collective PD in spite of that challenge is one of the most important themes of this study.

Source: Mauldin Collection, Library of Congress. Reprinted with permission.

Chapter 8

From Conciliation to Coercion

Collective interventionist PD initiatives are commonly resisted by one or more primary antagonists, and this resistance tests the will of the great powers to sustain them. This chapter is concerned with the issue of collective enforcement of great-power views: how, given local antagonist intransigeance to their PD proposals, the major states are attracted prior to the endgame to coercive as against conciliatory interventionist PD.[1]

This chapter argues, first of all, that the collective great-power decision to adopt coercive as against conciliatory interventionist PD is primarily affected by insulationist PD—that is, by the major states' ability to defuse the local conflict as an element of their own relations. In particular, insulationist PD accounts for an important variation among our cases in the timing of the adoption of coercive interventionist PD.

If one or more of the great powers has vital interests in intervening in the local conflict, as in the Belgian case, the line between conciliation and coercion can be quickly crossed. The importance for the major states in maintaining a collective PD framework that includes the more assertive great power then outweighs the perceived risks entailed in becoming more deeply engaged in local ethnic conflict. More commonly, when the major states lack important interests driving them to intervene in the local conflict, the shift to coercion is delayed, even after prolonged local resistance to great-power proposals. Such cases, conforming to Type III cases described in chapter 2, require a change in the collective will of the major states to affect the local conflict before a coercive approach can be adopted. The cause of this change is discussed in the next chapter; the point here is that the inadequacy of conciliatory interventionist PD does not in itself push the major states toward a coercive approach. Conciliation is often widely perceived as ineffective, yet the shift to coercive intervention does not occur. The delay in collective adoption of coercive intervention must be understood in light of the inertial effect of prior major-state insulationist PD.

A second preoccupation of this chapter is with local conflict developments that underscore the inadequacies of conciliatory intervention without, however, pushing the major states to collectively shift to a coercive approach. These are termed here "transition" developments, because they force upon the great-power agenda the issue of collective enforcement of collectively held major-state viewpoints. Transition developments include (1) humanitarian emergency, (2) military intervention in the local conflict by neighboring states and great powers, and (3) provocations against an international military presence in the local area introduced for force-dampening purposes.

This chapter argues that conciliatory intervention often persists prior to the endgame stage in spite of these developments, for two reasons. First, great-power consensus can be too weak to support a tougher response, a problem often seen in relation to humanitarian emergency and to provocations against international military forces. Second, divisions between great powers impede cooperation for collective coercion, a difficulty especially highlighted in the aftermath of unilateral great-power military intervention in the local conflict.

The Impact of Insulation on the Mode of Interventionist PD

The Belgian case alone illustrated the ability of the major states to apply coercive interventionist PD in the early stage of local conflict. They were able to do so within six months of that local conflict's inception. Such a response was not forthcoming in the early stages of the other conflicts, for one of two alternative reasons: either because a unified great-power concert was unable to summon the will to coerce the parties, or the concert was weakened by the inability of the major states to agree on whether the local antagonists should be coerced. In one other case (the Memel), the major states practiced accommodation to the parties because they attached a very low priority to the local conflict. Their conciliatory intervention approach was dictated by their relative indifference to a settlement between the German and Lithuan-

TABLE 8.1
Insulation and Conciliatory and Coercive Intervention

Category	*Cases*
Concert consensus permits prompt coercion	Belgium
Concert consensus precludes collective coercion	the Memel
Concert divisions impede coercion	Greece Armenia Bosnia I the Congo Cyprus Bosnia II

ian communities in the Memel. In the other six cases, coercive intervention was ruled out by differences between the major states over how intervention should proceed (Bosnia I and II, Greece, Armenia, Cyprus, the Congo). Great-power rivalry over the local conflict was more important for the major states in these instances than overcoming resistance of the primary antagonists to their PD proposals.

Table 8.1 describes these groupings, which will now be discussed in turn. The discussion is designed to show that in each of these categories the choice between coercive and conciliatory PD intervention is determined mainly by the character of relations between the major states. How the major powers defuse the local conflict as an issue between themselves, rather than the workability of conciliation or coercion in relation to the local antagonists, determines the choice of collective intervention in the local ethnic conflict.

Concert Consensus Promptly Permits Coercion

Only in the Belgian case were the great powers able within months to go beyond conciliation and to employ coercive tactics, their collective will to intervene being sufficiently strong to permit it. In February 1831, French mobilization on the Belgian frontier led the Dutch government to accept the first Basis of Separation proposal drafted by the great powers. Subsequently, when the Belgians delayed accepting this same agreement, on May 10 of that year the major states issued an ultimatum threatening to break off relations with Belgium unless the Belgians accepted the proposal by June 1. And the French twice intervened militarily in Belgium against the Dutch—once in

August 1831 when the Dutch renewed war against the Belgians, and again in December 1832 (together with Britain) to compel the Dutch to evacuate the Antwerp fortress.

Great-power insulation of this ethnic conflict was tied to strong and sustained intervention and mediation at the outset, and coercive tactics not surprisingly fit well into that approach. Moreover, England and France were both especially sensitive to political conditions in Belgium: the British wished to contain the French role there, and the French were determined to protect the Belgians against a reassertion of Dutch rule. Because of Belgian instability, both countries' interests could be satisfied *only if coercive measures were employed*, and the concert, protecting both countries' interests, in effect legitimated coercion within parameters ordained by the concert. On the other hand, the French prevented the concert from reacting as sharply to Belgian resistance as it had to obstacles posed by the Dutch. The concert was unable to effectively coerce the Belgians because the French were unwilling to be drawn into war against the revolutionists, unlike their belligerence toward the Dutch.

Collective Coercion Is Precluded by Weak Great-Power Unity

In regard to the Memel, the great powers cooperated closely yet demonstrated only weak collective will to address ethnic conflict, for two reasons. First, the Memel had small intrinsic importance for the Conference of Ambassadors, in which Britain and France played principal roles. Britain originally intended to establish the Memel as a free city on the model of Danzig, hoping to cede the territory later to a more politically, economically, and culturally strengthened Lithuania.

Second, more important Baltic regional concerns relating to the status of Poland and Lithuania, both newly created after the First World War, justified great-power caution on the Memel. Poland and Lithuania conflicted over Vilna, a territory claimed by Poland but ceded to Lithuania by Russian Bolsheviks in August 1920. Inflamed when Polish irregulars occupied Vilna in October 1920, this dispute caused consideration of a Memel settlement to be postponed. And great-power action on the Memel was made contingent upon Lithuanian recognition of the provisions of Versailles on internationalizing the Neimen River, which came about only in October 1922. Only that month, more than three years after the Memel had been severed from Germany in the Versailles Treaty, did the Conference of Ambassadors appoint a committee to report on the status of the Memel.

The causes of great-power delay also explain major-state unwillingness to intervene coercively in the Memel. However, even potential conciliatory intervention increased Lithuanian anxieties because internationalization of the territory, to which Lithuania was strongly opposed, remained a strong option. Fearing that the French administrator of the territory would persuade the French government to support a free-state solution for the Memel, Lithuania persisted in demanding control of the territory, yet after October 1922, "[i]t was commonly rumoured," according to an official British account, "that the Committee [appointed by the Conference of Ambassadors to consider the Memel question] would recommend the establishment of Memel as a Free State under the League of Nations."[2] Lithuanian nonuniformed military forces intervened in the Memel in January 1823, before the report of the committee recommending a free state solution could be made public.

Great-Power Divisions Impede Coercive Intervention

In the other six cases, great-power disputes ruled out coercion. In these cases conciliation was shown to be ineffective in the face of local antagonist resistance, but coercive intervention could only occur if the major states were in agreement about it. The effort to forge such agreement allowed and encouraged display of major-state differences impeding that coalition.

In the Greek case, Holy Alliance powers disagreed about how to react to strong Ottoman suppression of the Greek revolution. Russia wished to coerce the Turks to stop the suppression, using the threat of Russian conquest of Turkish holdings in the Danubian principalities as the primary means to do so. This would have used Turkish behavior against the Greeks as the pretext for a war of conquest against Turkey in the Balkan area. Metternich, on behalf of other Holy Alliance members, separated the Greek question from broader Russo-Turkish differences. He rejected war as a response to Turkish suppression and would have limited great-power involvement to providing advice to the Turks about how to bring the Greek insurrection to an end.[3]

England and Russia later divided over their approach to the Turks in this same case, with the Russians hoping that entente with the English would strengthen the case for coercing the Turks in the long run, while

England endeavored through entente to prevent the Russians from going to war with the Turks through unilateral coercion. Coercion of the Turks was impossible as long as Russia—whatever her military position—persisted in taking advantage of Turkish weakness, because the English were determined to contain Russia at the time the latter made war against Turkey and did not wish to see the Turks weakened further.

Austria and Russia divided in Bosnia I over coercing the Turks in the Slavic revolution in Bosnia-Herzegovina. The Russian government hoped, through association with Austria, to increase international pressures on the Turks over the long run, while the Austrians wished to avoid coercion in order to contain the vulnerability of the Austro-Hungarian Empire to Slavic pressure. The Austrians used collective mediation of the great powers to stress Turkish administrative reform, bringing pressure upon the Turks to honor commitments made earlier to their Christian peoples. This approach respected Turkish supremacy over the Christians and rejected interference in the internal Ottoman system. Russia by contrast pressed for autonomy for the Christian peoples in Bosnia-Herzegovina, posing as protector of the Ottoman Christians. It underscored Turkish responsibility for proper treatment of Christian peoples under Turkish control, holding in reserve coercion of the Turks for failure—which the Russians anticipated—to properly exercise it.

The British and Russians divided over a long period of time regarding coercing the Turks regarding the Armenian question. As the result of the Russo-Turkish War of 1877-1878, when Russia occupied Armenian territory in eastern Turkey, the Russians, encouraged by the Armenians, sought to coerce concessions from the Turks but were opposed by Great Britain. Later, following the 1878 Treaty of Berlin, the British took the lead to protect the Armenians, seeking to impose a program of Turkish reform after the Turks resisted, only to be opposed in this endeavor by Russia.

The major powers were ambivalent in the Congo case over coercing Tshombe to end his secessionist movement in Katanga, although agreeing to oppose it; this ambivalence contributed to deletion of the authorization to use force against foreign officers and mercenaries in Katanga in a key Security Council resolution of 21 February 1961. That resolution authorized the use of force in the Congo only in the last resort to prevent civil war, and not to coerce the parties to accept agreed-upon political terms.[4] (Such an approach also suited Hammarskjöld, for whom force was the least desirable technique to realize his objectives.)[5] The UN had a mandate to restore law and order in the Congo, but it was also obliged to avoid interference in the domestic affairs of the new country, a requirement that prevented UN personnel from upsetting the local power balance there.[6]

Hammarskjöld's initial timidity in acting to conciliate Lumumba and Tshombe was partly based on his unwillingness to violate this latter constraint. An even more important reason for this timidity, however, was that he viewed the importance of UN involvement in the Congo primarily in terms of ensuring that Congolese differences would not become an element of worldwide superpower Cold War competition. Great-power inability during the Cold War to act collectively—except during crises that raised the spector of superpower warfare—led him to push UN involvement there so as to contain superpower rivalry. In practice, Hammarskjöld's slowness in acting to reconcile the opponents and his refusal to affect the local power balance added to the likelihood that coercion would be needed later to deal with the Katanga secession. "Ironically enough," writes Catherine Hoskyns, "Hammarskjöld's sensitivity about intervention in [Congolese] internal affairs in 1960 meant that the situation could only be restored in 1961 by action which came very close to the intervention which he had tried to avoid. Though the outcome was in the end the same, the delay meant that the operation cost many more lives and was a great deal more controversial that it would have been had the problem been tackled earlier."[7]

The United States and the Soviet Union divided sharply over Cyprus. The UN, intervening in Cyprus as it had in the Congo to forestall superpower rivalry, named a mediator in 1964 to help conciliate the Greek and Turkish Cypriotes. Here, however, more than in the Congo, the conciliation effort clashed with rival superpower interests. In October 1964, with Archbishop Makarios confronted by a right-wing Greek government and adopting anti-Western policies, the Soviet Union entered into an alliance with Cyprus to offer "practical measures of assistance" to safeguard Cypriote freedom and territorial integrity. For their part, the Americans then supported the Greek government in attempting to undermine Makarios and to promote *enosis* with Greece. The UN–appointed mediator, Galo Plaza, by contrast recommended in March 1965 that Cyprus renounce its right to unite with Greece and that the island be demilitarized.

And finally, division in Bosnia II over coercing the Serbs in the wake of ethnic cleansing in Bosnia-Herzegovina divided the United States from its most important European allies, England and France. The British and French, whose military contingents comprised the most important part of the United Nations peacekeeping force in Bosnia-Herzegovina, rejected coercing the Serbs and favored an impartial approach to the civil conflict within Bosnia, while the United States insisted on punishing Serb aggression and on strengthening the ability of the Muslim-dominated government in Sarajevo to resist it.

In many of these cases, great-power advocates of coercion accommodate at first to those insisting upon conciliation, mediation, and nonintervention. England and Russia, by supporting the Turkish regime, alternatively prevented the imposition of a solution to the Armenian conflict. In Bosnia II, the Americans partly accommodated their NATO allies, abandoning their strike and lift proposal but not sanctions against Yugoslavia for its assistance to the Bosnian Serbs. In Greece, Metternich sought for two years, with Russian support, to gain voluntary agreement on the rights of Turkish subject peoples against which Turkish conduct could be judged.[8] Metternich launched this effort to ride out the Russian war fever directed at the Turks. The Anglo-Russian entente of 1826 was intended by the English to have the same effect. And Russia formally cooperated with the 1875 and 1876 Austrian-led mediation efforts in Bosnia I.

The decision of the great powers in each of these cases to at first favor conciliatory rather than coercive interventionist PD in the local conflict highlights two broader tendencies. The first is the durability of collective insulationist PD, as the preponderant great-power viewpoint favoring conciliation toward the local antagonists prevails over the coercive approach endorsed by an individual major state. The concert is not disposed to change its basis for agreement on intervention merely because one major state presses for a different one. The second point underscored by this experience is that differences between the major states accentuate the significance of insulation relative to intervention. In most of these cases (Greece, Bosnia I and II, Armenia), the major states act together to manage their differences over the local conflict, supporting weak conciliatory intervention as one aspect of conflict management between themselves. In the two cases (the Congo and Cyprus) in which the great powers are unable to act together, the UN acts independently to assist the major states with insulation and to provide an international framework for conciliating the local opponents.

For stronger primary antagonists, great-power conciliation in these cases is attractive because it screens out unwanted coercive measures known to be favored by at least one major state. The alternative to conciliation is great-power coercive intervention directed against that antagonist. Anticipating that coercion might otherwise be applied outside the concert association, the stronger antagonist is more willing to entertain measures of conciliation launched by the concert and not dismiss them out of hand.[9]

On the other hand, great-power conciliation paradoxically provides incentives to the primary antagonists *not* to bridge their differences. Since the stronger antagonist is in no immediate danger of being threatened by major-state intervention if it considers the initiatives and cooperates in principle, it looks to its great-power supporter as a diplomatic protector on the larger questions, standing pat on them even when willing to make small concessions. In each of these cases, the stronger antagonist capitalizes on the mild interventionist position of the major states to stretch out the negotiations while gradually moving against sharpened local resistance from its ethnic challenger with its military strength. But the weaker side, unaware of the great-power dispute, often looks beyond the stage of conciliation and counts on future potential support by its hard-line major-state supporter. The weaker antagonist's attraction to conciliation is thus also undermined, as in the Slavic resistance to Austrian mediation proposals in 1875 and 1876.

Transitions

The burden of the foregoing has been that insulationist PD, rather than local ethnic conflict developments, most affects the mode of interventionist PD initially adopted by the major states toward the local conflict. But the evolution of local conflict is not unimportant for the major powers. It affects the international importance of that conflict and the workability of the intervention mode that the major states have put in place. Shaping major-power attitudes towards the local ethnic conflict, local developments can bring into question prior major-state decisions and assumptions guiding collective interventionist PD.

The primary interest in elaborating on these developments here is with the perceived effectiveness of conciliatory interventionist PD, most commonly employed in our cases, in which threat-making was ruled out as an instrument of conflict management. The exceptional early decision in the Belgian case to employ coercive intervention significantly enlarged the tactic that could be employed to contain at least the military aspects of Belgian-Dutch conflict. The concern here is with how conciliatory intervention, sustained in seven other cases, is questioned by the major states as its limitations in affecting the local antagonists become apparent.

TABLE 8.2
The Incidence of Transition Developments

Cases	*Humanitarian Emergency*	*Actual or Threatened Military Intervention by Outside States*	*Provocations Against Internationally Authorized Forces*
Belgium		X	
Greece	X	X	X
Bosnia I		X	
Armenia	X	X	
The Memel		X	(a)
The Congo	X	X	X
Cyprus		X	(a)
Bosnia II	X	X	X

(a) The Lithuanian invasion of the Memel, the Grivas-led covert Greek invasion into Cyprus in the early 1970s, and the 1974 Turkish invasion of Cyprus each led to hostilities against international military forces. These instances, in which combat was brief and low level, are categorized in this study as examples of intervention rather than as localized provocation.

Three kinds of developments exacerbate local conflict and, in doing so, add to doubts about whether conciliatory intervention adopted by the major states toward the conflict is adequate: (1) a humanitarian emergency, in which a resurgence of violence puts at risk large numbers of noninvolved civilians (Greece, Armenia, and Bosnia II), (2) military intervention of outside states (all cases), and (3) provocations and depredations against an international military presence introduced into the area of the local dispute as a force-dampening measure (the Congo, Bosnia II, Greece). These are summarized in table 8.2. These developments, testing as did local resistance the will of the major states to persist with conciliation, are here termed "transitions." If sufficiently important, they could—and in our cases occasionally did—challenge conciliatory interventionist PD and strengthen arguments for shifting to a more deeply committed coercive form of intervention.

Humanitarian Emergencies

Repeated massacres of Greek and Armenian populations in the Ottoman Empire, an August 1960 massacre by the Congolese army in Kasai, and repeated atrocities by Serbs against Muslims in Bosnia-Herzegovina from

1992 to 1995 each clashed with international humanitarian norms. They ran counter to widely accepted beliefs that noncombatant populations should not be targeted in war, and were of sufficient scope that they could not be ignored by the major states.

The Greek case was apparently the first in which the violation of international humanitarian norms caused an unfavorable political reaction in international politics. "The age of nineteenth-century liberalism had begun," commented C. M. Woodhouse, "and Greece was among its first beneficiaries."[10] These norms were of fundamental importance to the Greeks, whose ability to prevail against their Turkish rulers depended upon attracting great-power support. Even where the Greeks suffered military setbacks, they were helped politically by Turkish brutality. By late 1822, a year after the Greek revolution began,

> Western Europe had been stirred to attention by the sacrifice of the Philhellenes at Peta, by the Turkish atrocities at Chios, and by the Greeks' capture of the historical citadel of Athens. European opinion was soon to be still more deeply stirred by the long siege of Mesolonghi, which had already begun. From the Turks' point of view nothing could be more unreasonable and inexplicable than Europe's reactions to these trivial events, these insignificant names. . . . The Sultan's court at least was compelled to take note of European reactions, and to soothe them with promises of good behaviour in the future.[11]

Atrocities against Armenians in Anatolia from 1894 to 1896 attracted the disapproval of the major states for the same reasons. In 1894, massacres in the Armenian homeland in the aftermath of Armenian protests against cruelties suffered at the hands of Kurds led to collective great-power intervention with the Sultan. European intervention became more strident when separate incidents occurred over the next two years in Constantinople, the first in the summer of 1895 when Armenian demonstrations led to violent Turkish reactions, and the second as Armenian nationalists' seizure of the Ottoman bank in Constantinople in 1896 again triggered a massacre. While violence in eastern Anatolia was regularly denied by the Ottoman government and usually viewed by European ambassadors from strategic vantage points, atrocities in Constantinople could not be denied and offended the moral proprieties of the ambassadors. According to one study, "The European ambassadors witnessed the murder of the Armenians in the streets of Constantinople; they saw them dragged out of the houses and clubbed to death. The reaction of the ambassadors was spontaneous and in

Constantinople itself at least effective. They threatened to use force unless the massacres were stopped. The Sultan now thought it expedient to pretend to be guided by their advice."[12]

The August 1960 massacre by the Congolese army in Kasai led to strong reaction by Hammarskjöld on the basis of the belief that, as Hammarskjöld explained, it was "a case of incipient genocide."[13] The army had landed in Kasai to prepare for a planned invasion of neighboring secessionist Katanga province but immediately became involved in a lesser instance of secession by the Baluba tribe in the town of Bakwanga. To this incident Hammarskjöld responded by overriding prior UN restraint in Congolese domestic disputes. "Prohibition against intervention in internal conflicts," he wrote, "cannot be considered to apply to senseless slaughter of civilians or fighting arising from tribal hostilities," and he authorized forceful interposition of UN troops to stop the massacre.[14]

In Bosnia II, atrocities by Serbs against Muslims were publicized by the newly independent Bosnian government following the invasion of Serbs and Croats into Muslim areas in April 1992. A long-term Serb siege of the Bosnian capital of Sarajevo began at the same time, and another against the western Bosnia Muslim enclave of Bihac shortly afterward, reinforced by indiscriminate bombardments. These led to widespread sympathy for the Muslim cause, to the major-power decision to launch an airlift for Sarajevo, and eventually to military intervention against the Bosnian Serb forces to end the sieges and the killings of Muslims. Although by August 1992 Bosnian Serb leaders gave assurances that ethnic cleaning against Muslims would be halted and concentration camps housing Muslims would be closed, these were slow to take effect. Over time, Croats and Muslims were also implicated in atrocities, but Serb excesses were most widespread and publicized, creating a widespread perception that Serb military action was the most serious problem to be dealt with in Bosnia.

Military Intervention from Outside

All eight cases studied here feature the use of force by outside secondary states or by major powers against one of the primary antagonists. Among the formal and open uses of force are Serb and Montenegrin intervention in Bosnia-Herzegovina in 1876; Russian intervention later in that same case and as an outgrowth of the Greek Revolution; Serb and Croat intervention in Bosnia in 1992; Lithuanian intervention in the Memel; Belgian intervention in the Belgian Congo; Turkish intervention in Cyprus; and unilateral French intervention (beyond that which was concert endorsed) in Belgium against the Dutch. Informal and covert intervention characterize Serb and Montenegrin military personnel early in the Slav Revolution of 1875 in Bosnia-Herzegovina; Greek military activity against the Makarios regime in Cyprus in 1966–67 and again in 1971–74; and American military assistance to the Muslim-led Sarajevo regime in Bosnia in 1993–95.

Military intervention from outside the local conflict in each of these cases complicates the prevailing conciliatory interventionist PD of the major states. By helping the aggrieved ethnic challenger in the local conflict, it stiffens the challenger's resistance to conciliatory proposals put forward or (as in the Memel case) being prepared for consideration by the major states. But military intervention by independent-minded major states especially forcefully challenges interventionist PD by questioning the insulationist PD underpinning it. This is especially significant when (as in cases other than Belgium and the Memel) the collective major-power decision will to become involved in a particular local ethnic conflict is changeable in the course of the evolution of the conflict.

Motivated by shared cultural attributes with Slav revolutionists in Bosnia-Herzegovina, Serb and Montenegrin intervention in Bosnia I appears to have been controlled by Russia. Prince Milan of Serbia was ready at the outset of the revolution to intervene of behalf of his brethren, but was constrained from doing so by Russian refusal at that time to provide him with military support.[15] He therefore dedicated himself to staying out of the war, against the wishes of his belligerent ministers. Even as war fever increased in Serbia in 1876 as a result of well-publicized Turkish atrocities in Bulgaria, Russian attitudes remained a dominant factor in Serb intentions. "There is little doubt," B. H. Sumner has written of Serb military intervention in Bosnia-Herzegovina in the summer of 1876, "that the outbreak of the Serbian war would not have occurred if the Serbian government had really believed the protestations of the foreign office at St. Petersburg to be sincere and effective, and if the Balkan Christians had not come to believe that the true policy of Russia was guided by Ignatiev and the panslavs."[16]

When the Turks defeated the two Slav states, Russia intervened with Austrian support to force a halt in the Turkish military advance and then to compel the Turks to agree to reforms toward the Slavs. These actions, which led to Russo-Turkish hostilities, inflamed relations with England

and brought the English into active diplomatic intervention as allies of the Turks. Russian military intervention against the Turks in 1828 similarly grew out of military action—the Battle of Navarino—in which the Turks, though militarily defeated at the hands of a great-power coalition, angrily refused to acknowledge it. Instead, they repudiated concessions made earlier in the Danubian principalities to Russia in the Treaty of Akkermann, and the Russians in reply proposed a joint blockade of the Dardanelles and the Bosphorus to isolate Constantinople. When the British, being unable to agree on a policy, failed to act either in support of or in opposition to Russia at this time, the Russians acted alone and the Turks went to war.

Beyond the aim of impressing the Turks, Russian ultimata in these cases were designed to catch the support of other great powers. In 1828 and again in 1877, Russian diplomats sought to neutralize opposition to Russian war-making abroad by inviting other major states, especially England, to participate in coercing the Turks. English participation in a display of force would have been expected to impress the Turks more than would Russia acting alone, making it more likely that the Turks would back down without war. Thus, the Russians sought to take advantage of the concert in order to bring about a collective coercive posture.

Lithuania in the Memel and Croatia and Serbia in Bosnia II fought weak opponents. Lithuania, intervening to forestall creation of an international zone in the Memel, quickly overwhelmed the small French force stationed there, the French electing not to resist the invasion militarily. In Bosnia II, where the newly declared independent government of Bosnia-Herzegovina had no standing army, its independent status was quickly placed in jeopardy by invading Serb and Croat forces. After their invasion, neither Croatia, itself newly independent from Yugoslavia, nor the Serb-dominated former Yugoslavia acknowledged until late 1995 the validity of their borders with Bosnia-Herzegovina.[17] Their joint offensive, though slowed by emplacement of international peacekeeping forces in Bosnia-Herzegovina, would in practice have prevented that country from exercising independent authority if the United States had not counteracted it by providing massive military assistance to Bosnia-Herzegovina on a covert basis. The United States provided this assistance as a means of pressuring the Serbs to give up Bosnian territory they had taken by force, even as it formally supported the UN policy of conciliating all the parties.

Shortly after Congolese independence was declared, Belgian intervention in the Congo to defend the interests of European settlers in the country greatly strengthened the Katanga secession. Turkish intervention in

Cyprus in 1974 was provoked by the successful Greek-led coup in Cyprus that temporarily toppled the Makarios government. Though a strong opponent of Makarios, Turkey demanded Makarios's return to power and invaded after the Americans failed to put pressure on Greece to reinstate him. The Americans were officially committed to negotiating about the coup against Makarios but not to his return, effectively opening the door to the Turkish invasion.

France, which acted on several occasions as the military agent of the concert in the Belgian case, also at times acted unilaterally. It mobilized forces on the Belgian frontier in February 1831 to coerce the Dutch to accept the first Basis of Separation agreement worked out by the concert, and in August 1831, immediately after the Ten Days War, it unilaterally kept its forces in Belgium for some weeks after they succeeded, with concert sanction, in forcing Dutch forces out of Belgium. Striving toward a protectorship of the Belgians, French leaders may have hoped that the concert, having delegated France to compel the Dutch to retreat militarily from Belgium, would sanction the stationing of a permanent French force there. Such force would be designed to deter future Dutch intervention in Belgium and make unnecessary the kind of coercive efforts undertaken in August 1831. The British government opposed this conception and was determined to limit the French presence in Belgium even if doing so led to war with France. In this instance, British opposition to French independent action in Belgium was derived from the same thinking that produced the concert's earlier decision in 1830 to resist and repel, even coercively, Dutch dominance over the Belgians—namely, the advantage of preserving an independent Belgium as an outpost against any empire building in Europe.

Military intervention by small states into the area of ethnic conflict in these cases—Serbia and Montenegro in Bosnia I; Belgium in the Congo; Turkey in Cyprus; Lithuania in the Memel; Croatia and Yugoslavia in Bosnia II—is stimulated by cultural affinity with one of the primary antagonists in the local conflict. But independent major-state military intervention, of greater significance to the present study, is impelled by broader considerations. French intervention in Belgium and Russian intervention in the Greek and Bosnia I cases were opportunistic, as a major power took advantage of a neighboring regime's misfortunes to extend its own influence. American covert assistance to the Sarajevo regime in Bosnia II was stimulated by moralistic opposition to Serb military excess. Each of these independent great-power actions constitutes an *apparent* defection from the conciliation-minded concert and collective PD, designed not to torpedo the great-power concert but to affect it, to push it in a coercive direction. Affecting the concert's interventionist PD in this way can, it appears, be done only when the independent-minded major state questions collective insulationist PD, risking a rupture with its great-power associates.

This point, it is argued here, shows the durability of concert association, adapting insulationist PD for common purposes. The independent-minded major state in such cases enlarges its leverage upon its concert associates as it knowingly antagonizes them, but unilateral great-power independent behavior only temporarily divides the allies. The concert, its conciliatory interventionist PD weakened, weathers the challenge.

Localized Provocations

In three cases (Greece, the Congo, and Bosnia II), international forces allocated by the great powers or by a great-power surrogate such as the United Nations to an area of localized ethnic conflict are challenged by one of the primary antagonists. The resulting military action is substantial. The three-power Pacific Blockade sent to Greek waters in September 1827 was intended to (1) prevent neutral and Turkish vessels from bringing supplies and reinforcements to the Turkish garrisons on the Greek mainland, where they were needed to suppress Greek resistance to Turkish rule; and (2) gain an armistice in the fighting on the mainland, the blockading forces being authorized to engage only the antagonists that rejected the armistice. The Greeks accepted an armistice, but the Turks did not. In practice, the captains of the three fleets had substantial leeway to pursue the blockade as they saw fit. The British captain accepted that "although the measures . . . are not adopted in a hostile spirit . . . the prevention of supplies . . . is ultimately to be enforced, if necessary, and when all other means are exhausted, by cannon-shot."[18] On 20 October 1827, following the fleets' failure to intercept a large resupply convoy from Egypt, the British captain entered the Bay of Navarino, where Turkish and Egyptian ships were anchored. He intended to discuss an armistice with the Turkish commander but was prepared to fight on the least pretext.[19] When the Turks initiated fire in reply to the Allied fleet entrance to the Bay, a general engagement occurred and the Ottoman force was destroyed by nightfall.[20]

The UN peacekeeping force in the Congo was designed to stop fighting in the country, contain superpower competition there, and provide conditions that would end the Congolese civil war. Following deployment of this force, the regular Belgian forces that had been brought into the Congo soon after its independence had been declared, to cope with breakdown of law and order but also to support the Katanga secession, had been removed by September 1960. But UN political and military officials in the Congo had been unable to persuade the Katanga regime and European representatives to remove the approximately five hundred foreign military officers and mercenaries whose presence in Katanga had enabled the insurrection there to persist. Hammarskjöld had concluded by the summer of 1961 that tougher measures were needed for this purpose, but was determined to prevent fighting between those forces and UN peacekeepers as well as provocations that could lead to fighting.[21] An operation by UN peacekeepers led to the nonviolent arrest of about three hundred of the European cadres on August 28, but because of what Brian Urquhart termed "the overcharged atmosphere of Elisabethville,"[22] leading UN civilian and military officials in the Congo believed that further drastic action was needed. Although Hammarskjöld explicitly informed the UN Congo mission of its very limited authority to use force, as we have seen, UN officials in the country nevertheless believed that forceful measures were needed. Having tipped off the mercenaries that arrests were imminent, UN peacekeepers came under attack from the Katanga mercenary-led gendarmerie when they began their follow-up operations on September 13. Inconclusive fighting ensued in Elisabethville, UN objectives in the Congo were set back, and the behavior of UN peacekeepers was condemned by Western governments.

UN forces interposed between Bosnian Serb contingents and the Moslem-dominated Bosnian government in Sarajevo in 1992 were augmented in 1993 to protect five Muslim enclaves in Serb-held territory. These forces held off the opposing contingents only to the degree that the latter did not deliberately intend to initiate hostilities—that is to say, they supported periods of respite in the ongoing civil war when the belligerents themselves desired a respite.[23] But because of the frequency of Serb, Muslim, and Croat operations against each other and against civilians, UN forces were often challenged by the belligerents. Peacekeepers were taken hostage, notably by Serbs in May 1995 (following NATO warplane retaliation for Serb violations of prior agreements restricting deployment of heavy weaponry around Sarajevo) but also by Bosnian government troops in January and June 1995. The initial UN response to such challenges was conciliatory, but in June 1995 it authorized and introduced a 12,500-man NATO Rapid Reaction Force to deter future hostage taking. International contingents were also threatened with and targeted by hostile fire, and they frequently returned fire to establish tactical military advantage, even if this went counter to agreed-upon rules of engagement. For example, international units detailed to guide food convoys through contested areas to Sarajevo assumed that all resistance to their mission was hostile. As one commanding office of a British regiment guarding these convoys explained, "We had to impress our will on the forces occupying the area with a mixture of coercion, threats, bluff, and bravado and, in the end, force. You have a mandate and if in the end someone pushes you over the edge, then you shoot people and I suppose that's why they called us 'Shootbat.'"[24] Though controversial at NATO headquarters and with NATO members, British regiments employing these tactics took through every convoy under their jurisdiction.[25]

Force-dampening in these cases, as with humanitarian emergencies and outside military intervention, weakens prevailing conciliatory interventionist PD of the major states. Force-dampening uniquely contributes to weakened conciliation, however, through the gap in philosophy between international political leaders forging a presence in a local conflict, on one hand, and their military representatives on the other. Home governments are motivated by the need for conciliation, patience, and avoidance of a rupture with the primary antagonists. Such an approach requires forestalling, slowing, or at least compensating for crises between the local antagonists that can become uncontrolled. This in turn requires focusing primarily on diplomatic negotiation, using international forces on the scene as trip wires of danger and as means of mutual reassurance. By contrast, military commanders in these cases are most concerned about security and military advantage under hostile conditions. They cannot afford to disregard tactical military requirements under conditions in which their troops are placed in harm's way, often plan for the worst, act aggressively to safeguard their troops and missions,[26] and lack patience or dedication to resist the drift of events. Coercion in these cases is thus conditioned less by the calculation of state interests than by the more specialized interests and needs of fighting forces.

The Aftermath of Transition Developments

These transition developments underscore the inadequacy of conciliatory PD but do not invariably establish or confirm the alternative of coercion.

At times this is because great-power consensus weakens: coercion must wait until consensus is again in place. In these cases a transition development—unilateral major-state intervention against a primary ethnic antagonist—exposes the weakness of conciliatory interventionist PD by interrupting great-power consensus. A second problem impeding the move to coercive intervention as an alternative to conciliatory PD is that even when great-power consensus persists and coercion is tried, support is not strong enough for coercive PD to be sustained. This problem, evident in the aftermath of humanitarian emergencies and of provocations against international forces, reflects the inertial effect of earlier major-state support for coercive interventionist PD.

The first problem shows how unilateral intervention by major states is far more disruptive of great-power unity in our cases than is intervention by small states. In all but one instance in the cases studied here, small-state intervention bolsters conciliatory interventionist PD. Croat and Serb intervention early in the Bosnia II case, the threat of Russian intervention in Armenian Turkey in 1912, Turkish intervention in Cyprus in 1974, Belgian intervention in the Congo in 1961, and Lithuanian intervention in the Memel in 1923: each stimulated conciliatory PD of the major antagonists. Only in Bosnia I, when the July 1876 decision by Serbia and Montenegro to intervene militarily in Bosnia-Herzegovina led Andrassy to terminate his campaign to conciliate the primary antagonists, did small-state intervention bring an end to the conciliatory approach.

On the other hand, major-state intervention invariably challenges the major-state consensus underpinning conciliation. Russian war-making in 1876 against Turkey in Bosnia I undermined the structure of the concert itself. England refused to cooperate with Russian belligerence and became a determined ally of the Turks through its suspicion of Russian intentions. Russian war-making earlier against Turkey in the Greek case also led to suspension by England of collective action against Turkey until Russian-Turkish belligerence ended. Unilateral French action in support of the Belgians against the Dutch interrupted concert unity until the French agreed to end their incursions. And American covert military support for the Muslim-dominated Bosnian regime brought about major tensions with England and France.

These four examples show how highly interested major states act independently to coerce a primary antagonist at the risk of rupturing relations with great-power associates. The actions are in part opportunistic but also designed as leverage to push for a tougher collective coercive position. With respect to the latter motive, a will to act independently provides essential leverage, and therefore a major power desiring to alter great-power consensus has incentive to act independently even if it knowingly antagonizes its allies when doing so. The actions each constituted only apparent defections from the concert activity, not full breakdowns of great-power unity; they were not designed to defect from the collective framework. Great-power cooperation was least interrupted in the Belgian case, when the unilaterally-minded great power was most easily persuaded to sacrifice its leverage in favor of concert objectives. The concert had in that case already decided to support Belgian independence against both Dutch assertion of control and the expansion of French influence, and the French, demanding Belgian independence, were unwilling to accept diplomatic isolation as the price for insisting on a special role for France in Belgium. In the Greek, Bosnia I and Bosnia II cases, however, major-state divisions were not immediately repaired, and collective interventionist PD was either weakened (as in Bosnia II) or delayed (as in Greece and Bosnia I).

But the move to collective coercive PD can be hindered by great-power consensus as well as by division. Consensus can in fact limit the use of coercion even after coercive PD is practiced. In the Greek, Congo, and Bosnia II cases, we have seen, military action was at times coercive. Yet the implementation of coercion was opposed by great-power political leaders, unwilling or unable to follow up on the military success. One difficulty here is that, having insulated the local conflict as an issue among themselves on the basis of conciliatory intervention, major-state leaders are unable or unwilling to reconsider the basis of insulationst PD. Another part of the problem, however, is that the introduction of military forces into the local conflict area lessens the control of the political superiors of those forces over PD policy.

This is not merely because of the independent-mindedness of the military commanders, but because of instabilities associated with the introduction of those forces. Designed as force-dampening, the international forces are likely to be perceived as provocative by the primary antagonist otherwise enjoying local military superiority.[27] As illustrated in the Greek, Congo, and Bosnia II cases, a standoff between international forces and the superior primary antagonist can be force-exacerbating, increasing the chances of a military clash even as great-power home governments desperately wish to avoid it. In short, the transition from conciliation to coercion cannot be smooth when home governments do not control the outlooks and behaviors of their military commanders on the scene of local ethnic conflict, and therefore cannot effectively minimize the dangers associated with stationing of opposed military forces in close proximity.[28]

Humanitarian emergencies also direct attention to the constraints upon coercive intervention associated with great-power consensus. Through much of the twentieth century, these emergencies rarely troubled existing state alignments. When they occurred, forceful collective major-state action was usually stymied by respect for sovereign prerogatives employed to abuse human rights, and by the poor position of the major states to combat the abuse of norms. Turkish atrocities in Greece, Congolese army depredations in Bakwanga, and Serb ethnic cleansing of Muslims in the initial state of Bosnia II did not suffice to bring a collective major-state coercive response. In only one of the four cases of humanitarian disaster studied here, Armenia, did the great powers threaten—on more than one occasion in the 1890s—coercive action against its perpetrators. In those instances, the major states collectively brought their weight to bear upon the Ottoman regime and the atrocities ceased. However, the great powers were unable to impose an Ottoman-Armenian settlement that would have prevented future such atrocities.[29]

Conclusions

This chapter has focussed especially on those cases in which great-power vital interests are not engaged, but where conciliatory PD is inadequate to surmount local antagonist resistance. When the great powers lack vital interests to intervene in the local conflict, they do not quickly cross the line between conciliatory and coercive intervention. And when conciliatory PD is inadequate because of local resistance, the major states do not easily choose a coercive interventionist approach likely to be more effective in overcoming primary antagonist resistance. In short, the preoccupation here is with those PD instances reflecting a discongruity between interventionist PD requirements and major-state objective capabilities.

Moving from conciliatory to coercive interventionist PD in these instances tests the cohesion and will of the major states in two respects. It tests, first, great-power ability to continue to act collectively even when conceding that conciliation is an ineffective mode of intervention. And it tests also great-power ability to shift away from conciliatory interventionist PD to an alternative coercive approach.

The results of each of these tests are strongly affected by the relationships of the great powers among themselves. We have already seen that those relationships have a priority for the major states over relations with the primary ethnic antagonists, but the perceived ineffectiveness of conciliatory PD reinforces this priority further. In short, problems in interventionist PD are experienced by the major states as a burden upon their ability to insulate the local conflict as an issue among themselves. They can persist in interventionist PD when challenged by the primary antagonists only if they can sustain insulationist PD.

With respect to the challenge of retaining a collective great-power PD posture, our cases offer encouraging evidence: the long-term durability of the great-power concert, despite its frustrations with the primary antagonists and divisions within the concert. We have seen that in those cases in which great-power vital interests are not engaged, early divisions between the major states over the mode of interventionist PD are invariably decided by a collective decision to persist with conciliatory PD, as the great-power advocating coercion then acquiesces in the collective conciliatory PD effort. Further, when the great-power advocate of coercive PD unilaterally intervenes against one of the primary antagonists, the consequence is to weaken and interrupt the concert, but not to break it down completely. Collective intervention is then postponed until the intervention ends, resuming afterward. These developments reflect the importance of the collective framework, and the mutual dependence of the major states on it.

The second test, over shifting to a collective coercive approach, reflects more problematic results. Transition developments distinguished here—humanitarian emergencies, unilateral intervention in the local conflict, and local provocations against international forces—while underscoring the inadequacies of conciliatory interventionist PD, do not stimulate a sustained coercive alternative. Following strong great-power protests against Ottoman outbursts in Constantinople against the Armenians in the mid-1890s, and UN deployment of troops in Sarajevo following Serb outbursts against the Muslims in Bosnia-Herzegovina in 1992, the major states returned to accommodating the primary antagonists. The major states do not follow up military successes with political coercion of the primary antagonists, instead persisting with the older conciliatory approach. And they refuse to be swayed from conciliatory PD by unilateral great-power coercive intervention, as in the Greek and Bosnia I cases. From the point of view of objective interventionist PD requirements, persisting conciliatory PD is not effective. It reflects, as did enduring great-power consensus, inertial major-state behavior.

As this indicates, the persistence of great-power consensus and collective great-power preference for conciliatory interventionist PD leaves the problems of interventionist PD unresolved and indeed increases them in those instances in which the primary antagonists are particularly hostile to each other. In the contemporary post–Cold War period (at least until September 11, 2001), when the major states have been unwilling to enlarge their PD commitments and have encountered severe difficulties in effectuating intervention in the local conflict, these frustrations are particularly acute, leading in the Bosnia-Herzegovina case to calls for abandoning the interventionist PD effort entirely. However, nothing in the case experience studied here suggests that the major states are collectively *incapable* of moving to a coercive interventionist PD. Rather, our study indicates that the move to coercion required in several of the cases needs to be stimulated by manifestly stronger developments than had intruded into the cases earlier. An understanding of those newer developments is the aim of the next chapter.

"Good heavens! I'd swear I heard one of the pieces groan!"

Source: Bill Mauldin, *Back Home.* New York: William Sloane, 1947. Reprinted with permission.

Chapter 9

The Endgame

This study has argued that the great powers have been more preoccupied with preventing local ethnic conflict from undermining their own relationships than with defusing conflict between the local antagonists. It has further maintained that collective major-state influence on the local antagonists is heavily conditioned by the character of great-power insulation of the local conflict. These arguments leave unexplained how the major states ultimately succeed in bringing the primary antagonists to accept peaceful conflict management.

Focussing on this latter problem, this chapter studies how and why the major states, without impairing relations among themselves, prevail upon the primary antagonists to accept a framework for managing contentious local issues. The period during which the mobilization of great-power influence upon the primary antagonists is accomplished is termed here the "endgame," which is concluded when interventionist PD succeeds. The process by which the result is accomplished is studied here in relation to military and political questions between the primary antagonists. Military issues deal with the balance of forces between the antagonists, while political issues relate to territorial demarcations and the structure of institutions.

The focus is on the strengths and weaknesses in great-power commitment to PD promotion in these issue areas, and to shifts in that commitment. Particular emphasis is given to (1) the impact of great-power insulation on interventionist PD, (2) the scope of the clash between the local primary antagonists, (3) great-power interests as a stimulant of interventionist PD, and (4) the special PD difficulties for the major states when they shift from conciliatory to coercive interventionist PD in aggravated ethnic conflict cases.

The analysis reaches four conclusions. First, conciliatory intervention will succeed if the local antagonists agree to remain within the same state or to separate, and if the great powers discover and persuade the local antagonists to accept a more equitable relationship between them. Second, conciliatory intervention will be inadequate when the local antagonists do not agree to remain in the same state or to separate from it. The effectiveness of coercive interventionist PD then depends on whether or not intervention in the local conflict is vital for the major states. If it is not vital for them, a mismatch between great-power PD objectives and resources sets in, and interventionist PD cannot succeed until the mismatch is overcome. Third, interventionist coercive PD that evolves from conciliation can succeed only if the great powers demonstrate decisively that they have shifted away from conciliation. This is because having been previously committed to conciliation, the great powers are mistakenly perceived by one or more of the local antagonists as unable to shift away from it; correcting this misperception is the key to successful interventionist PD in aggravated ethnic cases. Finally, when the misperception just referred to exists, the stronger primary antagonist, which could not be defeated by conciliatory PD, becomes the instrument of its own undoing. Its persisting resistance to the concert finally provokes concert members to mobilize resources collectively to push for settlement of the local conflict.

This chapter first distinguishes conciliatory and coercive interventionist PD as applied in the endgame stage, noting the distinctive features of each as they are reflected in the cases. It then seeks to demonstrate that the outcome of collective great-power interventionist PD depends heavily on whether great-power insulation of local conflict is accomplished easily or with difficulty, whether the local antagonists agree to remain in the same state, whether the major states have vital interests in intervening in the local conflict, and whether the great powers shift from a conciliatory to a coercive mode of interventionist PD. Finally, this chapter discusses endgame outcomes in light of the threefold typology of great-power motivations presented chapter 2.

Intervention by Conciliation

Table 9.1 displays the initial and ultimate interventionist PD techniques collectively adopted by the great powers in each of our cases (excluding the

Cyprus case, which as of April 2004 has reached the endgame stage but is not yet concluded). It shows that conciliation, the initial collective great-power interventionist technique of choice in all but one of the cases considered in this study, ultimately succeeded in whole or in part in five of our cases (Belgium, Greece, Bosnia I, Armenia, and the Memel). To succeed in these latter instances, conciliatory interventionist PD required that the major states identify an equitable arrangement between the local primary antagonists—the central government and its ethnic challenger—that each could voluntarily endorse. Satisfactory arrangements were typically discovered by the great powers through an iterative process in which the desires and interests of the primary antagonists were clarified.

Cases of successful conciliatory interventionist PD may be grouped into three categories according to their degree of local turbulence: (1) When the primary antagonists agreed throughout to remain in the same political entity, conciliation created new local institutions to form a counterpoise to the authority of the central regime (Armenia, the Memel). (2) When the antagonists at first did not agree to remain in the same state—that is, where one antagonist wished to separate and the other to prevent that separation—conciliation was effective only after a military test of strength between the local antagonists (Belgium, Greece, the Congo). (3) When the antagonists disagreed about remaining in the same state and were also affected by interventionist-minded neighboring states, conciliation could not be effective at all (Bosnia I and II).

The following discussion addresses successful as well as unsuccessful uses of conciliatory interventionist PD in our cases to understand the limits of conciliation as an interventionist PD tool. The discussion addresses first the propensity of the major states to apply conciliation to the local antagonism, and then the receptivity of the primary antagonists to conciliatory PD.

The Propensity of the Major States to Intervene

In the first type of conciliatory case, limited contentiousness between the primary antagonists reduces the urgency of the major states to intervene. Lithuanian and German groups in the Memel, cut adrift from Germany, were willing to remain together in the same political entity. Armenians were willing to be ruled by Turks. Because opposition between the antagonists was contained, pressure on the major states to intervene collectively

TABLE 9.1
Cases and Interventionist Techniques

Case	*Dates*	*Initial Interventionist PD Technique*	*Successful Interventionist PD Technique*
Belgian Revolt against the Dutch	(1830–1838)	Conciliation (P) Coercion (M)	Conciliation (P) Coercion (M)
Greek Revolt against Ottoman Empire	(1821–1832)	Conciliation	Coercion (M) Conciliation (P)
Bosnian Revolt against Ottoman Empire	(1875–1878)	Conciliation	Conciliation (M) Coercion (P)
Armenian Unrest in Ottoman Empire	(1878–1914)	Conciliation	Conciliation
German/Lithuanian conflict in the Memel	(1918–1939)	Conciliation	Conciliation
Belgian Congo conflict	(1960–1964)	Conciliation	Coercion
Croat/Muslim/Serb conflict in Bosnia-Herzegovina	(1992–1995)	Conciliation	Coercion

Notes: The Cyprus case, whose endgame thus far is not yet concluded, is excluded from this table; P = political issues; M = military issues.

was low and, indeed, the primary obstacle in the way of effective PD in these cases was the limited great-power will to press for it.

In the Memel, a conciliatory solution was decidedly a secondary question for the major states and they were slow to move toward one, especially since prevailing conditions in the Memel—until the Lithuanian invasion—were tranquil. In Armenia, which was also mostly peaceful, great-power rivalry was the major problem; the deadlock strengthened the hand of the Turks and made it difficult for the major states to weigh and plan for alternatives to the status quo. In these cases, the major states, having more important interests elsewhere, and having successfully insulated the Memel and Armenia as issues between themselves, postpone intervention, even as this means continued local deadlock and the dissatisfaction of one of the primary antagonists.

In the second type of conciliation case, ethnic antagonist disagreement in Belgium, Greece, and the Congo about whether to coexist in the same political entity makes local conflict more turbulent. The central government is determined in each of these cases to stamp out the challenge to its authority, and the ensuing military confrontation makes it more difficult for the great powers to avoid intervening in the dispute. In the Belgian and Greek cases the military advantage lay with the ruling regime, which controlled well-trained and well-armed military cadres while its ethnic challenger did not. By contrast, the Katanga secessionist movement, supported by well-trained mercenaries, held a military advantage over poorly disciplined troops of the new Congolese government. It was for this reason that Lumumba's Congo government called for UN assistance to bring the secession to an end.

Conciliation in these cases is delayed by the military test of strength between the central regime and its challenger. However, in none of the three cases were the major states prepared to fully stand aside in the military contest. In the Belgian case, the French were determined to support Belgian independence, and the other great powers ultimately prevailed upon the French to associate with a great-power concert to prevent the Dutch from holding on to the Belgians by force. Turkish use of force against the Greeks also was ultimately checked by the great powers, who acted collectively in 1826 to prevent the Turks from continuing to resupply their contingents in Greece. In the Congo, UN secretary general Dag Hammarskjöld's efforts to reconcile the central regime and the Katanga secessionists did not wait for a final battle between government and secessionist forces. The Congo peacekeeping force interpositioned itself between Lumumba's ragtag army and its Katanga opposition, preventing a military showdown between them. Lumumba was angry about UN determination to be evenhanded rather than committed to suppressing the Katanga opposition.

Why should outside mediators be so strongly motivated in these cases in an early stage, despite the local turbulence and before the military showdown is completed? Possibly the most important reason is that the great powers share the objective in all three cases of preventing unilateral action by any one great power on behalf of one or another primary antagonist. In Belgium the major states resisted French opportunism; in Greece, where the Russians had initially helped foment the Greek revolt, they tried to ward off Russian intervention; and in the Congo, the Americans and Soviets were wary of each other's involvement. To head off opportunistic involvement by any one great power in an ongoing civil war, the major states have strong incentive to form a concert framework. This motive is important even if the major states lack strong collective views on the internal political controversy. Even if they prefer to remain aloof early in that controversy—as in Belgium and Greece—the possibilities or the reality of outside meddling make it difficult for them to do so.

In the two Bosnia-Herzegovina cases, internal ethnic challenge was fomented by sympathetic outside states who, apart from providing arms and encouragement to the revolutionists, intervened militarily in the struggle on their own. In Bosnia I, support from Serbia, from Montenegro, and from Slavs in Austria-Hungary strengthened the Slavic revolution within Bosnia-Herzegovina against a Moslem regime ruling on behalf of the Turks; a year after the revolution began, Serbia and Montenegro intervened militarily in support of the revolution. In Bosnia II, the newly independent Moslem-dominated government of Bosnia-Herzegovina was rapidly opposed by a counterrevolution from Bosnian Slavs and Croats, each aided by a sympathetic neighboring state; the Serb-dominated former Yugoslavia and the newly independent state of Croatia covertly introduced regular military contingents against a Bosnia-Herzegovina regime unprepared for such an onslaught. In these cases, conciliation is urgent for the major states, but is rendered impossible by neighboring-state intervention.

On one hand, the local violence makes it impossible for the major states to remain aloof. In Bosnia I, mediation between the Slav revolutionists and the Turks was necessary to prevent (1) immediate Turkish military suppression of the revolt, (2) early military intervention by Serbia and Montenegro on behalf of the revolutionists, and (3) open Russian support of the revolutionists. While the need to avoid wider war was heightened by the linkage of neighboring states with a local ethnic antagonist, the rivalry between Austria and Russia in the Balkans meant that action to defuse the struggle in Bosnia-Herzegovina was a prerequisite for insulating that struggle as a great-power issue. In Bosnia II, while the dangers of the unilateral intervention by the major states was reduced by the ending of superpower cold war, the urgency of intervention was dictated by ethnic cleansing directed at the Moslems and by the tight Bosnian-Serb siege of Sarajevo. The great powers acted through the United Nations to approve a UN peacekeeping force to cope with the resulting humanitarian emergency, and intense UN- and EU-sanctioned mediation was soon begun to conciliate the opponents.

While violence makes the major states unable to avoid intervention, neighboring states undermine it. In Bosnia I, Serb and Montenegrin support of the revolutionists emboldened the latter to toughen their position over time, leading the Austrian-Hungarian foreign minister to tilt his proposals increasingly toward Slav demands. The Turks, having held back well-trained military contingents in the hope of a peaceful solution, could do so no longer in the spring of 1876, and subsequently (with support from the British) they rejected further Austrian mediation. In Bosnia II, successful mediation was stymied as long as Bosnian Serbs and Croats relied upon support from the former Yugoslavia and Croatia, respectively, assisting their aspirations to obtain better arrangements in a military showdown. In particular, Bosnian Serbs, militarily superior to the Moslems, renounced periodically negotiated cease-fires to heighten military pressure against their opponents.

Receptivity of the Primary Antagonists to Conciliation

Table 9.2 lists the successful application of conciliatory interventionist PD in our cases. In our least turbulent cases, in which the ethnic antagonists are willing to remain in the same state, the problem of applying great-power conciliatory intervention is most straightforward. Armenian willingness to be ruled by Turks raised only the issue of protecting Armenians from arbitrary Turkish rule. To this end the Turks agreed in February 1914 to ask the major states to recommend two foreign inspectors-general for Eastern Anatolia to help select judicial and political officials, and to create an elective council in two regions, each composed equally of Moslems and Christians. A power-sharing solution was also worked out for the Memel, defining how its inhabitants would independently determine their local leaders while providing protection for the minority German speakers in relation to the Lithuanian majority. The most difficult issue in these cases is reconciling power sharing with state sovereignty. In both cases, conciliation works because the primary antagonists have divergent interests: each antagonist can benefit from agreement by trading lesser priorities for more important ones.

In the second group of cases, in which the central government decides to stop the secession by force, that government opposes any conciliatory PD that it views as not designed primarily to have the same objective. This makes conciliation infeasible as long as the ethnic challenger insists on secession and the central regime, acting to prevent secession, refuses to

TABLE 9.2
Successful Conciliatory Interventionist PD

Cases	*Results*
The Memel	Power-sharing arrangement
Armenia	Agreement on local power sharing
Belgium	Separation of forces agreement
Greece	Recognition of Greek independence
The Congo	Tshombe becomes Congo president

recognize the secessionists as equals. In the Belgian, Greek, and Congo cases, a conciliatory solution for political issues was worked out only after the major powers blunted the military force of the superior primary antagonist. In the Belgian case, years after the Dutch were militarily repulsed, a settlement was arranged for the Belgians and Dutch to separate, as both antagonists became reconciled to the economic advantages of sharing commerce on the Scheldt River. Similarly, years after the Turks were prevented from strengthening their forces in Greece, they recognized the creation of Greece as a separate political entity. In the Congo, Moïse Tshombe, the leader of the Katanga revolt, was forced to terminate his challenge to Leopoldville authority and shortly afterward was appointed to head the government in Leopoldville. Despite the one-sided military result in these cases (to be further discussed below), the primary antagonists here are receptive, as they are in the Memel and in Armenia, to a political settlement by a process of trading concessions.

Finally, in the most difficult cases, a conciliatory solution was not possible in either Bosnia-Herzegovina conflict. This was because (1) the interested neighboring states had sufficient political and militarily military leverage to prevent their local ally from accepting a conciliatory solution; (2) those states were sufficiently strong to promote a military solution through superior military strength; and (3) the ethnic antagonists were so polarized that no equitable trading of concessions was possible. In short, conciliatory intervention proposals in both Bosnia I and II could not overcome the force committed to the Slavs by their neighboring allies. The endgame in these cases can be understood only by tracing the collective great-power PD shift from conciliation to coercion, a development studied in the next section.

Coercive Intervention

Coercion is as significant a form of interventionist PD as conciliation in our cases, succeeding in its entirety or in part in five of six cases (Belgium, Greece, the Congo, and Bosnia I and II). In all but the Belgian case, coercive intervention ultimately succeeds as the major states shift away from conciliation as a PD technique. Invariably, coercive interventionist PD contrasts with the equitable and voluntary character of conciliation in seeking to compel one or more of the primary antagonists to retreat from positions they previously adopted. It has already been noted that conciliatory PD tends to be favored by the major states when they lack vital interests in PD and consequently do not wish to risk war with the primary antagonists over PD objectives. Coercive PD, on the other hand, is decided upon by the major powers because they conclude that conciliation is inadequate for these purposes.

This does not occur merely because of primary-antagonist opposition to conciliatory-PD proposals; the gyroscopic character of conciliatory PD, once decided upon, ordinarily prevails even when PD is parried by the primary antagonists. Rather, the five cases studied here in which coercive PD is decided upon collectively by the major states show that the decision to discard conciliation and to choose coercion occurs either because great-power vital interests are perceived to be at stake, or because local circumstances lead the great powers to change their approach even as their interests remain nonvital. However, the shift to coercive PD is not always full blown. In two cases (Belgium and Greece) the major states adopted a coercive approach to force an end to a central regime's military suppression of an ethnic challenger, yet retained conciliation to cope with political issues posed by ethnic violence, including territorial boundaries and the shape of postwar political institutions. And in one case, Bosnia I, they employed the opposite combination.

Two contrasting dynamics for the emergence of coercive interventionist PD appear in the cases. First, when coercion is employed early in the local conflict—that is, within months of its intensification—the decision to do so is pushed primarily by one great power. The primary difficulty for coercive PD is then to establish parameters by which the major states can agree (Belgium). Second, when coercion is decided upon only later in the local conflict cycle, the decision reflects a widespread view that conciliation is inadequate to implement some PD objectives and that a coercive approach is required instead. The difficulties for the major states in shifting policy are then overshadowed by the problem of convincing skeptical primary antagonists of their determination to implement coercive action if primary antagonist cooperation is not forthcoming.

Coercive PD is addressed here first in connection with the great-power decision to launch collective coercive PD, and then in light of the impact of coercive PD upon the primary antagonists.

Initiating Collective Coercive PD

Collective coercive PD can be launched early in the local conflict cycle only because differences between great powers over the advisability of coercive behavior are resolved. In the Belgian case, the Dutch requested great-power assistance to uphold their control over Belgium, as provided for by treaty in 1815, but vital interests impelled France to act coercively and unilaterally to ensure Belgian independence from the Dutch. In this instance, the French acquiesced in a collective approach to the Belgian problem in which the other major powers acted to contain French expansion; in return, the French were rewarded by concert support of Belgian independence. The concert's compellent leverage against the French thus made possible collective compellence against the Dutch to permit Belgian independence.

By contrast, later initiation of coercive PD toward the local conflict comes about because the great powers recognize that conciliatory PD is not effective and that a tougher alternative is needed. The distinction between conciliation and coercion is not always sharply defined, however. In the Greek case, Britain and Russia, in the Anglo-Russian Protocol of April 1826, sought a mediated settlement in Greece but publicly indicated they would intervene "jointly or separately" between the parties if the latter rejected this proposal. This implied a Russian threat to use force, and a "joint blockade," later implemented with French support, was thereupon privately discussed. In the Congo, the United Nations and its secretary general were committed to mediate between the breakaway Katanga regime and the central government. However, when the Katangans proved adamant in their resistance, officers of the UN peacekeeping force stationed in the Congo grew impatient and decided on their own authority upon a coercive approach against mercenary forces supporting the secession.

In Bosnia I, the eastern states decided to aim at partitioning the Ottoman Empire, a solution later provided for at the 1878 Berlin Conference when Austria was allowed, over Ottoman objections, to occupy Bosnia-

Herzegovina. Finally, in Bosnia II, the failure of UN and European Union mediation efforts in Bosnia-Herzegovina and persistent Serb violations of the armistice between the antagonists led to the UN's transfer of military operations in Bosnia-Herzegovina to NATO and to a program of coercive bombing against Bosnian Serbs.

Conciliating the primary antagonists requires preventing the stronger antagonist from moving to impose its views upon the weaker one, but ongoing civil war between the antagonists makes realization of this objective very problematic. Failure of the joint blockade to prevent the Ottoman Turks from reinforcing their military and naval contingents in Greece led the Admirals of the blockading fleets to confront the Turks so as to defuse fighting there. After the resulting victory in Navarino Bay, the French were authorized to send an armed contingent to Greece to compel the Turks to abandon their military offensive against the Greeks. In the Congo, similarly, the UN peacekeeping force commander sought to deter actions by the Katanga mercenaries against the peacekeepers—as he put it, "to be able to react immediately and decisively if people get killed or badly hurt."[1] As in Navarino Bay, the proximity of UN and mercenary forces to each other in this instance undermined the goal of the deterring mercenary incidents against UN forces, while Hammarskjöld's instructions to avoid incidents provoking the mercenaries had no bearing upon the proximity problem or upon the broader UN objective of bringing about the removal of the mercenaries.

In Bosnia I, Austrian mediation had been designed to dampen chances of fighting between Slav revolutionists and Turkish forces, but it lacked a military option if deterrence failed. The failure to deter intensified fighting became clear in the summer of 1877, when regular Serb and Montenegrin forces intervened against the Turks in support of the revolutionists. Once the Turks were victorious over the Serbs and Montenegrins, the problem for the concert was to develop a means of coercing the Turks to surrender their battlefield gains. Finally, in Bosnia II, although the UN and NATO were publicly committed to a tougher approach toward the Bosnia Serbs on Bosnian peace terms, they were more preoccupied with deterring Serb attacks against isolated Muslim enclaves in Bosnia-Herzegovina than in forcing Bosnian Serb retreats.

In these cases, the major powers succeed in adopting a coercive posture only because they are otherwise unable to bring about satisfactory restraint in the local civil war.[2] They are in fact primarily interested at first in each instance in *preventing* and *deterring* the stronger primary antagonist from exploiting its superior force strength in relation to the weaker antagonist, rather than in *compelling* the former to retreat from gains it has already made. Perceived failure in the ability to deter the stronger antagonist from utilizing its local force advantages is a precondition in these cases to employing compellence against that antagonist, the failure demonstrating the stronger primary antagonist's flagrant resistance to great-power demands. Paradoxically, persisting ambitions of the stronger local antagonist brings about the collective great-power coercive posture that ultimately is its undoing, even as the great powers lack intrinsic vital interests supporting such a posture.

Impact on the Primary Antagonists

Examples of successful coercive interventionist PD in our cases are displayed in Table 9.3. Coercion is linked to vital interests in the Belgian case, in which the French, with the support of the other great powers, were firmly committed from the start to preventing the Dutch from using their military force to reimpose political authority over the Belgians, and also in Bosnia I, when Austria-Hungary sought, also with the support of the other major states, to coercively detach Bosnia-Herzegovina from the Ottoman Empire and occupy that territory itself. The French did not precede or couple force mobilization and intervention against the Dutch with overt threats; Austria relied on force mobilization and intervention against the Turks by its ally, Russia, which also did not make overt threats. Neither France nor Austria or Russia provided nonmilitary assurances to soften the impact of force activity—even as Dutch and Ottoman rulers were being asked to surrender *their* vital interests in exercising sovereignty over their respective territories. In these cases, a primary antagonist is intimidated as the great powers implement rules based upon their might. In short, coercive PD in these cases is simple and crude.

The Dutch acquiesced in the French demands, avoiding a direct clash with French forces. A major reason for the acquiescence was undoubtedly the support the concert provided to the French. The only demands made by the concert upon France were that it not undertake to station forces permanently in Belgium or to attempt to dominate the new government established there; the concert did not otherwise, so far as is known, critique the crude and uncompromising form of French coercive behavior. Without great-power opposition to French coercive action directed at them, the Dutch were in no position to resist the superior French military forces.[3]

TABLE 9.3
Successful Coercive Interventionist PD

Cases	*Results*
Belgium	Enforcing Belgian independence
Greece	Imposing controls on Turkish reinforcement forces
Bosnia I	Austro-Hungarian occupation of Bosnia-Herzegovina
The Congo	Ending of Katanga secession
Bosnia II	Serb military retreat and acceptance of "Road Map" plan

And in Bosnia I the Turks acquiesced in Austrian occupation of Bosnia-Herzegovina when even England, the closest Ottoman ally, failed to support them. Prior to and at the Berlin Conference, Austria successfully promoted an arrangement in which the other major states were provided with compensation for Austrian territorial gain, leaving Turkey isolated. Austria did not need to threaten the Turks prior to her occupation of Bosnia-Herzegovina in 1878 because it was permitted by the Treaty of Berlin—to which the Turks were a signatory—to gain its objective.

In the Greek, Congo, and Bosnia II cases, coercion is not linked to vital interests, and therefore mobilizing collective great-power will and resources to support it is problematic. After the annihilation of the Turkish fleet at Navarino Bay, the Turks even more strongly resisted allied PD. Differences between the great powers then made coercing the Turks impossible, and the concert nearly foundered on British opposition to the Russian decision in 1828 to make war against the Turks. Finally, following Russian military victory in that war, the British and French were able to persuade the Turks that Greek independence was the best way to forestall opportunistic great-power activity on behalf of the Greeks.

UN members were extremely divided over their objectives in the Congo, with no consensus evident on employing coercion to end the Katanga secession. Moreover, coercion was limited in this instance by American support for Tshombe, the Katanga secessionist leader. In December 1961, when UN peacekeepers (with American assistance) were forcing Tshombe to end his secession effort, the American ambassador escorted Tshombe on a presidential jet to a meeting with the Congolese prime minister, Cyrille Adoula.

In Bosnia II, coercion was impeded by major differences between the major states—the Russians supporting the Serbs, the Americans assisting the Muslim-dominated government in Sarajevo, and the British and French seeking an evenhanded approach to protect their soldiers in the UN Bosnia peacekeeping force. As the Bosnian Serbs, the strongest primary antagonist, rejected existing peace proposals requiring them to surrender territory taken by force in the war, the Contact Group would not support collective coercive action until negotiations on military and political questions were clearly shown to be futile. Negotiations collapsed in May 1995 following Serb rejection of the last-ditch American "road map" proposal, put forward to clarify once and for all whether primary antagonist disputes in Bosnia-Herzegovina were negotiable. By that time, military gains by the Sarajevo government and its Croat allies had forced the Serbs out of large portions of Bosnia that they previously controlled, and in August 1995 a NATO air campaign, responding to renewed Serb shelling of Sarajevo and the overrunning of Moslem enclaves in eastern Bosnia, compelled the Serbs to accept the "road map" plan. A peace agreement based on that plan was accepted by the three primary antagonists a few months later.

As in the Belgian and Bosnia I cases, these instances show how agreement between great powers is a prerequisite for coercing the stronger primary antagonist. Nevertheless, all five cases taken together point up the difficulties facing the concert in bringing influence to bear upon the stronger primary antagonist in ethnic conflict. The latter, understandably attracted to the possibility of imposing its own military and political settlement on its adversary and stiffening its terms to redeem its prior sacrifice, could find persuasive reasons to doubt the potential of the major states to collectively implement coercive PD. The Dutch in the Belgian case (even after French intervention in August 1831), the Turks in the Greek case (even after Navarino) and in Bosnia I (after the Turkish victory over the Serbs and Montenegrins), the Katangans (even after the earliest UN peacekeeper efforts to disarm the mercenaries), and the Bosnian Serbs in Bosnia II (even after Western power threats to retaliate for violations of cease-fires), could question the seriousness of the major states to act coercively, in spite of the objective superiority of the international forces assembled by the latter. Contextually, in other words, the stronger primary antagonist—deeply engaged in vital interests of its own, and having accommodated well to prior collective great-power conciliation directed to the local conflict—is desensitized to indications that the great powers finally are serious about imposing a military or political settlement in the local conflict.

The Congo and Bosnia II cases show the special difficulties besetting the great powers under these conditions when they need to act coercively in defense of nonvital interests. Acting to soften tensions between themselves and the stronger primary antagonists, they employ threats, emphasize their moderation, and provide inducements to forestall their use of force in defense of their objectives. However, because of the stronger primary antagonist's doubt about great-power intentions, these tactics fail. The major states are ultimately required in those cases to act counter to their preferences—that is, to implement coercion as a test of military strength—to compel the stronger primary antagonist to give way.

Analysis and Findings

Emphasizing variability in great-power interventionist PD, this study has given four sources of such variability particular attention: (1) the impact of great-power insulation upon interventionist PD, (2) the choice of interventionist approach, (3) the degree of importance of major-state interest in intervention, and (4) the scope of the clash between the local primary antagonists. The data from the cases presented here is now reexamined under these headings to seek regularities transcending time and place.

The Impact of Insulation

This chapter has hypothesized that intervention and insulation are linked as PD pursuits. The case material indeed points up how great-power relations condition the initiation of intervention and account for the success or failure of interventionist PD. The launching of collective intervention in most of our cases is primarily explained by the interests of great powers toward each other and not by their interests toward the primary local antagonists.

Collective suppression of Dutch military activity in Belgium was heavily affected by French insistence that Belgium become independent and by the Anglo-French desire for a cooperative great-power approach to this subject. Concert intervention on the Greek question in 1826 represented an effort to reconcile the broad British policy of collaborating with the Turks on one hand, with the traditional Russian antagonism to the Turks on the other. Austrian mediation toward the Slavs in Bosnia-Herzegovina in 1876 was designed to help defuse the Slav revolt as a great-power dispute. The Armenians, who counted on Western European and later Russian support against their Turkish rulers, and were regarded with suspicion by the Turks for this reason, were repeatedly disappointed as great powers employed the Ottoman regime as a bulwark against their rivals. Mediation by the UN secretary general and emplacement of a peacekeeping force in the Congo grew out of the Secretary General's desire to keep the Congo out of the Cold War. In Bosnia II, creation of the Contact Group in 1994 represented an effort to reconcile divergent American, Russian, and European perspectives on the civil war.

Only in the Memel case were great-power conflicts absent as intervention occurred. The great powers were largely indifferent to the fate of the Memel, postponing decision on that conflict. Pressure from the Lithuanians in particular finally led the major states to appoint a committee to recommend permanent arrangements for the Memel territory. Elsewhere, great-power confrontation delayed collective interventionist PD. Early action on the Belgian question was impeded by the French determination to act alone, which was opposed by the other major states. In the Greek case, British suspicions of the Russians even after Navarino made it impossible to collectively influence Turks and Greeks toward a settlement. British mistrust of cooperation between Germany, Austria, and Russia—and suspicion of Russian intentions in particular—weakened common great-power action in Bosnia I. In the Armenian case, Anglo-Russian rivalry brought about a long-term deadlock. The UN's influence in the Congo was to some extent stymied by the unwillingness of the superpowers to refrain from unilateral activity of their own in the Congo. Finally, in Bosnia II, the major states were sharply at odds over whether mediation should be disinterested, pro-Serb, or anti-Serb and pro-Muslim.

A formal concert of major states is not sufficient in any of these cases to defuse local ethnic conflict, or even to act quickly to bring international pressure to bear. However, the eventual success of interventionist PD in all these cases shows that the concert can be strengthened as a PD resource. If one accepts, as does the present writer, that collective interventionist PD has greater potential to bridge local antagonist differences than does one major state acting alone, the manner in which this strengthening occurs deserves careful study. In particular, it is necessary to highlight the contrast between the early formal concert, when both the ability to act rapidly and adequate authority in relation to the primary antagonists are lacking, and the role of the concert in the endgame, when rapid response and political authority are demonstrated.

The contrast between the early weak form of the concert and the later strong form is displayed in our cases in three contrasting ways. One is where fully successful intervention does not take place until many years after an acceptable concert framework is put in place. In the Belgian case, a concert arrangement that included France soon succeeded in imposing a military settlement that in practice ensured Belgian independence, but the political issues were not resolved until an appropriate mix of offers to satisfy the primary antagonists was made many years later. A second possibility, as in the Memel case, is where insulation comes into question only in the endgame, as a regional power or antagonist acts in opposition to the concert and places the local conflict on the great-power agenda for the first time as an urgent matter. A third type of case, reflected in the Greek, Bosnia I and II, and the Congo cases, is where the concert framework is so delicate that insulation remains continually in question prior to and into the endgame. Here the greater assertiveness and success of the concert is best explained by a shift in major-power attitudes that take into account earlier concert inadequacies and introduce a new effort to compensate for them. This shift, as we have seen (and will further comment on below), is partly in reaction to developments in the local conflict arena.

The three modes have in common that the successful application of interventionist PD is not the outcome of any graduated measure of concert activity and that the endgame can present complex issues for great-power action irrespective of great-power insulation of the local conflict. The main difference between these modes is to be found in the degree to which insulation of the local conflict as an issue among the great powers strengthens their ability to act effectively in the endgame.

The Scope of Local Conflict

It has been hypothesized here that the relative effectiveness of conciliation and coercion as interventionist PD instruments is conditioned by the scope of the differences between the local ethnic antagonists. When the ethnic challenger does not insist on full political separation from a central regime, the relatively small scope of local conflict that this entails narrows major-state interventionist burdens and enhances a conciliatory PD approach. On the other hand, when the challenging group insists on full separation, the larger scope of local conflict thereby brought about requires a tougher coercive approach to cope with the more polarized, hostile relationship between the local antagonists.

Conciliation indeed has the greatest potential in our cases when the scope of the conflict between the primary antagonists is relatively small. In the Memel and in Armenia, where the primary antagonists were reconciled to coexisting in the same political entity, disagreeing only on the distribution of rights and benefits between them, conciliatory interventionist PD was effective and coercion unnecessary. By contrast, coercion has greater value than conciliation when the scope of disagreement between the primary antagonists is larger, extending to the overall political relationship between them. In the Belgian, Greek, Congo, and Bosnia I and II cases, in each of which the ethnic challenger desired to disassociate itself from a political entity to which it was formally subjected, coercive PD was effectively employed. The added burdens on the great powers for influencing the primary antagonists required coercive PD in those instances.

Instances are also found in our cases in which, despite the larger scope of conflict between the primary antagonists—that is, where disagreement extended to separation by the ethnic challenger from a preexisting political entity—intervention is effectively accomplished by conciliatory means, as with political settlement in the Belgian and Greek cases and military settlement in Bosnia I. The most effective instrument of interventionist PD does not then conform to variation in the scope of primary antagonist conflict, but depends on other considerations, one being the limited resources available to the great powers, separately and together. In most of the cases studied here, the major states tend to favor conciliatory intervention because it is relatively low risk and nonconfrontational. In doing so, they protect their own positions conservatively when they do not perceive local issues to be important enough to risk war. Sometimes conciliation succeeds, and military or coercive backup is not required. In the Belgian, Greek, and Bosnia I cases, the primary antagonists understood their dependence upon great-power assistance in shaping a military or political settlement, and could therefore be moved by the great powers toward a settlement by incentives rather than by threats.

However, the frequently prominent interplay between the great powers when they decide on interventionist PD suggests that the requirements of insulating the local conflict as an aspect of great-power conflict are often likely to be in tension with the ideal or most efficient mode of interventionist PD, as determined by the scope of the local antagonists' differences.

This tension is particularly visible in the early stage of the local conflict when insulation, which we have seen has priority for the major states over intervention, is usually in doubt. The gyroscopic character of conciliatory interventionist PD is evidence of this tension, major states persisting with conciliation after the primary antagonists reject conciliatory proposals, as in Belgium, the Congo, and Bosnia I and II. In the Congo and Bosnia II, the scope of PD objectives increased, but the resources made available to support attainment of those objectives did not.[4] The tension between the requirements of insulation, on one hand, and the requirements of influencing the primary antagonists, on the other, would be expected to diminish by the later stages of the local conflict, as the major states have ample opportunity to become closely aware of the local antagonists' differences and to develop more effective ways of reconciling them.

Great-Power Interests

It has been hypothesized here that the choice of instruments employed to initiate interventionist PD depends on the relative importance of the great-power interests served by the intervention: when vital great-power interests are at stake, coercion is more likely than conciliation to be initially employed as collective interventionist PD; alternatively, when vital interests are absent, interventionist PD will at first tend to be conciliatory. The case material for the most part reflects this distinction. In three cases in which great-power vital interests are lacking, initial interventionist PD is conciliatory. In the Greek case, although Russia did originally favor a tougher approach toward the Turks, the other Holy Alliance members dissented, limiting early concert PD to conciliating the opponents. After the Holy Alliance dissipated, the British also adopted a conciliatory approach, and conciliation of the Greeks and Turks became the original rationale of the Anglo-Russian entente of 1826. None of these great powers had vital interests in this instance in pushing the Turks to permit Greek independence, although the Russians were prepared to use the Greek issue to strengthen their overall justification for weakening the Turks by force.

In the Congo, the United Nations initially worked to end the Katanga secession by conciliatory means, an approach consistent with Secretary General Dag Hammarskjöld's outlook and with UN members' nonvital interests in coping with the secession. Conciliatory PD in the Congo was also far more politically expedient than coercion, for a decision to implement coercion in the Congo would have magnified ongoing Cold War disputes about the scope of the Secretary General's authority and about conflicting commitments undertaken by the U.S. and the Soviet Union in the Congo. Finally, the UN's interventionist PD in Bosnia II was also at first conciliatory, reflecting the absence of vital major-state interests in the issue. The strongest expression of diplomatic interest there came from the regional European organizations such as the European Community and the Council for Security and Cooperation in Europe, which maintained that European states should take primary responsibility for resolving their own interstate and internal disputes. By the time civil war broke out in Bosnia-Herzegovina, the United States and the former Soviet Union, traditional rivals for influence, had become less engaged in the former Yugoslavia.

By contrast, early coercive interventionist PD in Belgium was accompanied by acceptance by the concert of the French vital interest that Belgium be made politically independent of the Netherlands. Conciliation of the Dutch would not have sufficed for the French on this question. The concert adopted a coercive approach toward the Dutch on Belgian independence in exchange for French agreement to abstain from efforts to control the new Belgian polity.

Bosnia I less clearly fits our hypothesis. In that instance, although the initial approach of the concert led by Austria-Hungary was conciliatory toward the primary antagonists, Austria had a vital interest that was defensive rather than expansionist: preventing Slavic revolt in Bosnia from spreading to the large Slavic population of Austria-Hungary, a development that would have undermined the multinational character of the Austrian empire. This interest later impelled Austria to seek to occupy Bosnia-Herzegovina as the outcome of the 1878 Berlin Conference. Early concert conciliation thus screened a vital Austrian interest that later led to a partial solution for the Balkans that included the imposition of Austrian authority in Bosnia.

The significance of the distinction between PD based on vital and nonvital interests is limited to aggravated cases of internal ethnic conflict in which, it is argued here, coercive interventionist PD is essential for effective PD. (In nonaggravated cases, conciliatory PD will suffice to gain a settlement between the primary antagonists.) When only nonvital major state interests are at stake, initial great-power pursuit of conciliatory PD will retard the decision to embark upon coercing the antagonists and thus delay effective PD in aggravated cases. This is because, under these conditions, a great-power interest/resource gap sharply reduces the leverage of the major states in relation to the primary antagonists if—as would be expected in aggravated cases—one or more primary antagonists resist collective great-power PD. PD is then unlikely to succeed unless the major states can be persuaded to harden their approach and act coercively. However, the major states then appear to have no clear incentive, on the basis of their own values or their own leverage, to change course and adopt coercive measures. That is, if conciliatory PD does not work, neither nonvital great-power interests nor the interest/resource gap justifies shifting to a coercive approach. The contrast in this respect between the discouraging prospects for nonvital-interest conciliatory PD, as illustrated in the aggravated Greek, Congo, and two Bosnia cases, and the strong position of France, defending vital interests, in the also aggravated Belgian case, is very impressive.

The Shift to Coercion

It has been hypothesized here that when the great-power concert employs coercive PD belatedly toward aggravated ethnic conflict, it will have difficulty bringing coercion to bear on the stronger ethnic antagonist, which underestimates the concert's will and resources to press for a settlement. The stronger local antagonist assumes that in the coercive stage the great-power concert remains as before unable and unwilling to support PD with resources larger than those the primary antagonist can mount to defeat them. Also suggested here, however, is that the stronger primary antagonist's misperception is ultimately its own undoing.

The stronger antagonist's misperception of the concert's will and strength helps to explain the ineffectiveness of coercive threats alone in the cases studied here. In the four instances in which collective coercive PD toward intrastate ethnic conflict grew out of conciliation, the concert was ultimately required to employ force in hostile fashion, or in a military demonstration, to compel the stronger antagonist to retreat. In the Greek case, following its victory at Navarino to enforce the joint blockade, the concert needed to dispatch a French force to the Peloponnese to compel the Turks to cease action against the Greeks. In Bosnia I, upon Montenegro's refusal to make peace on Turkish terms in the spring of 1877, the concert, on Russian urging, attempted to force Turkey to rectify Montenegrin frontiers as the price of peace with Montenegro; Russia mobilized for war against Turkey to bolster this demand. When Turkey rejected the demand, Russia waged war against Turkey. In the Congo, four separate military forays by UN peacekeepers against the Katanga mercenaries were required before the mercenaries were fully subdued. And in Bosnia II, the UN and NATO, threatening to retaliate against Bosnian Serb armistice violations and ethnic cleansing activity against the Muslims, were repeatedly challenged by the Serbs until heavy NATO attacks were implemented against Bosnian Serb positions in the summer of 1995.

The stronger antagonist's unwillingness to retreat in these cases reflects a deep commitment to its political objectives. The Ottoman government in the Greek and Bosnia I cases, the Katanga secessionist government, and the Bosnian Serbs each were strongly determined to resist outside intervention. That disposition was not likely to change or be reexamined as a result of the concert's initial coercive efforts; more likely, the stronger antagonist's perceptions of the concert would selectively conform to its predispositions. Such a reaction is not irrational or even implausible, for a number of reasons.

First, the concert had been slow to shift to coercive PD because it was determined to minimize the risks and dangers to concert members of intervening in the local conflict. To be sure, not all concert members wished to minimize the dangers of intervention; Russia, for example, was willing to take considerable risk to weaken the Ottoman Empire in the Greek and Bosnia I cases, while Austria and England were not. But where the major-state consensus strongly favored lessening these risks, as in the Congo and in Bosnia II, lessening risks of war was in tension with projecting the desire to defend certain interests even in war. That is, the need to provide incentives and assurances to the stronger primary antagonist to obtain its retreat, while avoiding war and a military test of strength, conflicted with projecting resolution to that same antagonist.

Second, coercive threats were weakened to the degree that deterrence objectives were simultaneously sought; deterrence was often more important to the concert than the coercion when civil war was underway in the local conflict. In the Greek case, the concert immediately wished to prevent Turkey from bolstering its force in the Peloponnese, but its larger goal was to roll back Turkish influence there; the latter could not be accomplished until the former was implemented. In Bosnia I, the most pressing issue was to bring the Turkish-Montenegrin war to a close, but the Austrians and Russians were primarily interested in using the armistice negotiations as a pretext for weakening Turkey. In the Congo, the primary United Nations objective was to prevent a military confrontation between the central government and the Katanga secessionists; that objective was, after all, the primary reason for stationing UN peacekeepers in the country. And the UN's most important concern in Bosnia-Herzegovina was also deterrence—

strengthening the willingness of the local antagonists to comply with a UN-negotiated armistice; compelling the Bosnia-Serbs to give up land taken in the civil war had lower priority.

Finally, lacking vital interests in intervening in the local conflict, the concert had an interest/resource gap that would have become apparent to the stronger primary antagonist. Because of the persisting interest/resource gap, the concert was at first no more prepared to implement coercive threats than it had earlier been in the conciliatory PD stage, when its preference not to employ force was a major reason why it had been discouraged from shifting to coercive interventionist PD.

In the end, however, the stronger primary antagonist's persistent pursuit of its interests in the face of international opposition becomes in these cases the most important reason for its undoing. Flaunting its strong will, it ultimately provokes the concert to overcome the interest/resource gap and mobilize the requisite strength to directly challenge it, placing it at a decisive disadvantage. When faced with the primary antagonist's continued recalcitrance, the concert finally defends its reputation and exerts its superior military strength. In Bosnia I, Russian military victory over the Turks in 1877 led to a British effort to roll back Russian military gains and to the holding of the Berlin conference, at which Turkey was compelled to retreat from Bosnia-Herzegovina. In the Congo, UN victory over the Katanga mercenaries forcibly ended the secession effort. And in Bosnia II, the UN bombing effort against the Bosnian Serbs, supplementing the newfound military strength of the Sarajevo government acting in alliance with Croatia, compelled the Bosnian Serbs to accept a peace framework in which Bosnia-Herzegovina was internationally recognized as a state.

Conclusions

We conclude this chapter by recapitulating the major points made above in light of the threefold typology of insulationist PD outlined in chapter 2. The purpose is to document linkages between insulationist and interventionist PD and, through these linkages, to better understand the interplay between great powers and the primary antagonists. As already indicated, such linkages and interplay are major preoccupations of this study.

In Type I cases, we recall, great-power motivation to become involved in the local ethnic conflict is low throughout the development of the conflict. Given this low motivation, the obstacles in the local conflict area to great-power efforts to defuse the conflict are highly significant. With the major states poorly motivated or postured to intervene, even routine, perfunctory opposition to great-power proposals by one or more local antagonists is likely to stymie them, the major states being unable to contemplate a coercive interventionist approach. In the Memel, for example, Lithuanian opposition to a great-power-appointed committee proposal recommending that the Memel territory be made into an international zone was sufficient to defeat the proposal. In this instance, successful interventionist PD paradoxically depended on a decision by Lithuania to invade the Memel territory, challenging the regime placed there by the major states. When, unlike in the Memel, ethnic conflict is aggravated, the antagonists being unwilling to coexist in the same state, the problem for intervention-minded weakly motivated great powers is likely to be far more difficult. In short, Type I cases do not seem promising for successful collective interventionist PD unless local conditions are wholly favorable.

In Type II cases, in which the great-power motivation to intervene is high, the potential for collective interventionist PD is larger than in Type I if the major states employ compellence against the primary antagonists to push their proposals. Highly motivated great powers used coercive interventionist PD in the Belgian and Bosnia I cases, stimulated by the interest of one major power in each instance—France in the Belgian case, and Russia in Bosnia I—to intervene unilaterally. In Belgium, the major states sought to collectively protect Belgian independence by forcing the Dutch to remove their military forces from Belgium, and in Bosnia I, they imposed Austro-Hungarian occupation of Bosnia-Herzegovina on the Turks as part of a great-power territorial compensation scheme. The major powers could not readily overcome local obstacles to collective interventionist PD in these instances: a political agreement between the Belgians and the Dutch was not reached for nearly seven years after the great powers established Belgian independence from the Netherlands; and rising demands from the Slavs in Bosnia-Herzegovina, along with Serb and Montenegrin military intervention into Bosnia-Herzegovina a year after the outbreak of the Slavic revolt, put an end to Andrassy's mediation in that case.

At other times, as during the Soviet-American Cold War, differences between the major states hampered their ability to collectively intervene in local conflict, even as their motivation for intervening was high. Although the superpowers lacked vital interests in pursuing unilateral advantages in the Congo case and early in the Cyprus case, their high motivation to gain such advantage made it impossible to collectively affect the primary antagonists, except to prevent local warfare from escalating to hostilities between them. Apart from crisis management, the superpowers retarded collective interventionist PD by allying with and fortifying opposing primary antagonists, who could look to their great-power protector for support while rejecting proposals for managing their conflict. As a result, the outlook for collective interventionist PD was more problematic during the Cold War period than in the Belgian and Bosnia I cases. In the Congo, successful coercive intervention by UN peacekeepers against the secessionist Katanga regime depended on two sets of fortuitous developments. First, in the wake of Lumumba's death, both superpowers supported termination of the mercenary-supported Katanga regime. And second, the UN military commander in the Congo chose to use his forces coercively against the secessionists in spite of Hammarskjöld's clear preference for conciliation.

In Type III cases, the will of the major states to intervene in the local conflict grows, even as those states lack vital interests to intervene. Because local developments bring about that new willingness to become involved, Type III cases strongly illustrate the interplay between local conflict developments and great-power motivations. Our cases illustrate two alternative stimuli for this shift in motivations. In the Greek and Bosnia II cases, the determination of the militarily stronger primary antagonist to subdue its opponent eventually provoked a military confrontation with the major states, whose combined power eventually forced the stronger antagonist to retreat. The retreat was both military and political in the Bosnia II case, as the great-power use of force corrected an earlier mismatch between Contact Group proposals for a political settlement in Bosnia-Herzegovina and an unwillingness to act coercively against the Serbs. In the Greek case, the retreat was limited to the balance of forces. In that instance, the great powers were unable to capitalize on their military victory over the Turks at Navarino Bay because of differences between them over the terms of a Greek settlement and because of Russo-Turkish hostilities that began a few months later.

By contrast, the major powers became more motivated to intervene in Turkish Armenia in 1912 not because of the primary antagonists but because of Russia, which threatened to intervene there if violence were to recur between the Ottoman regime and the Armenian population in eastern Turkey. The larger willingness of the major states to intervene did not alter the commitment to a conciliatory approach toward the Turkish-Armenian conflict, but spurred the major states to create a framework for improved Armenian-Turkish relations so as to diminish the likelihood of Armenian restiveness in eastern Turkey.

Part IV

Conclusions

Chapter 10

Implications for Policy

This study has been designed, as indicated, to facilitate collective insulationist and interventionist PD. To assist this objective, the major themes of this study are now linked to the needs of policymakers and policy planners, in two respects: first, by providing diagnoses of recurring policy problems, and second, by outlining prescriptions for policy behavior.[1]

Diagnoses pertain to the causes of PD successes and failures that can, if taken into account, ease the burden of contemporary collective PD. Analyses of these causes can help orient policymakers and policy planners proactively, so that they prepare ahead of time for anticipated stresses and decision points. Diagnosis should identify immediate as well as distant policy concerns deserving of attention. It is argued here that policymakers in the cases analyzed in this study were reactive rather than proactive when they dealt with small-power ethnic conflict; a proactive approach would have greatly enhanced interventionist PD effectiveness. Prescriptions, on the other hand, move beyond the level of explanations. They address how contemporary policymakers and planners should enhance the chances of success and reduce the chances of failure when dealing proactively with specific problems of small-state ethnic conflict.

Diagnoses as well as prescriptions are derived in this chapter from a focus on great-power–primary-antagonist interactions. PD requirements have been understood in terms of the strengths and intentions of highly motivated primary antagonists to resist great-power initiatives and the value of collective great-power PD to overcome primary-antagonist resistance. Proactive great-power planning for PD must take account of both of these elements. Diagnoses and generalizations are also assisted by the variety of insulationist and interventionist PD experience documented in this study. This diversity obliges those seeking proactive PD to question any standard PD type of policy approach.

In one respect, however, the basis for diagnostic evaluation is quite different than for prescription. Diagnoses can be based on analysis of *preponderant* or *prevailing* tendencies in the case material, independent of any particular case type. Prescriptions, on the other hand, cannot be based on such universal tendencies but must be linked to more particular case features. To generate prescriptions, this chapter builds on the typology of cases elaborated in chapter 2 that is based on differences in great-power motivation toward interventionist PD.

Two kinds of conclusions are put forward in this chapter. "First-cut" conclusions, taken up first, address prevailing case tendencies detected in previous chapters. These conclusions generate policy diagnoses, but not policy prescription. One important first-cut conclusion is the extensive great-power cooperation on insulationist and interventionist PD, particularly to dampen unilateral great-power intervention in local conflicts in which major-state interests are in conflict. This cooperation enhances the value of collective PD as a policy option. Another conclusion is the absence in our cases of policy planning to lessen the diplomatic and operational problems of collective PD. This conclusion enhances the importance of studies seeking more effective PD policy approaches. "Second-cut," or contingent conclusions, utilizing the typology of cases outlined in chapter 2, are used to support policy prescriptions as well as diagnoses. Type I cases, in which the motivation of the major states to intervene in local ethnic conflict is low, appear to constitute the most policy-relevant category of cases at the present time.

The Great Powers: A First Cut

This section and the next discuss conclusions supported by a preponderance of the case evidence presented in this study. This section addresses great-power behavior; the next one deals with the primary antagonists. A preoccupation with collective great-power behavior underscores (1) major-state cooperation over insulationist PD, (2) major-state cooperation over interventionist PD, and (3) the reactive rather than the proactive character of that cooperation. These will be dealt with in turn.

Cooperation over Insulationist PD

Cooperation over insulationist PD is best reflected in the frequent restraint of individual great powers who would act unilaterally in local conflict to support one primary antagonist over another, seeking opportunistic, one-sided advantages. When the major states are strongly divided by rivalry in the local conflict arena, they cooperate to avoid a war that could grow out of that rivalry. This motive is significant in the Belgian, Greek, Bosnia I, Armenian, Cyprus, and Congo cases.

Persisting major-state solidarity cannot, however, be explained primarily by the fear of the consequences of great-power war. While mostly conciliatory, insulationist PD is especially noteworthy for major-state willingness—especially when sharp divisions prevailed about local conflict—to allow time to probe for convergent solutions. The great powers invest a huge amount of energy to apply problem-solving methods to their own divisions, even as they understand that successful problem solving can only be temporary and transitory, given their different outlooks.[2]

This problem-solving approach is strengthened by the determination of the unilateral-minded major state to exact a price for cooperation with the concert. In the Belgian and Bosnia I cases unilateral aims and activity by the French and Russians, respectively, are dampened not because the unilateral-minded great power compromises its views but because it is able to use its will to intervene in the local conflict to gain leverage on the terms of cooperation with other major states. And in the Congo, Cyprus, and Bosnia II cases, individual major states adhere to some restraint because others do so; UN action facilitates this restraint by preempting, to a degree, competitive great-power intervention.

In these cases, and in Greece, the major states are persistently attentive and sensitive to each other's interests in the local conflict, the most assertive among them dampening their activity so as to not break the formal solidarity of the major states. A common motivation behind great-power insulationist PD in these instances is the attraction of each great power to the prospect of being part of a cooperative major-state solution, avoiding isolation. A great power participating in PD statecraft can shape PD solutions and gain from the larger rewards obtained from defending international values.

A major advantage suggested by this experience for collective PD, compared with PD initiated by great powers independently, is that insulation creates value.[3] The major states find it more difficult to disengage from insulationist PD once considerable collective effort has been expended upon it. To be sure, this cooperation is frequently held down by great-power hostility and suspicion. At times, cooperation between the major states is sharply weakened by great-power disputes, as in the Cold War cases, Armenia, and Bosnia II. At worst, cooperation is terminated by unilateral action, as when, in the Greek and Bosnia I cases, Russia decided to make war against the Ottoman Empire, provoking sharp hostility with Britain and terminating collective interventionist PD until hostilities ended. Recognizing that cooperation between great powers is frequently built on major conflicts of interest, and that bargaining and negotiation usually do not alter these divisions but deflect them, great-power insulationist solidarity is nevertheless impressive in these cases.

Great-Power Cooperation over Interventionist PD

Interventionist PD cooperation is also impressive in these cases for its persistence and—in the seven cases with a completed endgame—for its effectiveness. Collective intervention is linked to collective insulation, especially in relation to the more aggravated, violent cases of local ethnic conflict. Three features of this linkage should be underscored. First, the strength of the staying power of collective insulationist PD, just noted, strengthens interventionist PD against primary antagonists that flaunt international values by persisting in violence against their ethnic challenger or against international forces. The ability of insulationist statecraft to create value ensures that such local antagonists will ultimately be met by forceful coercive measures that they cannot withstand. The collective great-power enterprise is in such cases more effective than is any one great power employing PD independently. Second, in the short-term, the link between intervention and insulation ensures that the largest investment of interventionist PD energy will be expended when insulationist PD is most problematic. This short-term linkage is produced by bargaining among great powers: sharply divided over how to cope with the local conflict, the major states insulate the local conflict as an element of their own relations only on condition that they agree on a program of intervention in it. Because the major states link intervention to insulation, they accept the need to consider and act upon interventionist PD when its prospects—after the local conflict has become more aggravated—are more problematic. That is, even if the major states have been unable to bring their collective influence to bear effectively *early* in the local conflict, they may continue to be energized by the conflict later on. Far from being deterred by prior PD failure, the great powers—spurred by insulationist PD needs to intervene in the conflict—are sufficiently energized to continue to aim at defusing the local conflict. Continual engagement affords the major states the opportunity to be more effective in later interventionist PD than they were earlier.

Third, just as cooperation over insulation is best reflected in unilateral great-power restraint toward local conflict, interventionist PD also depends heavily on it. Unilateral intervention—usually indispensable for the interests and capabilities of the local antagonists—is the most important obstacle to defusing the local conflict, and especially to international efforts to manage it. Limiting or diminishing outside assistance to the primary antagonists must be a key priority for a PD-minded coalition, especially in aggravated local conflict, when the primary antagonists most need outside assistance. Yet only great powers can, in association with each other, provide the necessary leverage to dissuade other major states from providing significant help to primary antagonists to whom they are linked. And primary antagonists denied such assistance will tend to be more receptive to collective interventionist PD.

The benefits and urgency of interventionist PD are stimulated and parallel insulationist needs only if the benefits of insulation are taken into account in decision-making. Much of the present study has argued for the need for decision-makers to take account of these benefits. When they do, as in the cases analyzed in this study, a powerful collective great-power motive for interventionist PD is introduced that appears at present to be neglected in the PD literature and downplayed by advocates of unilateral rather than multilateral great-power action. In practice, factoring insulation into the PD picture eases the burden of policy justification somewhat for advocates of interventionist PD. Interventionist PD that might not be approved if the policy issue were defined in terms of the merits of intervention itself—perhaps because the incentives for intervening in relation to the primary antagonists is not perceived to be sufficiently high to justify the costs and risks of engagement in the local conflict—are more likely to be authorized if debate includes the benefits of insulationist PD accruing from it. For example, debate about intervention is appropriately linked to durability and adaptability of the great-power concert. But factoring in this linkage requires policymakers and policy planners to be predisposed to the importance of insulation.

Interventionist PD is also limited by its linkage with insulation. When neither primary antagonist flaunts international values, as in the Memel and the later stages of the Cyprus and Belgian cases, the major states will tend to attach lower urgency to the local conflict, and will as a result be more weakly supportive of interventionist PD. Then the great-power concert will be less influential in relation to the local antagonists, whose views will carry more weight. In relation to aggravated local conflict, when international values are at stake, collective interventionist PD is limited in the opposite way: it is then forcefully shaped by great-power politics. In such cases, collective major-state management of the local dispute is essential to the stability of relations among the great powers, and so collective intervention is required, but intervention initiatives are dictated by the great-power ability (or inability) to agree. Particularly when the great powers initiate conciliatory interventionist PD toward aggravated local conflict, the practice of interventionist PD tends to be gyroscopic, the major states being unwilling or unable to alter it despite the refusal of the primary antagonists to cooperate. Limited by their own insulationist priorities, the great powers are not well positioned to capitalize on ripening conditions in the immediate region of the local ethnic conflict—such as a hurting stalemate between the opposing parties—that might otherwise offer opportunities for imposing a settlement.[4] Their ability to *effectively* manage the local conflict—that is, to satisfactorily incorporate the views of the primary antagonists into a framework that both sides can accept—is weakened because they attach greater importance to the views of great-power states than to those of the primary antagonists.

Reactive rather than Proactive Responses

In each of our cases, interventionist PD does not anticipate the outbreak of local ethnic violence but reacts to it. As such, it forfeits the advantage of intervening before relations between the local antagonists become polarized. The delay has little to do with the presence or absence of warning of adverse local developments.[5] In half the cases, warning of tension-raising developments in the local conflict arena was available to the major states (Armenia, Cyprus, and Bosnia I and II); in the other cases, information required for early interventionist PD was not available (Belgium, Greece, the Memel, and the Congo). The major states did not act collectively in the former instances and, so far as can be determined, they would not have been likely to act together in the latter instances even if the information about anticipated ethnic difficulties had been provided. Rather, the delay is due to the interests and norms of the major states.[6]

First, interventionist PD cannot be collectively pursued, as we have seen, until the major states insulate the local conflict as a problem in their own relations. However, there is no great-power regime facilitating expedient, prompt insulation of the local conflicts in our cases. In its absence, the time required to handle ad hoc insulationist PD in practice prevents collective action on the basis of warnings of worsened ethnic conflict.

Second, the interests and norms of the major states especially strongly stimulate collective interventionist PD when those states exercised crisis management among themselves. We have seen how crisis circumstances are mainly produced in this context by widely projected negative consequences of unilateral major-state opportunistic intervention in the local conflict. These points underscore inefficiencies and weaknesses of collective interventionist PD. PD will generally be directed to local conflicts in which major states do not act collectively merely because local ethnic violence is projected to worsen.[7] Whatever the advantage of their intervention, the major states when acting collectively will therefore be required to confront worsening ethnic conflict later on, *unless they can anticipate problematic developments in such conflict beforehand.* That is, collective interventionist PD initiatives directed to aggravated cases to forestall unilateral major-state opportunistic intervention risk being ineffective in relation to the primary antagonists. The ineffectiveness of interventionist PD in defusing local tensions and in reconciling the primary antagonists in turn depresses the great-power will to persist in applying it. We will return to the question of great-power proactive behavior below.

The Primary Antagonists: A First Cut

Local antagonist dependence on outside actors is understood here in terms of two general conclusions: (1) political and economic grievances are consistently more important than nationalism in fuelling ethnic challenges; and (2) the central regime can withstand the political challenger's resistance for long periods without accommodating to it.

The Challenger's Grievances

Political and economic grievances of local ethnic groups against their government stimulate ethnic conflict more than does the cultural identity of the challenging group, which is generally missing in these cases. Lacking cultural identity, the political challenger is less able to resist the central regime on its own, and becomes more dependent on outside assistance to redress its political and economic grievances. Outside states are significantly engaged in instigating or intensifying local ethnic conflict, and their engagement has international as well as local effects.

Internationally, the linkage between political challenger and outside sponsors enhances the influence of the challenger and helps shape the great-power PD agenda. In most of our cases, the challenger's mode of resisting the central regime was controlled by outside supporters (Bosnia I and II, the Congo) or primarily designed to gain international allies (Greece, Armenia). The stronger the political challenger's attachment to outside supporters, the more important are those outside supporters for determining whether a hurting stalemate exists between challenger and central regime. In effect, outside support, or the commitment to obtain or provide it, retards the onset of a hurting stalemate in which local antagonists conclude they are unable to prevail militarily. Even if a hurting stalemate prevailed beforehand, the prospect of outside intervention by the ethnic challenger's sympathizers transforms the conflict into one in which the challenger, through ostensibly weaker than the central regime, counts on international support to redress the gap.

The linkage between the political challenger and its outside sympathizers adds to the imperatives of interventionist PD but also to its difficulties. The imperatives of collective intervention are increased because the involvement of outside states in the local conflict arena increases the dangers of the conflict, especially for the indigenous parties but also for other neighboring states. Interventionist PD is then more likely.[8] On the other hand, the linkage increases the difficulty of making PD effective. First, great-power engagement in defense of the ethnic challenger's political goals complicates the forging of great-power consensus for interventionist PD: the great powers must weigh their individual ties to the ethnic challenger against the need for collective management of the local conflict. Second, the ability of the great powers to agree on interventionist PD does not preclude the political challenger from continuing to seek international assistance. When the challenger continues to count on such assistance, hurtful stalemate is blocked and the great powers will face greater obstacles influencing the local antagonists to defuse their conflict.

Outside ties to the political challenger also interfere with interventionist PD by exacerbating local conflict. The challenger's use of those ties to more boldly resist the central regime adds to local polarization and, as the political challenger seeks to provoke the central regime to act repressively, to the militarization of the local conflict (Greece, Armenia). The central regime can be expected to categorically oppose outside assistance to the political challenger and, if such assistance is forthcoming, is likely to interpret challenger resistance in more threatening fashion.[9]

The Weight of the Central Regime

The central regime is also motivated to seek outside assistance in the local conflict by its inability to prevail on its own against its domestic opponent. However, the central regime has higher standing among states than does its nonstate challenger, and therefore more potential for obtaining international support. Its international support potential has little to do with its domestic authority in relation to its challenger, and much to do with international norms and with the interests of neighboring countries.

To obtain international support, the central regime ordinarily does not have to demonstrate that it is surmounting its domestic challenge. In the Greek, Bosnia I and II, Armenia, Cyprus, and Congo cases, central regimes obtained support from external allies despite the great difficulty they experienced in coping with their ethnic antagonists. In some cases, the attractiveness of the embattled regime as an international ally increased precisely *because* of outside perceptions of its domestic weaknesses: the Ottoman regime, the Muslim-dominated government of Bosnia-Herzegovina, and the Lumumba regime in the Congo were advantaged internationally by the anxiety of outside states and international actors over whether their collapse, under pressure of ethnic conflict, could be exploited by other states.

The central regime often utilizes international norms and links to specific states to strengthen its domestic position. International norms recognize even highly weak and unstable regimes as formally supreme within their area of jurisdiction. When the authority of a regime is challenged, those norms grant it the perogative to determine, at least initially, how to meet that challenge, and to prevent outside intervention that diminishes its authority. Only flagrant abuse by a state of its authority, according to theses norms, justifies questioning the right of a state to keep outsiders at bay.

The central regime can also use other states to assist its domestic position, even as its ability to deal with its domestic rival is in doubt. When the regime's institutions are newly created—as in the early days of the Congo or of the Muslim-dominated government in Bosnia-Herzegovina—or else incompetent and paralyzed by inertia and corruption—as in the Ottoman regime—the prospect of regime collapse can galvanize international support even as it emboldens ethnic challengers. The regime then exploits other states' fears about its threatened demise to reduce or eliminate external pressures upon it to reform its political institutions and make accommodations with its adversary. For example, England and Russia competed for the favor of the Ottoman Empire, offering it leverage against pressures to reform. Each sought to neutralize the other's standing with the regime, while the latter encouraged the competition between them to avoid having to ameliorate the condition of the Armenians in the empire.

We have noted that international linkages assisting the political challenger strengthen the imperatives of collective interventionist PD and also the difficulties of implementing it. The central regime's ability to garner external assistance increases the difficulties of implementing PD even more than does the ethnic challenger's search for it. *Whatever the international support afforded to the ethnic challenger,* support for the central regime—even by one great power—stimulates optimism in the central regime's leadership about sustaining the conflict against its challenger. Confusing international support with a force multiplier, the regime is likely to persist in refusing to negotiate with the challenger, to accept impartial mediation by a great-power coalition, or to widen the terms of mediation. In short, it is likely to stymie great-power endeavors to reconcile the ethnic opponents.

The central regime's ability to serve as a gatekeeper, regulating major-power interventionist PD, is substantial but not always decisive. When the regime does not contend with great-power challengers to its authority, it can make use of external support to discourage and ultimately reject collective interventionist PD. An international great-power coalition's incentive to exercise good offices to defuse the local conflict is then diminished. On the other hand, external support for the central regime can be linked to an international challenge to its authority. When outside challenge to the central regime's authority rallies external support for the regime, it increases the urgency of collective interventionist PD because of the danger of great-power war. The need for great-power crisis management was considerable in the Greek and Bosnia I cases because of Anglo-Russian rivalry; it was smaller in the Armenian case as England and Russia routinely but warily coexisted as Armenian rivals. Crisis management also importantly stimulated interventionist PD in Belgium, the Congo, and Cyprus.

Contingent Conclusions: A Second Cut

This study has derived general conclusions by abstracting broad tendencies from particular circumstances. General insights have limited value for policymakers, however. First, policy-relevant prescriptions cannot be generated from general observations alone. Tensions and possibilities in the interplay between great powers and primary antagonists to local conflict make it impossible to prescribe in the abstract how to forge effective collective interventionist PD. Second, policymakers lack time to form a more differentiated view of a policy problem and tend on their own to adopt simplified generalized approaches based on their predispositions and their sense of historical parallels.[10] Contingent conclusions generated by focused comparisons are needed to check this tendency—that is, to discourage policymakers from treating similarly cases whose dissimilarities seem highly important. When alert to key dissimilarities between cases, policymakers can enhance the chances of policy success by linking particular types of policy problems to corresponding remedies and acting proactively to anticipate and forestall them.

Case analysis in this study has highlighted (1) a variety of types of PD experience to which policymakers should be alert, (2) a checklist of variables important in each type of experience that policy decisions and planning can affect, and (3) linkages between variables that seem significant in some instances of PD but not in others. Because no single approach to PD can be a key to all PD instances, policy planners should consider and adapt to their needs alternate sets of circumstances.

To enhance policy effectiveness, the present writer has distinguished types of PD cases by the manner of interplay between great powers and primary antagonists in local conflict, and by the behavior of the great powers in collectively dealing with such conflict. Each type of great-power interventionist PD yields conclusions appropriate for cases fitting that type. Each appears important enough to affect appropriate policy choices and the chances of policy success. These types are the focus for the following discussion of contingent conclusions about the interplay between great-power behavior and the local primary antagonists. That is to say, depending on whether the great powers have low motivation to intervene in the local conflict, high motivation to do so, or changeable motivation, distinctive diagnoses can be made about PD problems encountered by the great powers. Moreover, prescriptions for great-power behavior can be generated based on those diagnoses.

In what follows, distinctive diagnoses and prescriptions are discussed for each type of interventionist PD. In addition, the problems of detection and of relevance are raised for each type. With respect to detection, the distinction between the three types must be sufficiently clear-cut to be practical for those with planning and intelligence responsibilities. A key assumption underpinning the discussion is that it is feasible to discriminate between these types and to be sensitized to the distinctive problems each raises. The distinctions must also be linked to contemporary circumstances, which provide the immediate requirement for carrying out the preparations for insulationist and interventionist PD recommended here.

Type I: Low Great-Power Motivation

Type I cases present some of the most difficult problems for insulationist and interventionist PD. In this type, the great powers have little or no concern for local ethnic conflict, defining their vital interests apart from those conflicts. They are unwilling to take major risks collectively in relation to small-state ethnic conflict, just as they are unwilling to take major risks unilaterally in this respect. Given this individual diffidence of the major states, a major issue is the scope of permissible collective action.

Two possibilities should be distinguished. One, reflected in the Memel case, is that insulationist and interventionist PD take place but intervention is limited to conciliation. Conciliatory interventionist PD may influence the local antagonists when their conflict is relatively tranquil; it will not be effective when their local conflict is violent and aggravated. Because collective interventionist PD in Type I cases cannot be coercive, the most active interventionist PD in aggravated Type I cases will still entail a mismatch between great-power capabilities and the local requirements for defusing tensions. Even when directed to tranquil ethnic conflict, its effectiveness is likely to be undermined by the slow and halting manner with which it is initiated, raising questions on the part of the primary antagonists about the depth of commitment of the major powers to it. A second, more extreme Type I possibility is that the great powers are unable to agree on interventionist PD at all—they cannot, in other words, employ collective action to compensate for their unwillingness to take risks individually. The greatest danger in Type I cases is great-power neglect, the major states excluding from their agenda long-standing and possibly worsening local ethnic conflict.

Very limited here in their ability to prevent mature, visible ethnic conflict from worsening, the great powers need to employ *early* collective intervention in the local conflict, prior to the onset of polarized relations between the primary antagonists. But the low will to become involved in the local case will impede early collective intervention *unless* the major states have available a previously created early-warning regime enabling them to sensitize themselves to the potential emergence of local tensions and to legitimate collective involvement with the primary antagonists at an early stage. The Organization for Security and Cooperation in Europe appears to be a prototype for such a regime on the regional basis, and a panel of experts has proposed that a policy planning staff be created at UN headquarters to direct attention to early PD intervention.[11]

Type I cases are the most relevant for contemporary world politics, in which the great powers generally limit their risks and engagements in local ethnic conflict. The Type I emphasis should be on quiet, patient, judicious diplomacy, relying as much as possible on collective sanction to enhance its legitimacy and its weight, dispersing credit for PD success as well as the risk of PD failure. Such diplomacy would aim to maximize the relatively little leverage of the great powers, using a great-power concert to compensate for the disincentives of the major states to act alone.

Type II: High Great-Power Motivation

When one or more great powers is highly motivated to intervene for unilateral advantage in a neighboring-state ethnic conflict, other major states will tend to resist. Because of the conflict between major states, insulationist PD in Type II cases is an alternative to mutually undesired great-power warfare. Insulationist PD typically functions as containment by engagement, unilateral-minded great powers being compensated for restraint and for agreement to cooperate with collective great-power interventionist PD. Interventionist PD, an outgrowth of insulation, is primarily driven by the need of the major states to sustain their coalition. Heavily affected by the primacy of great-power interests, insulationist and interventionist PD in Type II cases are subject to a dilemma inherent in that primacy: successful interventionist PD is critical for international stability, but the effectiveness of interventionist PD proposals and thereby of insulationist PD is in doubt. Persistence of this dilemma helps explain why Type II cases are problematic for the great powers despite their collective engagement.

On one hand, the Type II emphasis on insulationist PD insures that interventionist PD will primarily mirror great-power needs rather than those of the primary antagonists. Collective great-power interests are best advanced if the primary antagonists accept intervention proposals, yet, because those proposals are so heavily conditioned by great-power needs, they are not likely to be optimum from the point of view of the primary antagonists. The more delicate the crisis management experienced by the major states as an outgrowth of the local conflict—the delicateness being affected by how vital is the search for advantage by the independent-minded great power—the less optimum will their interventionist PD proposals in that conflict tend to be. On the other hand, ineffective intervention directed to aggravated ethnic conflict will ultimately threaten great-power cohesion as the primary antagonists persist in resisting interventionist PD proposals, and as outside states—including great powers—view the resulting local instability as an attractive source of unilateral advantage. Having defined their responsibility in maintaining international peace and security to require intervention in the local conflict, the great powers are likely to encounter difficulties, from recalcitrant primary antagonists and from each other, when collective interventionist PD fails to defuse the local conflict.

As to how the major states can cope with this dilemma, the following two prescriptions presume that the great powers will, in these cases, pursue great-power-driven solutions to local ethnic conflict. First, having agreed on neutralizing the local conflict as an element of their own relations, the great powers should not hesitate to bolster their leverage with the primary antagonists for their interventionist PD proposals. Thus, in the Bosnia I case, the great powers should have backed Andrassy's mediation effort with the threat of military intervention, on the assumption that the mediation was as important for them as was insulation. This prescription will be unattractive to those great powers, such as Austria-Hungary in the Bosnia I case, that use interventionist PD as a screen for territorial expansion. The prescription presumes that the great powers can define their major objectives rather than leaving them diffuse and unspecified. A second prescription for dealing with this problem is that the great powers act as soon as possible after reaching a consensus. They did so at the 1878 Berlin Conference when, the Ottoman Empire being represented, Austro-Hungarian occupation of Bosnia-Herzegovina was imposed over Ottoman objections.[12]

Of the three types of interventionist PD cases distinguished in this study, Type II cases are least likely in the contemporary period for two reasons. The first is that the major states at present do not compete for influence in Third World states, in which intrastate ethnic conflict is most severe; to the contrary, they attempt to avoid heavy political engagement in unstable states because they wish to avoid responsibility for exercising political authority in them.[13] Second, the volume of intrastate ethnic conflict at present discourages the major powers from placing local ethnic conflict on their political agenda. Even if they did compete for influence in local ethnic conflict, the major states would be hard pressed to be selective about the location of such conflict.

Type III: Shifting Great-Power Motivation

Type III cases, in which the great powers increase their motivation to intervene in local ethnic conflict over time, are the most frustrating and difficult for the major states. In such cases, great powers and primary antagonists misunderstand each other. The great powers underestimate the will of the stronger local antagonist to dominate its opponent militarily and politically. They also underestimate the stronger primary antagonist's willingness to take risks that could potentially draw in the major states to assist its opponent. These mistakes are largely attributed to the wholly different position and outlook of the great powers and the stronger local antagonist. The great powers seek to defuse the local conflict, while the stronger antagonist aims at a one-sided solution. The great powers lack vital interests in affecting the result of the local conflict, whereas the primary antagonists have preeminent interests in the results. The major states, finally, are unwilling to take large risks in becoming involved in the local conflict, while the primary antagonists are committed to taking major risks.

The militarily stronger local antagonist also misjudges the will and capability of the great-power coalition. It assumes, also plausibly but incorrectly, that the initial accommodationist response of the major states reflects an unwillingness to consider tougher policies, and that the major states, lacking vital interests in intervening in the local conflict, will draw back from confrontation with one or more primary antagonists. It also assumes that frustration of collective *conciliatory* interventionist PD signifies the coalition's inability to effectuate *any* kind of interventionist PD. The result is that the stronger primary antagonist becomes the agent of its own reversal at the hands of the great powers. Its use of force, against its local opponent as well as against forces allocated by the great powers to the local conflict arena, provokes the great-power coalition to shift from conciliatory to coercive interventionist PD, and ultimately to a use of force on a scale that the militarily stronger local antagonist cannot withstand.

These problems of mutual misunderstanding arise from a Type III case dilemma: the major states persist in intervening in aggravated ethnic conflict, but they are also unwilling to deepen their engagement in that conflict because they fear losing control over the scope of their involvement if they do so. Yet their persistence in intervening increases their risk of losing control over the level of their engagement. This is because their level of engagement and their agenda are inevitably affected by transition developments—humanitarian emergencies, threatened military intervention by outside states, and provocations directed against international forces—that stimulate still deeper engagement in that conflict. The dilemma becomes more acute as the major states become more militarily and politically engaged in the local conflict. Then their involvement effectively assists the militarily and politically weaker of the primary antagonists and challenges the local superiority of the stronger primary antagonist, and they must anticipate that the stronger antagonist will come to regard them as an adversary. For example, should they introduce military forces into the region, the stronger antagonist for this reason would be more likely to target those forces.

Great-power leaders' awareness of these problems has made them more anxious to control their level of commitment in local ethnic conflicts, and slower to take on new obligations. But hesitation by the major states for any reason weakens their bargaining leverage with the primary antagonists when the great powers *eventually* increase the scope of the engagement in aggravated local conflict. Moreover, major-state anticipation of this weakened position reinforces initial major-state commitment avoidance. Hesitation by the great powers in taking on commitments in turn strengthens the stronger political local antagonist in its belief that the major-state coalition is permanently handicapped in its ability to influence the local antagonists. Type III collective PD can succeed only if this belief is undermined.

Great-power PD diffidence should be challenged on policy and on planning grounds. First, a PD approach that seeks to play it safe is likely to be unsatisfactory from a major-state policy standpoint. Great-power abdication of responsibility for dispute management in these aggravated ethnic conflict cases will erode great-power influence potential also *in those cases in which the major states have strong reasons to become engaged,* as small states generally question great-power intentions and leadership. Second, proactive policy planning can and should improve the outlook for collective interventionist PD as great-power engagement in local conflict increases. Only a very small number of local intrastate ethnic conflicts are at issue here, it must be emphasized. Type III cases include only those instances in which early interventionist PD is ineffective, but because of the aggravated character of the local conflict, strong yet nonvital interventionist PD interests remain.

Policy planning for such cases should have two working assumptions. The first is that the major states are much more likely to be able to limit the costs of deepened engagement in local ethnic conflict if they can anticipate the conditions in which that engagement will take place. The second assumption is that the decision on whether to shift from low to high motivation to intervene in the local conflict should not be made on the basis of a simple either-or choice. That is, the decision should not be conceived as being between commitment-avoidance and all-out intervention: policy planning can and should introduce other possibilities that allow interventionist PD to be potentially useful while successfully controlling its risks.

Two prescriptions for such planning are generated from this study. First, even when it is difficult or impossible to prevent polarized ethnic opponents from resorting to military force, the great powers can collectively prevent exacerbation of local conflict. The most important aggravating factor to local conflict, it has been argued here, is the intervention of states located adjacent to a local intrastate conflict area that are sympathetic to one or another of the primary antagonists. Forestalling such intervention assists insulationist PD. Another aggravating factor is the inability of the great powers to insulate violent, polarized local conflict as an issue among themselves. As the Bosnia-Herzegovina and Kosovo cases have recently demonstrated, worsening local ethnic conflict challenges the major states to readdress the local conflict as an issue among themselves, but they may experience severe difficulty in doing so. If they cannot insulate the conflict, collective interventionist PD will be impossible. But the great powers can plan ahead to seek bases for insulation, anticipating aggravation of specific local conflicts.

A second prescription for Type III cases is not to overrate the strategic importance of early great-power PD frustrations in those cases. Great-power planning regarding them should be initiated that distinguishes *short term* great-power intervention difficulties from *longer-term* great-power potential. Persistent great-power frustrations are likely to be experienced as a record of failure that the major states are unlikely to permanently accept, especially when primary antagonists have, or appear to have, totalistic war aims. The more ambitious the goals and strengths of the stronger local primary antagonist, the more difficult it will be for the latter to steer clear of hurtful great-power responses in opposition. Two of the eight cases examined here—in Greece and in Bosnia II—show that deepened local hostilities between the primary antagonists can provoke wider hostilities between a primary antagonist and a great-power coalition. Policy planning should anticipate that aggravated local conflict in which the great powers have persisting collective interventionist PD interests will, in similar fashion, provoke a shift from low to high motivation to intervene in that conflict.

Notes

Notes to Chapter 1

1. "[T]oday's typical war is civil, started by rebels who want to change the country's constitution, alter the balance of power between races, or secede." *The Economist,* 12 March 1988, cited in Frederic S. Pearson and J. Martin Rochester, *International Relations: The Global Condition in the Late Twentieth Century,* 3rd ed. (New York: McGraw-Hill, 1992), 277.

2. See, on this point, William W. Kaufmann, "The Organization of Responsibility," *World Politics* 1 (July 1949):510–532.

3. More recent studies on this topic include Kevin M. Cahill (ed.), *Preventive Diplomacy: Stopping Wars Before They Start* (New York: Basic Books, 1996); Carnegie Commission on Preventing Deadly Conflict, *Preventing Deadly Conflict: Final Report* (Washington, D.C.: Carnegie Commission on Preventing Deadly Conflict, 1997); Michael S. Lund, *Preventing Violent Conflicts* (Washington, D.C.: United States Institute of Peace, 1996); Bruce W. Jentleson (ed.), *Opportunities Missed, Opportunities Seized* (Lanham, Md.: Rowman & Littlefield, 2000); I. William Zartman (ed.), *Preventive Negotiation* (Lanham, Md.: Rowman & Littlefield, 2001); David Cortright, *The Price of Peace* (Lanham, Md.: Rowman & Littlefield, 1997); Michael E. Brown (ed.), *Ethnic Conflict and International Security* (Princeton, N.J.: Princeton University Press, 1993); Michael E. Brown (ed.), *The International Dimensions of Internal Conflict* (Cambridge, Mass.: MIT Press, 1996); Stephen John Stedman, Donald Rothchild, and Elizabeth M. Cousins (eds.), *Ending Civil War: The Implementation of Peace Agreements* (Boulder, Colo.: Lynne Rienner, 2002); David Carment and Patrick James (eds.), *Peace in the Midst of Wars* (Columbia, S.C.: University of South Carolina Press, 1998); Robert I. Rotberg (ed.), *Vigilance and Vengeance* (Washington: Brookings, 1996); Janie Leatherman et al., *Breaking Cycles of Violence* (West Hartford, Conn.: Kumarian Press, 1999); I. William Zartman (ed.), *Elusive Peace* (Washington, D.C.: Brookings, 1995); Patrick M. Regan, *Civil Wars and Foreign Powers* (Ann Arbor, Mich.: University of Michigan Press, 2000); and David A. Lake and Donald Rothchild (eds.), *The International Spread of Ethnic Conflict* (Princeton, N.J.: Princeton University Press, 1998).

Earlier analyses include Alexander L. George (ed.), *Managing U.S.-Soviet Rivalry: Problems of Crisis Prevention* (Boulder, Colo.: Westview Press, 1983); and René Albrecht-Carrié (ed.), *The Concert of Europe* (New York: Walker & Company, 1968).

4. Boutros Boutros-Ghali, *Agenda for Peace* (June 1992), reproduced in Adam Roberts and Benedict Kingsbury (eds.), *United Nations, Divided World: The U.N.'s Roles in International Relations,* 2nd ed. (Oxford: Clarendon Press, 1993), 475. A critique of the Boutros-Ghali report is "The United Nations and International Security," by Adam Roberts, in Brown, *Ethnic Conflict and International Security,* 208–235.

5. Lakhdar Brahimi et al., *Report of the Panel on United Nations Peace Operations,* 23 August 2000, UN document A/55/305-S/2000/809 (New York: United Nations, 2000), accessed online at http://www.un.org/peace/reports/peace_operations/docs/ 3, 10.

6. Lund, *Preventing Violent Conflicts,* 80, 171, 181.

7. Ibid., 112, 182. See also note 24.

8. Ibid., 163. Emphasis in original.

9. Ibid., 167.

10. "[A] complete analysis of strategic bargaining about ethnic conflict would require explicitly incorporating the international system as a causal variable." Ashley J. Tellis, Thomas S. Szayna and James A. Winnefeld, *Anticipating Ethnic Conflict* (Santa Monica, Calif.: RAND, 1997), 107.

11. On the system as a cause of state behavior, see Martin Hollis and Steve Smith, "The International System," in *The Theory and Practice of International Relations,* edited by William C. Olsen, 9th ed. (Englewood Cliffs, N.J.: Prentice-Hall, 1994), 192–200; and Kenneth N. Waltz, *Theory of International Politics* (Reading, Mass.: Addison-Wesley, 1979), chap. 3. The present study employs the "bottom-up" rather than the "top-down" conceptualization of the international system.

12. The frequent influence of the primary antagonists over the major states in the early stages of internationalized ethnic conflict encountered in this study was at odds with this expectation.

13. Expressing what he feels is a paradox, Michael E. Brown writes that "international motivations to take action are weakest in the early stages of internal conflicts, when levels of violence are low and windows of opportunity are open. . . . [I]nternational motivations to act are weakest when options are strongest, and motivations to act are strongest when options are weakest." "Internal Conflict and International Action," in Brown, *International Dimensions of Internal Conflict,* 615. The present writer believes this may be only an apparent paradox, once regularities in great-power behavior are understood. On this point, see also chapter 2.

14. Alexander L. George, *Bridging the Gap* (Washington, D.C.: United States Institute of Peace, 1996), 112.

15. Barry Buzan, *People, States and Fear,* 2nd ed. (Boulder, Colo.: Lynne Rienner, 1991), 99.

16. It will be argued, however, that the propensity of major states to intervene will depend more on great-power interests, and the likelihood of unilateral great-power action, than upon small-state conditions. See below, chapters 2 and 6.

17. Elaine Sciolino, "New U.S. Peacekeeping Policy De-emphasizes Role of the U.N.," *New York Times,* 6 May 1994. This article should be compared with "U.N. Peace-Keeping Operations," *Washington Post,* 19 June 1993. A brief discussion of the policy guidance, Policy Decision Directive 25 (1994), is in Amos A. Jordan et al. (eds.), *American National Security*, 5th ed. (Baltimore, Md.: Johns Hopkins Press, 1999), 522. At a panel meeting at the International Studies Association's Annual Convention in San Diego, California, in April 1996, an informed panelist characterized this Presidential Decision Document as a "parking garage disclaimer."

18. Brown, "Introduction," in *International Dimensions of Internal Conflict,* 13.

19. Ibid., 3–12.

20. The distinction between highly motivated and poorly motivated collective PD helps to clarify the distinction, elaborated upon by Alexander George and others, between gross capabilities and usable options (see note 14, above). As with any other foreign policy strategy, interventionist PD is most enhanced when usable options comprise a larger rather than a smaller proportion of gross capabilities. The proportion of usable options to gross capabilities will be larger as the major states are more motivated to act collectively, and smaller as the major states are less motivated to intervene. When great powers are more highly motivated, they will tend to respond to local antagonist resistance by a willingness to employ larger resources to overcome the resistance.

21. Lori Fisler Damrosch (ed.), *Enforcing Restraint: Collective Intervention in Internal Conflicts* (New York: Council on Foreign Relations, 1993), 9.

22. The Chairman of a U.N. working committee on rights in the U.N. General Assembly, Danilo Turk, was quoted in 1994 as saying, "The framework of domestic jurisdiction has narrowed. Things that were considered domestic 30 to 40 years ago are now international jurisdiction, and we could act on them." Barbara Crossette, "What is a Nation?", *New York Times,* 26 February 1994. See also Ted Robert Gurr and Barbara Harff, *Ethnic Conflict in World Politics* (Boulder, Colo.: Westview Press, 1994), 147–151.

23. Zartman, *Elusive Peace,* 10; Zartman, "The Hurting Stalemate and Beyond," in Paul C. Stern and Daniel Druckman (eds.), *International Conflict Resolution After the Cold War,* Committee on International Conflict Resolution, The National Research Council (Washington, D.C.: National Academy Press, 2000), 225–250.

24. Brown, "Introduction," 29. This point is affirmed by Michael Lund (*Preventing Violent Conflict*) and Ted Robert Gurr (*Minorities at Risk: A Global View of Ethnopolitical Conflicts* [Washington, D.C.: United States Institute of Peace, 1993], 313).

Those emphasing early intervention in intrastate ethnic conflict argue, contrary to the view articulated here, that early PD *is* "do or die," since PD failure at that stage permits and may contribute to much worse conflict later. By contrast, the present study takes into account the practical difficulties of making early intervention effective and argues, realistically, that there should be a backup to failure at that stage. The difficulties of early intervention as well as the opportunities for later intervention are importantly found, it is argued here, in the character of great-power relationships.

25. Brown, *Ethnic Conflict and International Security,* 5. Other comparative studies of ethnic conflict are Joseph V. Montville (ed.), *Conflict and Peacemaking in Multiethnic Societies* (New York: Lexington Books, 1991); Manus I. Midlarsky (ed.), *The Internationalization of Communal Strife* (London: Routledge, 1993); Donald L. Horowitz, *Ethnic Groups in Conflict* (Berkeley, Calif.: University of California Press, 1985); Joseph Rothschild, *Ethnopolitics: A Conceptual Framework* (New York: Columbia University Press, 1982); Walker Connor, *Ethnonationalism: The Quest for Understanding* (Princeton, N.J.: Princeton University Press, 1994); Gurr and Harff, *Ethnic Conflict in World Politics*; Gurr, *Minorities at Risk*; Harold R. Isaacs, *Idols of the Tribe* (New York: Harper & Row, 1974); Michael Ignatieff, *Blood and Belonging* (New York: Farrar, Straus and Giroux, 1993); David A. Lake and Donald Rothchild, "Containing Fear: The Origins and Management of Ethnic Conflict," *International Security* 21 (Fall 1996):41–75; and David Carment and Patrick James, "International Constraints and Interstate Ethnic Conflict," *Journal of Conflict Resolution* 39 (March 1995):82–109.

26. For such an approach to ethnic conflict see, for example, Gurr, *Minorities at Risk.*

27. Gurr and Harff, *Ethnic Conflict in World Politics,* 13. Six years after this 1994 assessment, one of its authors concluded that "the rash of ethnic warfare peaked in the early 1990s," highlighted by "a sharp decline in new ethnic wars, the settlement of many old ones, and proactive efforts by states and international organizations to recognize group rights and channel ethnic disputes into conventional politics." Ted Robert Gurr, "Ethnic Warfare on the Wane," *Foreign Affairs* 89 (May/June 2000):52.

28. Connor, *Ethnonationalism,* 22. "For most people," Connor wrote in 1967, "ethnic consciousness still lies in the future." Ibid., 18. For a primordial view of ethnicity, which is rejected in the present study, see Isaacs, *Idols of the Tribe.*

29. On the importance of elites as "catalysts that turn potentially volatile situations into violent confrontations," see Brown, "Introduction," 23.

30. On the relative violence-prone character of ethnic conflict, and especially intrastate ethnic conflict, see ibid., 3–7. On the role of the security dilemma in such conflict, see Barry R. Posen, "The Security Dilemma and Ethnic Conflict," in *Ethnic Conflict and International Security,* 103–124; and Barbara F. Walter, "The Critical Barrier to Civil War Settlement," *International Organization* 51 (Summer 1997):335–364.

31. Brown argues that "if preventive actions fail and violence does break out, the next key act is keeping opportunistic neighboring states out of the conflict." Brown, "Introduction," 29. While this correctly affirms the importance of insulation, which is usually neglected in this context, the present study diverges from Brown in treating insulation as an aspect of prevention rather than as a byproduct problem.

32. Alexander L. George, "Case Studies and Theory Development: The Method of Structured, Focused Comparison," in Paul Gordon Lauren (ed.), *Diplomacy: New Approaches in History, Theory, and Policy* (New York: Free Press, 1979), 51. Emphasis in original.

33. Ibid., 52. Emphasis in original.

34. The following discussion is indebted to Gary King et al., *Designing Social Inquiry* (Princeton, N.J.: Princeton University Press, 1994).

35. For a discussion of different levels of great-power cooperation, see Gordon A. Craig and Alexander L. George, *Force and Statecraft*, 3rd ed. (New York: Oxford University Press, 1995), 247.

36. The subject has been discussed normatively. "To the extent that multiple international actors are involved, as often is the case, coordination is very important. Major powers and international organizations need to work together." Jentleson, *Opportunities Missed, Opportunities Seized*, 336. But Jentleson does not seek regularities, observing only that how the great powers work together and the identity of those states "will vary from case to case."

37. George, "Case Studies and Theory Development," 60. Emphasis in original.

38. Gurr, *Minorities at Risk*, x. Gurr identified 233 communal groups politically active since the end of the Second World War, each sharing a culture-based collective identity.

39. As many more cases were identified than could be studied with the focused comparison approach, cases were selected with the intention of varying the primary antagonist states, the historical eras, and the length of the local conflict life cycles in the case sample.

40. George, "Case Studies and Theory Development," 60. Emphasis in original.

NOTES TO CHAPTER 2

1. Other conceptual frameworks addressing the PD problem are Janie Leatherman et al., *Breaking Cycles of Violence*; Bruce W. Jentleson, "Preventive Diplomacy: A Conceptual and Analytical Framework," in Jentleson, *Opportunities Missed, Opportunities Seized*; Kalypso Nicolaïdis, "International Preventive Action: Developing a Strategic Framework," in *Vigilance and Vengeance: NGOs Preventing Ethnic Conflict in Divided Societies*, edited by Robert I. Rotberg (Washington, D.C.: Brookings, 1996); I. William Zartman, "Preventive Diplomacy: Setting the Stage," in Zartman, *Preventive Negotiation*; Brown, "Introduction"; and David Carment and Patrick James, "Ethnic Conflict at the International Level: Causation, Prevention, and Peacekeeping," in *Peace in the Midst of Wars*. None of these studies focuses especially upon collective great power PD. None, therefore, distinguishes between insulation and intervention as PD objectives.

2. The second set of circumstances is the concern of those who note, as in a recent analysis of the PD problem, that "prevention of great-power involvement in a crisis has traditionally been at the core of preventive diplomacy." Leatherman et al., *Breaking Cycles of Violence*, 109. A pioneering examination of this question, to be discussed in chapter 3, is by Paul Gordon Lauren, "Crisis Prevention in Nineteenth-Century Diplomacy," in *Managing U.S.-Soviet Rivalry*.

3. An illustration of the former condition is afforded by the contemporary Bosnia-Herzegovina civil war; the latter is illustrated by the Turkish-Armenian dispute. Both cases are examined in detail in this study.

4. Brown, "Internal Conflict and International Action," 625.

5. Ibid., 615. See also Nicolaïdis, "International Preventive Action," 33; Lund, *Preventing Violent Conflicts*; and Zartman, *Preventive Negotiation.*

6. Lund, *Preventing Violent Conflicts,* 190.

7. Brown, "Internal Conflict and International Action," 615.

8. See chapter 3.

9. A major state will be motivated to intervene in a small state if it has a vital interest in doing so, if it has a sphere of influence in the area, if it aspires to expand its sphere of influence into the area, or if it wishes to forestall another major state from doing so.

10. In these cases, larger regional issues are perceived by the great powers to be linked to the intrastate conflict. For an analysis that emphasizes the importance of these regional concerns, see Brown, *International Dimensions of Internal Conflict,* 600–601.

11. Alexander L. George and Jane E. Holl, *The Warning-Response Problem and Missed Opportunities in Preventive Diplomacy,* a report to the Carnegie Commission on Preventing Deadly Conflict (New York: Carnegie Corporation of New York, 1997). Michael Lund writes, "Preventive diplomacy must come to terms with the lack of national and international political will to act decisively and concertedly in launching and persisting with preventive efforts." *Preventing Violent Conflicts,* 163.

12. This distinction is developed in George and Holl, *Warning-Response Problem.*

13. Such planning is associated with a policy of "watching and waiting," which has been documented elsewhere. See, for example, Barry H. Steiner, "On Controlling the Soviet-American Nuclear Arms Competition," *Armed Forces and Society* 5 (November 1978):57 and note 20. For an argument that "wait-and-see also has its costs and risks," see Jentleson, *Opportunities Missed, Opportunities Seized,* 8.

14. See chapter 9.

15. Stedman, "Negotiation and Mediation in Internal Conflict," in Brown, *International Dimensions of Internal Conflict,* 363.

16. Ibid., 369.

17. Brown, "Internal Conflict and International Action," 605. A difference of view exists in the Brown volume over whether conditions of local conflict in its early stage would permit international action. Brown, who strongly advocates early international intervention in the local conflict as a "top priority" (ibid.), argues, "There is a lot that the international community can do to help people who want to make peace. . . . The key is making sure that one is dealing with people who genuinely want peace." Stedman, more skeptical about the value of such international action, writes, "Some analysts argue that the international community should assess the will of the combatants before it agrees to implement a peace agreement in a civil war. This assumes that the will of the parties to make peace is easy to ascertain. *In practice, this is generally very difficult.*" "Negotiation and Mediation in Internal Conflict," 365 (emphasis added).

18. Stedman, "Negotiation and Mediation in Internal Conflict," 359.

19. Ibid., 361.

20. Ibid., 363.

21. Ibid., 351. Emphasis added.

22. Ibid., 360.

23. See, for example, Geoffrey Blainey, *The Causes of War*, 3rd ed. (New York: Free Press, 1973).

24. Cited in Bruce W. Jentleson, "Preventive Diplomacy and Ethnic Conflict: Possible, Difficult, Necessary," in Lake and Rothchild, *The International Spread of Ethnic Conflict*, 309.

25. Stedman, "Negotiation and Mediation in Internal Conflict," 351.

26. References to American policy guidance on military aspects of PD, Policy Decision Directive 25 (1994), are in chapter 1, note 17.

27. For an argument that domestic impediments to intervention are not as severe as commonly understood, see Bruce W. Jentleson, *Coercive Prevention: Normative, Political, and Policy Dilemmas* (*Peaceworks Report* no. 35, October 2000) (Washington: United States Institute of Peace, 2000), 24ff.

28. An analysis of such problems is found in Richard K. Betts, "Compromised Command: Inside NATO's First War," *Foreign Affairs* 80 (July/August 2001):126–132.

29. Jentleson, *Opportunities Missed, Opportunities Seized*, 13.

Notes to Chapter 3

1. Cited in F. H. Hinsley, *Power and the Pursuit of Peace* (Cambridge: Cambridge University Press, 1967), 216. On the European concert, see Albrecht-Carrié, *Concert of Europe*.

2. On tacit regimes, see Alexander L. George, "U.S.-Soviet Efforts to Cooperate in Crisis Management and Crisis Avoidance," in Alexander L. George, Philip J. Farley, and Alexander Dallin, eds., *U.S.-Soviet Security Cooperation: Achievements, Failures, Lessons*, 585.

3. The distinction between cooperation by reciprocity and by bargaining is in Alexander L. George, "Strategies for Facilitating Cooperation," in George, Farley, and Dallin, *U.S.-Soviet Security Cooperation*, 693.

4. Lauren, "Crisis Prevention in Nineteenth-Century Diplomacy," 35.

5. Trachtenberg, "Intervention in Historical Perspective," in Laura W. Reed and Carl Kaysen (eds.), *Emerging Norms of Justified Intervention* (Cambridge, Mass.: American Academy of Arts and Sciences, 1993), 16ff.

6. William L. Ury, and Richard Smoke, *Beyond the Hotline: Controlling a Nuclear Crisis* (Cambridge: Harvard Nuclear Negotiation Project, 1984), 73.

7. "[T]he fear of disorder," as Hinsley has put it, "exerted a powerful effect . . . in bringing about . . . the restraint which prevailed among the Great Powers during these years [and] the system of diplomacy by conference." *Power and the Pursuit of Peace,* 223.

8. Lauren, "Crisis Prevention in Nineteenth-Century Diplomacy."

9. "Epilogue: Perspectives," in George, Farley, and Dallin, *U.S.-Soviet Security Cooperation,* 713–714.

10. Craig and George, *Force and Statecraft,* x.

11. See, for example, ibid., 285ff.

12. For a discussion of dependence and vulnerability in relation to Soviet-American bipolarity, see Alexander L. George, "Incentives for U.S.-Soviet Security Cooperation and Mutual Adjustment," in George, Farley, and Dallin, *U.S.-Soviet Security Cooperation,* 645ff.

13. On ententes as a recurring phenomenon in world politics, see Craig and George, *Force and Statecraft,* chapter 18.

14. This problem was magnified in the first half of the nineteenth century by the general belief among the great powers that local conflict would probably lead to general war. See F. R. Bridge and Roger Bullen, *The Great Powers and the European States System: 1815–1914* (London: Longman, 1980), 10–11.

15. Hinsley, *Power and the Pursuit of Peace,* 218.

16. Intransigence of Greek and Turkish Cypriotes has not been affected by the end of Soviet-American cold war and bipolarity.

17. George, "Incentives for U.S.-Soviet Security Cooperation," 646.

18. "Bipolarity encourages each giant to focus upon crises," Kenneth N. Waltz has written, "while rendering most of them of relative inconsequence." "The Stability of a Bipolar World," *Daedalus, 93* (Summer 1964):903. By contrast, Waltz argues that under multipolarity "[u]ncertainties about who threatens whom, about who will oppose whom, and about who will gain or lose from the actions of other states accelerate as the number of states increases. Even if one assumes that the goals of most states are worthy, the timing and content of the actions required to reach them become more and more difficult to calculate." *Theory of International Politics,* 165.

19. Leatherman et al., *Breaking Cycles of Violence,* 14.

20. George, "Incentives for U.S.-Soviet Security Cooperation," 646ff.

21. Gordon A. Craig and Alexander L. George refer to a "diplomatic revolution" brought about by a number of mostly twentieth-century trends, including the rise of special interest groups and popularly elected heads of state (*Force and Statecraft,* 286). Other studies of the newer developments are Seyom Brown, *New Forces, Old Forces, and the Future of World Politics* (New York: HarperCollins, 1994), and James Rosenau, *Turbulence in World Politics: A Theory of Change and Continuity* (Princeton, N.J.: Princeton University Press, 1990). Traditional state practice is highlighted in John J. Mearsheimer, *The Tragedy of Great Power Politics* (New York: W. W. Norton, 2001).

22. See, on this phenomenon, Warren P. Strobel, "The Media and U.S. Policies Toward Intervention: A Closer Look at the 'CNN Effect,'" in *Managing Global Chaos: Sources of the Responses to International Conflict*, edited by Chester A. Crocker and Fen Osler Hampson with Pamela Aall (Washington, D.C.: United States Institute of Peace, 1995).

23. Elaine Sciolino, "New U.S. Peacekeeping Policy De-emphasizes Role of the U.N."

24. Recent discussion of the problem of missed opportunities in PD largely focuses on states in this respect. See Jentleson, *Opportunities Missed, Opportunities Seized*; George and Holl, *Warning-Response Problem*, 16–17. How much missed PD opportunities can be ascribed to recent nonstate developments is an important question that requires further inquiry.

25. William DeMars, "Waiting for Early Warning: Humanitarian Action After the Cold War," *Journal of Refugee Studies* 8 (1995):390–410; DeMars, "Uncharted Territory: Humanitarian Action and Intelligence in Civil Wars," paper delivered at the Annual Convention of the International Studies Association, San Diego, California, 17 April 1996.

26. "Waiting for Early Warning," 399, 401.

27. George and Holl (*Warning-Response Problem*, 10ff) are particularly concerned with the gap between warning and response. They note that "in many ethnic and religious conflicts . . . *timely or accurate warning may not be the problem at all*" (11; emphasis in original).

28. The variety of U.N. political roles is analyzed in Roberts and Kingsbury, *United Nations, Divided World*. See also Augustus R. Norton and Thomas G. Weiss, "Superpowers and Peacekeepers," *Survival* 32 (May/June 1990):212–220.

29. Chester Crocker, "Southern Africa Peace-Making," *Survival* 32 (May/June 1990): 223.

30. It might be suggested that even a great-power warning regime, utilizing preexisting great-power norms, would be inadequate to overcome the present diffidence of the major states toward interventionist PD. However, such a regime is still desirable because, apart from encouraging insulationist PD, it can legitimate early intervention in intrastate ethnic conflict when weakness in great power motivation to intervene (in what are categorized here as Type I cases) generates a special need to intervene early. For this argument, see below, 207.

31. Mearsheimer, *The Tragedy of Great Power Politics*, 49.

32. See, on this point, Hinsley, *Power and the Pursuit of Peace*, 4.

Notes to Chapter 4

1. John W. Rooney, Jr., *Revolt in the Netherlands: Brussels—1830* (Lawrence, Kans: Coronado Press, 1982), 128.

2. Ibid., 130.

3. Rooney, *Revolt in the Netherlands*; Clive H. Church, *Europe in 1830: Revolution and Political Change* (London: Allen & Unwin, 1983); J.S. Fishman, *Diplomacy and Revolution: The London Conference of 1830 and the Belgian Revolt* (Amsterdam: CHEV, 1988); and Charles Webster, *The Foreign Policy of Palmerston: 1830–1841* (London: G. Bell & Sons, 1951).

4. C. M. Woodhouse, *The Greek War of Independence* (London: Hutchinson University Library, 1952), 57.

5. C. W. Crawley, *The Question of Greek Independence* (Cambridge: Cambridge University Press, 1930); Woodhouse, *The Greek War of Independence*; and Matthew Anderson, "Russia and the Eastern Question, 1821–41," in *Europe's Balance of Power: 1815–1848,* edited by Alan Sked (London: Macmillan, 1979).

6. Cited in Albrecht-Carrié, *Concert of Europe,* 263.

7. Mihailo D. Stojanovic, *Great Powers and the Balkans: 1875–1878* (Cambridge: Cambridge University Press, [1939] 1969); B. H. Sumner, *Russia and the Balkans: 1870–1880* (Hamden, Conn.: Archon Books, [1937] 1962); and R. W. Seton-Watson, *Disraeli, Gladstone and the Eastern Question* (London: Macmillan, 1935).

8. A. O. Sarkissian, *History of the Armenian Question to 1885* (Urbana, Ill.: University of Illinois Press, 1938); W. N. Medlicott, *The Congress of Berlin and After,* 2nd ed. (London: Archon Books, 1963); G. P. Gooch and Harold Temperley (eds.), *British Documents on the Origins of the War, 1898–1914* (London: His Majesty's Stationery Office, 1936); and Roderic Davison, "The Armenian Crisis, 1912–1914," *American Historical Review* 52 (April 1948):481–505.

9. Thorsten V. Kalijarvi, *The Memel Statute: Its Origin, Legal Nature, and Observation to the Present Day* (London: R. Hale, 1937); W. N. Medlicott and Douglas Dakin (eds.), *Documents on British Foreign Policy: 1919–1939,* First Series, vol. 23 ("Poland and the Baltic States: March 1921–December 1923") (London: Her Majesty's Stationery Office, 1981); Jean Meuvret, *Le Territoire de Memel et la politique Européene* (Paris: Centre d'Etudes de Politique Etrangère, 1936); and "Convention and Transitory Provision Concerning Memel, . . . May 8, 1924," printed separately as Extract no. 28 from the *Official Journal* of the League of Nations.

10. Catherine Hoskyns, *The Congo Since Independence* (London: Oxford University Press, 1965); Brian Urquhart, *Hammarskjöld* (New York: Knopf, 1972); Conor Cruise O'Brien, *To Katanga and Back* (London: Hutchinson, 1962); and Ernest W. Lefever, *Uncertain Mandate: Politics of the U.N. Congo Operation* (Baltimore: Johns Hopkins Press, 1967).

11. UN document S/5575, 4 March 1964, cited by Leland M. Goodrich, in "The Maintenance of Peace and Security," in *International Organization* 19 (Summer 1965):440.

12. Joseph S. Joseph, *Cyprus: Ethnic Conflict and International Concern* (New York: P. Lang, 1985); Theodore A. Couloumbis, *The United States, Greece and Turkey: The Troubled Triangle* (New York: Praeger, 1983); John Reddaway, *Burdened with Cyprus: The British Connection* (London: Weidenfeld & Nicholson, 1986); and Ronald J. Fisher, "Cyprus: The Failure of Mediation and the Escalation of an Identity-Based Conflict to an Adversarial Impasse," *Journal of Peace Research* 38 (May 2001):307–326.

13. David Owen, *Balkan Odyssey* (New York: Harcourt Brace, 1995); Richard Holbrook, *To End a War: From Sarajevo to Dayton—And Beyond* (New York: Random House, 1998); James Gow, *Lack of Will: International Diplomacy and the Yugoslav War* (New York: Columbia University Press, 1997); and a file of clippings from the *New York Times* maintained by the present writer.

Notes to Chapter 5

1. Martin O. Heisler, "Hyphenating Belgium: Changing State and Regime to Cope with Cultural Division," in Montville, *Conflict and Peacemaking in Multiethnic Societies,* 178–179.

2. Woodhouse, *Greek War of Independence,* 23. "It was . . . to some degree a matter of chance whether a Greek remained an oppressed peasant or rose to heights of wealth and power, sometimes beyond the reach of his Turkish contemporaries. The hardship and difficulty of life under Ottoman rule lay chiefly in its lack of a uniform and predictable system." Ibid., 24.

3. Kalijarvi, *Memel Statute,* 29.

4. Hoskyns, *Congo Since Independence,* 37.

5. Connor, *Ethnonationalism,* 40–41. For other discussions of the basis of nationalism, see Ernest Gellner, *Nations and Nationality* (Ithaca, N.Y.: Cornell University Press, 1983); Anthony D. S. Smith, *The Ethnic Origin of Nations* (Oxford: Basil Blackwell, 1986); Smith, *Nationalism in the Twentieth Century* (New York: New York University Press, 1979); and Issacs, *Idols of the Tribe.*

6. This idea was brought to the attention of the present writer by William Sumner. According to Sumner, Serb nationalism first developed in the Austro-Hungarian province of Voivodina with the emergence of the Serb commercial middle class in the early nineteenth century; the Serb national culture in that province was centered in towns in which there flourished a Serbian college, printing presses, and newspapers. A Serb middle class was lacking in Bosnia-Herzegovina at the time of the 1875 uprising against Turkish rule. *Russia and the Balkans,* 128–129.

7. Woodhouse, *Greek War of Independence,* 40–41. And when the development of a middle class helped introduce nationalism, as among middle-class Serbs in the Voivodina region of the relatively modernized, liberal-minded Austro-Hungarian empire, the results were initially benign. Serb nationalism in Voivodina in the 1870s was far more pacific than was Serb resistance, under feudal conditions, to the Ottoman Empire in Herzegovina. Sumner, *Russia and the Balkans,* 141.

8. Connor, *Ethnonationalism,* 39.

9. By contrast, modernity appears to have lead to less benign cultural adjustment when economic and political grievances were present, as in the formation of a Palestinian consciousness in areas occupied by Israel after the Six-Day War in 1967, and the development of an

Indian consciousness under British domination of the Asian subcontinent. This phenomenon was not studied here. On the Indian case, see John Strachey's discussion of the formation of the Indian National Congress in *End of Empire* (New York: Random House, 1960), 77–78.

10. Cited in Polyvios G. Polyviou, *Cyprus: The Tragedy and the Challenge* (Washington: American Hellenic Institute, 1975), 10.

11. Woodhouse, *Greek War of Independence,* 195.

12. William Zartman has noted the tendency of the challenger's unity to deteriorate during the life cycle of ethnic conflict. See his "Negotiations and Prenegotiations in Ethnic Conflict: The Beginning, The Middle, and the Ends," in Montville, *Conflict and Peacemaking in Multiethnic Societies,* 514. However, Zartman has not linked this phenomenon to cross-border intervention in the conflict.

13. This shift is discussed in ibid., 513ff. Intensifying effects of arbitrary economic and political restrictions were evident in those instances, such as the Greek, Bosnia I, Armenia, and the Congo cases, in which the restrictions were especially onerous or long-lasting. In such cases, institutionalized inequality exacerbated hatreds between the central government and its ethnic challenger.

14. Woodhouse, *Greek War of Independence,* 29–31. With a population in Greece only one-ninth that of the Greeks, the Turks had eighteen times more land per capita, and no Turkish land could pass into Greek hands. Ibid., 36.

15. Susan L. Woodward, "The Balkans and Europe: Euro-Atlantic Security and Values," in Robert L. Pfaltzgraff, Jr. and Richard H. Schultz, Jr. (eds.), *Ethnic Conflict and Regional Instability: Implications for US Policy and Army Roles and Missions* (Carlisle Barracks, Penn.: US Army War College, n.d.), 234.

16. William L. Langer (ed.), *An Encyclopedia of World History,* 4th ed. (Boston: Houghton Mifflin, 1968), 672.

17. Sumner, *Russia and the Balkans,* 141.

18. The term "consolidation" is developed in Zartman, "Negotiations and Prenegotiations in Ethnic Conflict," 513.

19. Remarkably, detailed histories of the first Bosnia revolt fail to identify a single Bosnian-Herzegovinan individual who led the revolt.

20. Connor, *Ethnonationalism,* 171.

21. Ibid.

22. Hoskyns, *Congo Since Independence,* 28. On European decolonization as a catalyst for ethnic challenge, see Connor, *Ethnonationalism,* 173.

23. Kalijarvi, *Memel Statute,* 32, 36.

24. Woodhouse, *Greek War of Independence,* 88–89.

25. William Zartman has noted: "As ethnic conflict is an internal matter by definition . . . governments are loath to regard external intervention of any kind as friendly—all the

more so because mediatory intervention necessarily implies some compromise on the part of the government (as well as the dissidents) and some criticism of government practices" ("Negotiations and Prenegotiations in Ethnic Conflict," 512).

26. See Medlicott and Dakin, *Documents on British Foreign Policy: 1919–1939,* 649ff.

27. On force-of-events considerations as problems in crisis management, see Craig and George, *Force and Statecraft,* 224–225.

28. On the strengths and weaknesses of power sharing, see Arend Lijphart, "The Power-Sharing Approach," in Montville, *Conflict and Peacemaking in Multiethnic Societies,* 491–509.

29. Given the divided character of Cyprus, a problem-solving solution for the island would probably take the combination form implemented in Bosnia II, in contrast to the power-sharing agreement devised for the island in 1959.

30. Woodhouse, *Greek War of Independence,* 88.

Notes to Chapter 6

1. This list is based in part on a lengthier one put forward by Paul Gordon Lauren in "Crisis Prevention in Nineteenth-Century Diplomacy." One additional PD objective, establishing an international zone of authority, was reflected only in the Memel case of the eight studied here and is not further discussed in this study.

2. These dynamics seem similar to those outlined by Robert O. Keohane in his discussion of interstate regimes. For example, they helped coordinate behaviors and expectations. See Keohane's *After Hegemony: Cooperation and Discord in the World Political Economy* (Princeton, N.J.: Princeton University Press, 1984), 56. I choose to call the institutionalization arrangements flowing from shared PD objectives "frameworks" rather than "regimes."

The delicacy of the frameworks studied here is well captured by Robert Jervis, who conceives of "cooperation [as] enforced by the possibility of defection." "Realism, Game Theory, and Cooperation," *World Politics* 40 (April 1988):330. However, Jervis focuses on the ambiguities of this connection, whereas it appears to this writer that the connection in the cases studied here is clear-cut. Further, Jervis emphasizes international anarchy, and therefore the problem of defection. In these cases, the mutual fear of defection was considerable, and cooperation was therefore greater, and more stable, than predicted by a focus on international anarchy. See also David A. Lake, "Beyond Anarchy: The Importance of Security Institutions," *International Security* 26 (Summer 2001):129–160.

3. Keohane has written, "Regimes rarely emerge from chaos; on the contrary, they are built on one another. We should therefore think as much about the evolution of regimes as about their creation *ex nihilo.*" Ibid., 79.

4. Albrecht-Carrié, *Concert of Europe,* 58.

5. On Soviet-American crisis management, see Craig and George, *Force and Statecraft,* chapter 9.

6. Sumner, *Russia and the Balkans,* 309 and 408.

7. "The correspondence between the Russian Consul in Dubrovnik (Ragusa) and the Prince of Montenegro leaves no doubt that the Slav Committee of Moscow not only assisted the insurgents but directed in fact the whole action in Herzegovina." Stojanovic, *Great Powers and the Balkans,* 82. On the status and activities of the Slav Committees, see also Sumner, *Russia and the Balkans,* 158–159; 194. In addition, two thousand Russian volunteers fought with Serbia against Turkey in 1876 (Stojanovic, *Great Powers and the Balkans,* 91).

8. On the subsidy and Austro-Hungarian protection, see Stojanovic, *Great Powers and the Balkans,* 93; on the military supply, see Sumner, *Russia and the Balkans,* 184f.

9. Stojanovic, *Great Powers and the Balkans,* 32.

10. Crises that assisted great-power self-restraint occurred in the Bosnia cases and the Belgian case. In Bosnia I, Austro-Russian disagreements followed the failure to mediate successfully between Slavs in Bosnia-Herzegovina and the Turks. Rejection by the insurgents of the Andrassy reforms in April 1876 worsened Austro-Russian disagreements and brought a Russian invitation to a new three-power meeting at Berlin. This in turn led to the Berlin Memorandum and a new proposal for direct Slav-Turk negotiations. The immediate danger perceived at that time was a Turkish intention to attack Montenegro (ibid., 58–61; Sumner, *Russia and the Balkans,* 161). Another Anglo-Russian diplomatic crisis took place after Serbia and Montenegro went to war against Turkey in June 1876. The decision was taken to hold another three-power conference in Reichstadt. "Reichstadt was as necessary for Austria as for Russia," wrote Sumner. "[Austria] could not delay close probing of Russian policy, now that she had failed to prevent the Serbs drawing the sword, even though (and partly just because) she considered that the Russian foreign office had played a double game in its lukewarm cöoperation in putting a curb on Belgrade" (Ibid., 177).

In the Belgian case, French behavior led to confrontation with England over the French-proposed appointment of the Duc de Nemours as Belgian king, and over the tardy removal of French forces from Belgium in August 1831. And in Bosnia II the American "strike and lift" proposal provoked a diplomatic crisis with American NATO allies in April 1993.

The danger posed by these diplomatic crises depended on fears about unilateral great-power involvement in the small-power dispute. In the first two cases those fears were substantial, while in Bosnia II they were small.

11. In the Belgian case the link was afforded first by the appointment as French ambassador in London of Tallyrand, who was on very good terms with the English, and second, by holding a virtually continuous conference on Belgium from November 1830 to 1833.

12. In the Greek case, Charles X of France associated his country with the Anglo-Russian pacific blockade of the Greek islands in 1826 because of his unwillingness to stand apart and lose the benefits of participation; he was determined to outbid Russia for the alliance of England. Crawley, *Question of Greek Independence,* 68.

13. On the difficulties faced by outside mediators in internal conflict, see Stedman, "Negotiation and Mediation in Internal Conflict," 341–376; and Zartman, "Negotiations and Prenegotiations in Ethnic Conflict," 530ff.

14. Following the Bosnia-Herzegovina revolt, the British Ambassador to Constantinople, Sir Henry George Elliot, relayed grievances from Bosnia-Herzegovina to Ottoman officials. In September 1875, Elliot was asked by those officials to draw up a memorandum on this subject, and a Turkish imperial decree on reform issued the following month largely followed his suggestions. David Harris, *A Diplomatic History of the Balkan Crisis of 1875–1878* (Palo Alto, Calif.: Stanford University Press, 1936), 138–139 and 139f. The British tried to stimulate Turkish initiation of reforms in Bosnia-Herzegovina in order to preempt intervention of the Eastern powers.

15. On United States support for "double *enosis*," see Stavros Panteli, *A New History of Cyprus* (London: East-West Publications, 1984), 385–386; and Joseph, *Cyprus*, 143.

16. On the differences between the United States and the UN and European mediators see especially Owen, *Balkan Odyssey*.

17. On the Holy Alliance and Russian positions, see Crawley, *Question of Greek Independence*, 31 and 39–41.

18. "The fact that England exercised an uneasy sway over the Ionian Islands brought home still more to the [British] Government the urgent need of finding a settlement; the 'Septinsular Republic' was nominally under the protection of England, but it could in fact only be treated as a Crown Colony . . ." (Ibid., 13). "After the autumn of 1821 British neutrality [on the Greek question] had been enforced on the whole impartially in very difficult circumstances by the Ionian Government . . ." (Ibid., 29).

19. These suspicions persisted despite the Anglo-Russian entente agreement of 1907, which did not extend substantively to Turkish Armenia.

20. The primary antagonists could help develop a substitute proposal when the major powers were extended, frustrated, and yet determined to construct a new agreed-upon foundation for PD. Such intervention occurred during Bosnia II when, after the Americans publicly criticized the Vance-Owen plan, the major alternative to that plan then under consideration was a three-part confederation proposal for Bosnia-Herzegovina put forward by Serbia and Croatia. The primary antagonists may not make the most of this opportunity, however; in Bosnia I, the Turks, rather than capitalize on British resistance to Russian proposals by making proposals of their own, were instead demoralized and in a mood to make concessions.

Notes to Chapter 7

1. Except for the Dutch regime in the Belgian case and the Moslem-dominated regime in Sarajevo in Bosnia II, the central regime was militarily stronger on its own in these cases than its ethnic challenger.

2. Harris, *A Diplomatic History of the Balkan Crisis of 1875–1878*, 255.

3. Christopher Cviic, "Yugoslavia: The Unmaking of a Federation," in F. Stephen Larrabee (ed.), *The Volatile Powder Keg* (Washington, D.C.: American University Press, 1994), 104.

4. I. William Zartman, "Ripening Conflict, Ripe Moment, Formula, and Mediation," in Diane B. Bendahmane and John W. McDonald, Jr. (eds.), *Perspectives on Negotiation: Four Case Studies and Interpretations* (Washington, D.C.: U.S. Department of State, 1986), 213–215.

5. Ibid., 211.

6. Ibid., 214.

7. For the idea that sacrifice in war "creates value," see Craig and George, *Force and Statecraft,* 232. The connection between sacrifice and value also seems to apply in the conflicts between ethnicities, such as those discussed in this study, in which an oppressive relationship is presumed to exist.

8. This was the point of departure for Lester Pearson's conception of peacekeeping forces, for example. See John A. Munro and Alex I. Inglis (eds.), *Mike: The Memoirs of the Right Honourable Lester B. Pearson,* vol. 2 (1948–1957) (Toronto: University of Toronto Press, 1973). Pearson distinguished UN peacekeeping from enforcement steps. The same idea seems to have underpinned Henry Kissinger's mediation efforts in the Arab-Israeli dispute following the Yom Kippur War. According to William R. Brown, Kissinger generally only raised issues in that dispute that related to actions required to avoid renewed fighting. In March 1975, when the Sinai Accord talks were suspended, he criticized both sides for "not being concerned over the possibility of imminent conflict." *The Last Crusade: A Negotiator's Middle East Handbook* (Chicago: Nelson-Hall, 1980), 283.

9. Hoskyns, *Congo Since Independence,* 392ff and 477.

10. Ibid., 477.

11. Ibid., 223.

12. Ibid., 476. While Hoskyns argues that Hammarskjöld should have attempted to conciliate the Congolese factions to each other earlier, the argument can be countered by the manner in which outside mediation is employed by the primary antagonists for self-interested reasons. See above, 123–126, on this latter issue.

13. For additional analysis of this point, see chapter 8.

14. Crawley, *Question of Greek Independence,* 60–62. The American government was not evidently aware of this action when it blockaded Cuba during the Cuban missile crisis.

15. For the distinction between warning and threat, see, for example, Herman Kahn, *On Escalation: Metaphors and Scenarios* (New York: Praeger, 1965), 277–278.

16. According to Crawley (*Question of Greek Independence,* 91), the Allied fleet was inferior to the Turkish force in numbers of ships but had far more guns.

17. Brian Urquhart, "The U.N. and International Security after the Cold War," in Roberts and Kingsbury, *United Nations, Divided World,* 100. Herman Kahn wrote similarly that "it is often valuable to be able, in escalation and crisis situations, to initiate impressive and significant actions, not only for prudential and preparatory reasons but as messages to the

opponent—i.e., for bargaining purposes." *On Escalation,* 254. The usual course for international force-dampening, by contrast, is for ad hoc actions, as in the Congo and Bosnia II.

18. Kahn, *On Escalation,* 251. Impressed as he was by nuclear weapons technologies in the contemporary period, Kahn urged preparation of an ability to act quickly in crisis. Such an ability was completely lacking in the Greek case.

19. By contrast, the trip-wire American deterrent force sent to Macedonia in 1993 has been more efficacious, particularly in light of American war-making against Serb forces in Bosnia and Kosovo. On the Macedonian case, see Michael S. Lund, "Preventive Diplomacy for Macedonia, 1992–1999: From Containment to Nation Building," in Jentleson, *Opportunities Missed, Opportunities Seized,* 173–208.

20. Crawley, *Question of Greek Independence,* 90; 115. In addition, the blockade was never enforced against Austro-Hungarian merchantmen, who regularly supplied the Egyptians with provisions under military protection. Ibid., 132–133.

21. During the 1960s, the United States, opposed to the Cypriote regime because of its warming to the Soviet Union, worked to partition the island between Greece and Turkey. The so-called Acheson Plan for the island, put forward in 1964, entailed partition. Panteli, *New History of Cyprus,* 365, 385–86. The United States also took the position that the 1960 Treaties of Guarantee gave Greece and Turkey the right to militarily intervene unilaterally or jointly on the island. Joseph, *Cyprus,* 129–130.

22. Hoskyns, *Congo Since Independence,* 329, 351.

23. By comparison, the British had 15,000 military personnel stationed on Cyprus in 1967 and were seeking permanent status for them. Christopher Hitchens, *Cyprus* (London: Quartet Books, 1984), 91.

24. Owen, *Balkan Odyssey,* 45. The Serbs obtained arms from the Russian black market. Ibid., 253.

25. Another motive for foreign military assistance is to balance the military capabilities of the ethnic antagonists, to create a mutually hurting stalemate in which the antagonists are moved to negotiate. Such a strategy does not always work and can instead exacerbate conflict. I am indebted to I. William Zartman for suggesting this point.

I am not able to cite any examples of this motive for military assistance from the cases studied here. One possible reason may be that during and following the Soviet-American Cold War period, when foreign military assistance became an important diplomatic tool of superpower governments in particular, such assistance was given to strengthen those opposed to negotiations between the primary antagonists.

26. The same condition applied in the Greek case, in which idealistic Englishmen traveled to fight with the Greeks against the Turks.

27. Parker T. Hart, *Two NATO Allies at the Threshold of War* (Durham, N.C.: Duke University Press, 1990), 114–115.

28. Owen, *Balkan Odyssey,* 253. Emphasis added.

29. For example, it is not systematically dealt with by Adam Roberts and Benedict Kingsbury in their otherwise thorough discussion of the UN's international role, *United Nations, Divided World.* However that study does make reference (194, 215–16) to transitionary roles for the UN in West Irian (1962–63) and in Namibia (1989–90) which did entail police roles, and it does discuss (215–16) the increasingly important UN role in election monitoring.

30. According to W. N. Medlicott, police assistance in Asiatic Turkey was an issue raised in the Andrassy note and in diplomatic discussions thereafter. *The Congress of Berlin and After,* 293.

31. Ibid.

32. After considerable delay, in February 1880 the Ottoman government appointed two reform commissions, one for the northern and the other for the southern Armenian districts, and accepted the British ambassador's suggestion that English officers accompany the commissions unofficially. These commissions were to select vice-presidents and members of the civil and criminal courts, replace old members of provincial administrative councils with elected ones, and dismiss incompetent or corrupt officials. Here as in virtually all cases to the present time, the police functions exercised by international personnel were quite restricted and untraditional, being limited to monitoring, advising, and enhancing the stature of other international personnel such as ambassadors and consuls. In the Armenian case, the commissions were soon discontinued when the Ottoman regime changed its mind about them and acted to sharply circumscribe their authority. Ibid., 324ff.

33. Ibid., 326.

34. "Police are Critical to the Peace Process," *PeaceWatch* 2 (June 1996):1–2. Police were provided in the city of Mostar by the Western European Union when the city became administered by the EU in 1994. See "Balkan Berlin," *The Economist* (22 January 1996).

35. "Police are Critical to the Peace Process." Present trends suggest that the supplying of police monitors when the UN intervenes with the permission of local factions to facilitate a political transition may become routine. For example, in addition to police assistance provided by the UN in Bosnia-Herzegovina, the third UN Angola Verification Mission (UNAVEM III) established in 1995 included three police monitors. UNAVEM II was deployed in June 1991 with 90 police observers, a number increased to 126 in 1994. *A Report on the Fifth Annual Peacekeeping Mission, November 2–11, 1995* (New York: United Nations Association of the U.S.A., January 1996), 24, 26.

36. It appears to be mostly for this reason that agreement was not reached to supply a European gendarmerie to the Armenian provinces of Turkey, although such action was discussed in connection with a program of European-guaranteed reforms for the provinces that did bring agreement in 1914.

37. On the application of the security dilemma concept to localized ethnic conflict, see Posen, "The Security Dilemma and Ethnic Conflict," 103–124.

38. See chapter 6 of this study.

39. See note 8 above.

40. For a similar argument, see Jentleson, *Coercive Prevention.*

41. Zartman, "Ripeness: The Hurting Stalemate and Beyond," 228.

NOTES TO CHAPTER 8

1. On the opportunities and limitations of coercive methods, see, for example, Alexander L. George, *Forceful Persuasion* (Washington: United States Institute of Peace, 1991); Alexander L. George and William E. Simons (eds.), *The Limits of Coercive Diplomacy*, 2nd ed. (Boulder, Colo.: Westview Press, 1994); Lawrence Freedman (ed.), *Strategic Coercion: Concepts and Cases* (Oxford: Oxford University Press, 1998); Thoms C. Schelling, *Arms and Influence* (New Haven, Conn.: Yale University Press, 1966); and Arnold Kanter and Linton F. Brooks (eds.), *U.S. Intervention Policy for the Post-Cold War World: New Challenges and New Responses* (New York: Norton, 1994).

Neither the George studies nor most of the contributors in Freedman's work deal with multilateral great-power coercion, and the Kanter-Linton volume does not include case studies. Multilateral great-power coercive PD is subject to constraints and opportunities different from those of single-state coercive diplomacy, it is argued here, because, as George emphasizes, coercive diplomacy is very context dependent.

As illustrated in the Memel and (thus far) in Cyprus, coercive interventionist PD is in some cases not attempted at all. Examples from the Memel and Cyprus cases are nevertheless introduced in this chapter as they suggest broader trends in PD.

2. Medlicott and Dakin, *Documents on British Foreign Policy,* viii.

3. He had in mind providing autonomy to the Greeks and withdrawing Turkish forces from the Greek peninsula. Crawley, *Question of Greek Independence,* 18–19.

4. On this resolution, see Urquhart, *Hammarskjöld,* 513; and Hoskyns, *Congo Since Independence,* 328ff.

5. As Brian Urquhart, a close confidant of Hammarskjöld, has written, "The real strength of a peacekeeping operation lies not in the capacity to use force, but precisely in its *not* using force and thereby remaining above the conflict and preserving its unique position and prestige. The moment a peacekeeping force starts killing people it becomes a part of the conflict it is supposed to be controlling, and therefore a part of the problem. It loses the one quality which distinguishes it from, and sets it above, the people it is dealing with."*A Life in Peace and War* (New York: Harper & Row, 1987), 178–179 (emphasis in original).

6. Hoskyns, *Congo Since Independence,* 223.

7. Ibid., 476.

8. Crawley, *Question of Greek Independence,* 18.

9. In these circumstances, conciliation could be sustained by a "good cop-bad cop" relationship, with conciliation being enhanced by the implied danger of the alternative.

10. Woodhouse, *Greek War of Independence,* 142. Writing of this period after the Battle of Navarino, a victory over the Turks that the Allies failed to follow up on diplomatically, Crawley wrote, "It is possibly true that the Powers could have pacified the East more speedily by abandoning the Greeks altogether, as Metternich wished; it was not the forces on the spot, but European opinion which prevented that." *Question of Greek Independence,* 97.

11. Woodhouse, *Greek War of Independence,* 93. The Chios incident in February 1822 was perhaps the most shocking for European opinion. "The prosperous island of Chios had been occupied, rather against the will of its pacific inhabitants, and claimed for the cause of independence by a force of Greek adventurers from Samos, acting without orders from any higher authority. The Turks easily recovered the island and carried out an atrocious revenge, murdering or selling into slavery all but about two thousand inhabitants out of about a hundred thousand." Ibid., 87.

12. J. A. S. Grenville, *Lord Salisbury and Foreign Policy* (London: Athlone Press, 1964), 46.

13. Urquhart, *Hammarskjöld,* 475.

14. Ibid.

15. When he inquired about such support, "Milan was told that he could not count on Russian help and he would have to shoulder all the consequences of a war with Turkey." Sumner, *Russia and the Balkans,* 178.

16. Ibid., 177.

17. Owen, *Balkan Odyssey,* 348.

18. Crawley, *Question of Greek Independence,* 84.

19. Ibid., 91–92.

20. The Allied Admirals distinguished three alternatives before entering Navarino Bay: (1) maintaining the blockade, which was expensive and difficult in the winter months; (2) anchoring in Navarino and remaining there, which would confine the fleet and expose it to the Egyptian fleet; and (3) confronting the Egyptian squadrons with propositions advantageous to the Turks. Ibid., 90.

21. Urquhart, *Hammarskjöld,* 561–564. UN forces had previously been vilified and embarrassed in the Congo. In August 1960 Congolese troops "began to insult and harass United Nations personnel. This culminated in a serious incident at Leopoldville airport when Congolese soldiers man-handled United Nations Canadians who they accused of being Belgian spies." And shooting incidents occurred between Congolese troops and UN Sudanese contingents in March 1961, following which the Sudanese were disarmed by the Congolese. Hoskyns, *Congo Since Independence,* 174, 341–342.

22. Ibid., 562.

23. This condition paralleled the situation in Cyprus, in which UN forces also served as buffers between the antagonists.

24. Gwyn Prins, *The Applicability of the 'NATO Model' to United Nations Peace Support Operations Under the Security Council*, UNA-USA International Dialogue on the Enforcement of Security Council Resolutions, paper no. 2 (New York: United Nations Association of the U.S.A., July 1996), 20. General Philippe Morillon, commander of UN peacekeepers in Sarajevo in 1992–93 and later commander in Paris of the French component of the NATO Rapid Reaction Force authorized for Bosnia-Herzegovina in June 1995, is quoted by Prins as telling the French field commander for the Rapid Reaction Force, "Don't be concerned about the rules of engagement. You have to establish the tactical advantage and use it. . . ." Ibid.

25. Ibid.

26. UN "wider peacekeeping" in Bosnia-Herzegovina permitted using force beyond self-defense. It aimed at achieving the overall consent of the primary antagonists for military operations, distinguishing between "operational" and "tactical" consent as follows: "Through continual negotiations with the appropriate leadership at the theater level, overall consent for an operation must be sought at all times. Accordingly, 'wider peacekeeping' ruled out the *strategic* use of force. At the same time, within a framework of operational consent, the *tactical* use of force is permitted in defense of the mission as well as in self-defense. Moreover, when force is used for these purposes it must be 'appropriate, proportionate, demonstrably reasonable and confined in effect to the specific and legitimate target intended.'" John Gerard Ruggie, *The United Nations and the Collective Use of Force: Whither—or Whether*, UNA-USA International Dialogue on the Enforcement of Security Council Resolutions, paper no. 1 (New York: United Nations Association of the U.S.A., June 1996), 9 (emphasis in original). Ruggie draws on unpublished writing by Colonel Allan Mallinson of the British Army.

27. The sensitivity of political leaders to the provocative effect of an international force stimulates political micromanagement of that force, as in the recent NATO use of force against Yugoslavia over Kosovo. Tensions between the military and civilian leadership in this instance is incisively studied by Richard K. Betts in "Compromised Command: Inside NATO's First War," *Foreign Affairs* 80 (July/August 2001):126–132.

28. This standoff raises a security dilemma as difficult as that between the ethnic antagonists themselves. See Posen, "Security Dilemma and Ethnic Conflict," 103–124. Preparations by international forces for offensive action is one response to the security dilemma. See John O. B. Sewall, "Adapting Conventional Military Forces to the New Environment," in *U.S. Intervention Policy in the Post-Cold War World*, 91ff.

29. They came close on one occasion. Late in 1896, Britain, Russia, and other major European powers, anxious to prevent further atrocities, agreed on a program of reform that they intended to jointly force the Ottoman regime to accept. The proposal initially made by Great Britain in October 1896 entailed that (1) European ambassadors in Constantinople would be instructed to work out a reform program for Turkey to ensure the survival of the Ottoman Empire; and (2) their governments would agree beforehand to enforce any reform scheme they had unanimously agreed to. This proposal was apparently forgotten when a Greco-Turkish war broke out the following year. Grenville, *Lord Salisbury and Foreign Policy*, 83–89.

Notes to Chapter 9

1. Urquhart, *Hammarskjöld,* 561.

2. The possibility that small-power antagonist activity can transform major-power difficulties in the local conflict seems not to be taken into account by those who criticize the so-called "mission creep" experienced by outside states in such situations. Col. Harry G. Summers, for example, has written that "'mission creep' seems to be the very hallmark of peacekeeping operations." *The New World Strategy: A Military Policy for America's Future* (New York: Simon & Schuster, 1995), 175. Summers referred to how introduction of American forces into Beirut in 1982 and into Mogadishu in 1994, originally designed as force-dampening initiatives, soon evolved into deeper involvement with catastrophic results. From these examples, he cautioned that the move of peacekeepers away from a position of neutrality between the primary antagonists and conciliation of them toward interestedness and coercion was likely to lead to disaster. It is argued here, on the other hand, that deepening hostilities between the primary antagonists can stimulate the development of interested and coercive postures by states that contributed peacekeeping forces.

3. As to why, given the clear-cut French military superiority over Dutch forces and Dutch unwillingness to go to war with the French, the Dutch nevertheless provoked French mobilization and incursion into Belgian territory, the answer is to be found in the considerable patriotic fervor in the Netherlands that led to renewal of war against the Belgians in the summer of 1831 and to the Dutch refusal in November 1832 to evacuate their Antwerp fortress. This fervor, and not the fear of French or concert retribution, dominated Dutch decision-making.

4. In the Congo, Lumumba's death emboldened African and Asian Security Council members to widen the UN's legitimate objectives in the Congo. In place of its reference in September 1960 to "military personnel," a Security Council resolution of 21 February 1961 referred to "foreign military and para-military personnel and political advisors not under the United Nations Command, and mercenaries"; the resolution called for the removal of these and made a mandatory request for preventing the departure of mercenaries headed toward the Congo. It also asked for recalling the Congolese parliament and for reorganizing of the Congolese army. All of this was expected to be done by conciliatory measures, the authority for using force for those purposes having been deleted from the resolution.

A similar problem characterized UN efforts in the 1990s Bosnia-Herzegovina civil war. There the original purpose for UN intervention was to supply food to the population of Sarajevo besieged by the Bosnian Serbs. But the vulnerability of the Muslim population in Bosnia-Herzegovina to Serb shelling and ethnic cleansing later brought a broader mandate for protecting Muslim "safe zones," enlarging the UN peacekeeping force in the region but without altering the basic conciliatory posture of the UN. In addition, since conciliation could not occur unless the UN held an impartial role between Muslims and Serbs, the UN role came to be conceived as protecting a Muslim Bosnian state against the Serb onslaught. Whatever the justification for these new objectives, the UN was powerless against the militarily superior Bosnian Serb army as long as it relied on conciliation alone. As the UN increasingly sought to protect the Muslim-dominated Bosnian government, it became more vulnerable to that army.

NOTES TO CHAPTER 10

1. On the importance of diagnoses and prescriptions, see George, *Bridging the Gap,* xx, 132.

2. I. William Zartman has written, "Preventive diplomacy is a problem-solving effort." *Preventive Negotiation,* 307.

3. See chapter 7, note 7.

4. On the concept of the hurting stalemate, see the citations in chapter 1, note 23.

5. On the so-called "warning-response gap," see George and Holl, *The Warning-Response Problem.*

6. In the four cases in which warning was present, the major states showed little or no receptivity to local developments, preferring not to make difficult decisions in relation to them. England avoided difficult decisions and refrained from deepening involvement in Bosnia I, Armenia, and Cyprus because of its alliance commitments, whereas the United States held to the same orientation in Bosnia II because of the more fluid international condition following the end of Soviet-American Cold War. In these instances, less important perceived threats and crises could not receive adequate attention in the absence of changes in state interests or in international relationships.

In the Belgian, Greek, Memel, and Congo cases, low policy priorities not only dulled initial major-state receptivity to local ethnic conflict but also, by dulling the sensitivity of great-power officials to it, were an obstacle to the gathering and analysis of information. Outside governments thereby lacked understanding of signals that might otherwise have allowed and encouraged the challenge of low policy priorities in advance of the outbreak of explosive local conflict. In none of these cases did developments prior to the outbreak of conflict suggest the imminence of violent activity, which evolved suddenly and rapidly.

7. The case material studied here reinforces the observation made by George and Holl that "in many ethnic and religious conflicts, humanitarian crises, or severe human rights abuses, *timely or accurate* warning may not be the problem at all. . . . [N]o serious response is likely to be taken solely on the basis of early warning simply because a simmering situation that threatens to boil over may not be deemed important enough to warrant the type and scale of effort deemed necessary to prevent the hypothetical catastrophe." *The Warning-Response Problem,* 11; emphasis in original. See also Jentleson, *Opportunities Missed, Opportunities Seized,* 324, for strong support for this same conclusion.

On the other hand, it cannot be argued on the basis of the data presented in this study that warning is unimportant. As Zartman has noted, "some warning must have been compelling in the many cases in which early prevention was practiced." *Preventive Diplomacy,* 5. And Jentleson strongly prescribes that "the [PD] action taken be *early, early, early.*" *Opportunities Missed, Opportunities Seized,* 337; emphasis in original. Nevertheless, given the presumed link between early warning and early intervention, Jentleson's emphasis upon the need for early intervention in local conflict is deflated by his argument that early warning was not the problem in numerous cases in which opportunities for early intervention were missed.

The argument made here is that the difficulties of insulationist PD weaken the potential for collective interventionist PD even when warning is present. The importance of early intervention is stressed below in connection with Type I cases.

8. Zartman has pointed out, "Even where violence is not the impending characteristic, the prospect of a worsening or damaging cycle of conflict provides the occasion—and potentially the motivation—for negotiations to manage, de-escalate, reduce, and possibly resolve the conflict." He also notes Jentleson's observation that most work on PD has dealt with high-intensity cases. *Preventive Diplomacy,* 4.

The prospect of worsening conflict between the local antagonists does not make the great powers more interested in collective interventionist PD, the major states being reactive rather than proactive in this respect, as we have seen. However, the prospect of outside sympathizer involvement in the local conflict tends to be understood by the major states as more threatening to international stability, and hence more likely to spur proactive collective interventionist PD.

9. This argument builds on Posen, "The Security Dilemma and Ethnic Conflict," 103–24.

10. On how "a consensus, even an erroneous one, that nothing could have been done in a past crisis can curtail the consideration of options in a future one," see Chaim Kaufmann, "See No Evil," *Foreign Affairs* (July/August 2002):145ff.

11. Brahimi, *Report of the Panel on United Nations Peace Operations,* 11 and 54.

12. A "near-miss" for applying coercive interventionist PD took place in the Armenian case in 1896–97. See chapter 8, note 29. For a recent defense of coercive interventionist PD, see Jentleson, *Coercive Prevention.*

13. See Thomas L. Friedman, "The New Iron Curtain," *New York Times,* 10 March 1997.

Selected Bibliography

Albrecht-Carrié, René (ed.). *The Concert of Europe*. New York: Walker & Company, 1968.

Anderson, Matthew. "Russia and the Eastern Question, 1821–41." In *Europe's Balance of Power: 1815–1848*, edited by Alan Sked. London: Macmillan, 1979.

Betts, Richard K. "Compromised Command: Inside NATO's First War." *Foreign Affairs* 80 (July/August 2001), 126–132.

Blainey, Geoffrey. *The Causes of War*. 3rd ed. New York: Free Press, 1973.

Boutros-Ghali, Boutros. *Agenda for Peace*. New York: United Nations, 1992. Reprinted in *United Nations, Divided World: The UN's Roles in International Relations*, edited by Adam Roberts and Benedict Kingsbury. 2nd ed. Oxford: Clarendon Press, 1993.

Brahimi, Lakhdar, et al. *Report of the Panel on United Nations Peace Operations*, 23 August 2000. UN document A/55/305-S/2000/809, *http://www.un.org/peace/reports/peace_operations/docs/*. New York: United Nations, 2000.

Bridge, F. R., and Roger Bullen. *The Great Powers and the European States System: 1815–1914*. London: Longman, 1980.

Brown, Michael E. (ed.). *Ethnic Conflict and International Security*. Princeton, N.J.: Princeton University Press, 1993.

———. *The International Dimensions of Internal Conflict*. Cambridge, Mass.: MIT Press, 1996.

Brown, Seyom. *New Forces, Old Forces, and the Future of World Politics*. Post-Cold War edition. New York: HarperCollins, 1994.

Brown, Willliam R. *The Last Crusade: A Negotiator's Middle East Handbook*. Chicago: Nelson-Hall, 1980.

Buzan, Barry. *People, States and Fear*. 2nd ed. Boulder, Colo.: Lynne Rienner, 1991.

Cahill, Kevin, M. (ed.). *Preventive Diplomacy: Stopping Wars Before They Start*. New York: Basic Books, 1996.

Carment, David, and Patrick James. "Ethnic Conflict at the International Level: Causation, Prevention, and Peacemaking." In *Peace in the Midst of Wars*, edited by David Carment and Patrick James. Columbia, S.C.: University of South Carolina Press, 1998.

———. "International Constraints and Interstate Ethnic Conflict." *Journal of Conflict Resolution* 39 (March 1995), 82–109.

Carment, David, and Patrick James (eds.). *Peace in the Midst of Wars.* Columbia, S.C.: University of South Carolina Press, 1998.

Carnegie Commission on Preventing Deadly Conflict. *Preventing Deadly Conflict: Final Report.* Washington, D.C.: Carnegie Commission on Preventing Deadly Conflict, 1997.

Church, Clive H. *Europe in 1830: Revolution and Political Change.* London: Allen & Unwin, 1983.

Connor, Walker. *Ethnonationalism: The Quest for Understanding.* Princeton, N.J.: Princeton University Press, 1994.

"Convention and Transitory Provision Concerning Memel signed at Paris, May 8th, 1924." In Extract no. 28 from the *Official Journal [League of Nations*]. [Geneva: League of Nations, 1924.]

Cortright, David. *The Price of Peace.* Lanham, Md.: Rowman & Littlefield, 1997.

Couloumbis, Theodore A. *The United States, Greece and Turkey: The Troubled Triangle.* New York: Praeger, 1983.

Craig, Gordon A., and Alexander L. George. *Force and Statecraft.* 3rd ed. New York: Oxford University Press, 1995.

Crawley, C. W. *The Question of Greek Independence.* Cambridge: Cambridge University Press, 1930.

Crocker, Chester. "Southern Africa Peace-Making." *Survival* 32 (May/June 1990), 221–232.

Crossette, Barbara. "What is a Nation?" *New York Times,* 26 February 1994.

Cviic, Christopher. "Yugoslavia: The Unmaking of a Federation." In *The Volatile Powder Keg,* edited by F. Stephen Larrabee. Washington, D.C.: American University Press, 1994.

Damrosch, Lori Fisler (ed.). *Enforcing Restraint: Collective Intervention in Internal Conflicts.* New York: Council on Foreign Relations, 1993.

Davison, Roderic. "The Armenian Crisis: 1912–1914." *American Historical Review* 53 (April 1948), 481–505.

DeMars, William. "Uncharted Territory: Humanitarian Action and Intelligence in Civil Wars." Paper presented at the Annual Meeting of the International Studies Association, San Diego, California, 17 April 1996.

———. "Waiting for Early Warning: Humanitarian Action After the Cold War." *Journal of Refugee Studies* 8 (1995), 390–410.

Durch, William J. (ed.). *UN Peacekeeping, American Policy, and the Uncivil Wars of the 1990s.* New York: St. Martin's Press, 1996.

Fisher, Ronald J. "Cyprus: The Failure of Mediation and the Escalation of an Identity-Based Conflict to an Adversarial Impasse." *Journal of Peace Research* 38 (May 2001), 307–326.

Fishman, J. S. *Diplomacy and Revolution: The London Conference of 1830 and the Belgian Revolt.* Amsterdam: CHEV, 1988.

Freedman, Lawrence (ed.). *Strategic Coercion: Concepts and Cases.* Oxford: Oxford University Press, 1998.

Friedman, Thomas L. "The New Iron Curtain." *New York Times,* 10 March 1997.

Gellner, Ernest. *Nations and Nationality.* Ithaca, N.Y.: Cornell University Press, 1983.

George, Alexander L. *Bridging the Gap.* Washington, D.C.: United States Institute of Peace, 1996.

———. "Case Studies and Theory Development: The Method of Structured, Focused Comparison." In *Diplomacy: New Approaches in History, Theory, and Policy,* edited by Paul Gordon Lauren. New York: Free Press, 1979.

———. *Forceful Persuasion.* Washington, D.C.: United States Institute of Peace, 1991.

George, Alexander L. (ed.). *Managing U.S.-Soviet Rivalry: Problems of Crisis Prevention.* Boulder, Colo.: Westview Press, 1983.

George, Alexander L., Philip J. Farley, and Alexander Dallin (eds.). *U.S.-Soviet Security Co-operation: Achievements, Failures, Lessons.* New York: Oxford University Press, 1988.

George, Alexander L., and Jane E. Holl. *The Warning-Response Problem and Missed Opportunities in Preventive Diplomacy.* Washington, D.C.: Carnegie Commission on Preventing Deadly Conflict, 1997.

George, Alexander L., and William E. Simons (eds.). *The Limits of Coercive Diplomacy.* 2nd ed. Boulder, Colo.: Westview Press, 1994.

Gooch, G. P., and Harold Temperley (eds.). *British Documents on the Origins of the War: 1898–1914.* Vol. X, pt. 1, *The Near and Middle East on the Eve of War.* London: His Majesty's Stationery Office, 1936.

Gow, James. *Lack of Will: International Diplomacy and the Yugoslav War.* New York: Columbia University Press, 1997.

Grenville, J. A. S. *Lord Salisbury and Foreign Policy.* London: Athlone Press, 1964.

Gurr, Ted Robert. "Ethnic Warfare on the Wane." *Foreign Affairs* 89 (May/June 2000), 52–64.

———. *Minorities at Risk: A Global View of Ethnopolitical Conflicts.* Washington, D.C.: United States Institute of Peace, 1993.

Gurr, Ted Robert, and Barbara Harff. *Ethnic Conflict in World Politics.* Boulder, Colo.: Westview Press, 1994.

Harris, David. *A Diplomatic History of the Balkan Crisis of 1875–1878.* Palo Alto, Calif.: Stanford University Press, 1936.

Hart, Parker T. *Two NATO Allies at the Threshold of War.* Durham, N.C.: Duke University Press, 1990.

Heisler, Martin O. "Hyphenating Belgium: Changing State and Regime to Cope with Cultural Division." In *Conflict and Peacemaking in Multiethnic Societies,* edited by Joseph V. Montville. New York: Lexington Books, 1991.

Hinsley, F. H. *Power and the Pursuit of Peace.* Cambridge: Cambridge University Press, 1967.

Holbrooke, Richard. *To End a War: From Sarajevo to Dayton—And Beyond.* New York: Random House, 1998.

Hollis, Martin, and Steve Smith. "The International System." In *The Theory and Practice of International Relations,* edited by William C. Olsen. 9th ed. Englewood Cliffs, N.J.: Prentice-Hall, 1994.

Horowitz, Donald L. *Ethnic Groups in Conflict.* Los Angeles and Berkeley, Calif.: University of California Press, 1985.

Hoskyns, Catherine. *The Congo Since Independence.* London: Oxford University Press, 1965.

Ignatieff, Michael. *Blood and Belonging.* New York: Farrar, Straus and Giroux, 1993.

———. *The Warrior's Honor.* New York: Henry Holt, 1997.

Isaacs, Harold R. *Idols of the Tribe.* New York: Harper & Row, 1974.

Jentleson, Bruce W. *Coercive Prevention: Normative, Political, and Policy Dilemmas.* Peaceworks Report no. 35. Washington, D.C.: United States Institute of Peace, 2000.

———. "Preventive Diplomacy and Ethnic Conflict: Possible, Difficult, Necessary." In *The International Spread of Ethnic Conflict,* edited by David A. Lake and Donald Rothchild. Princeton, N.J.: Princeton University Press, 1998.

Jentleson, Bruce W. (ed.). *Opportunities Missed, Opportunities Seized.* Lanham, Md.: Rowman & Littlefield, 2000.

Jervis, Robert. "Realism, Game Theory, and Cooperation." *World Politics* 40 (April 1988), 317–349.

Joseph, Joseph S. *Cyprus: Ethnic Conflict and International Concern.* New York: P. Lang, 1985.

Kahn, Herman. *On Escalation: Metaphors and Scenarios.* New York: Praeger, 1965.

Kalijarvi, Thorsten V. *The Memel Statute: Its Origin, Legal Nature, and Observation to the Present Day.* London: R. Hale, 1937.

Kanter, Arnold, and Linton F. Brooks (eds.). *U.S. Intervention Policy for the Post-Cold War World: New Challenges and New Responses.* New York: Norton, 1994.

Kaufmann, Chaim. "Possible and Impossible Solutions to Ethnic Civil War." *International Security* 20 (Spring 1996), 136–175.

———. "See No Evil." *Foreign Affairs* 81 (July/August 2002), 141–149.

Kaufmann, William W. "The Organization of Responsibility." *World Politics* 1 (July 1949), 510–532.

Keohane, Robert O. *After Hegemony: Cooperation and Discord in the World Political Economy*. Princeton, N.J.: Princeton University Press, 1984.

King, Gary, Robert O. Keohane, and Sidney Verba. *Designing Social Inquiry*. Princeton, N.J.: Princeton University Press, 1994.

Lake, David A. "Beyond Anarchy: The Importance of Security Institutions." *International Security* 26 (Summer 2001), 129–160.

Lake, David A., and Donald Rothchild (eds.). *The International Spread of Ethnic Conflict*. Princeton, N.J.: Princeton University Press, 1998.

Langer, William L. (ed.). *An Encyclopedia of World History*. 4th ed. Boston, Mass.: Houghton Mifflin, 1968.

Lauren, Paul Gordon. "Crisis Prevention in Nineteenth-Century Diplomacy." In *Managing U.S.-Soviet Rivalry: Problems of Crisis Prevention*, edited by Alexander L. George. Boulder, Colo.: Westview Press, 1983.

Leatherman, Janie, et al. *Breaking Cycles of Violence*. West Hartford, Conn.: Kumarian Press, 1999.

Lefever, Ernest W. *Uncertain Mandate: Politics of the U.N. Congo Operation*. Baltimore, Md.: Johns Hopkins Press, 1967.

Luard, Evan (ed.). *The International Regulation of Civil Wars*. New York: New York University Press, 1972.

Lund, Michael S. *Preventing Violent Conflicts*. Washington, D.C.: United States Institute of Peace, 1996.

———. "Preventive Diplomacy for Macedonia, 1992–1999: From Containment to Nation Building." In *Opportunities Missed, Opportunities Seized*, edited by Bruce W. Jentleson. Lanham, Md.: Rowman & Littlefield, 2000.

Mearsheimer, John J. *The Tragedy of Great Power Politics*. New York: Norton, 2001.

Medlicott, W. N. *The Congress of Berlin and After*. 2nd ed. Hamden, Conn.: Archon Books, 1963.

Medlicott, W. N., and Douglas Dakin (eds.). *Documents on British Foreign Policy: 1919–1939*. First Series, vol. 23, *Poland and the Baltic States: March 1921–December 1923*. London: Her Majesty's Stationery Office, 1981.

Meuvret, Jean. *Le Territoire de Memel et la politique Européene*. Paris: Centre d'Etudes de Politique Etrangère, 1936.

Midlarsky, Manus I. (ed.). *The Internationalization of Communal Strife*. London: Routledge, 1993.

Montville, Joseph V. (ed.). *Conflict and Peacemaking in Multiethnic Societies.* New York: Lexington Books, 1991.

Munro, John A., and Alex I. Inglis (eds.). *Mike: The Memoirs of the Right Honourable Lester B. Pearson.* Vol. 2. Toronto: University of Toronto Press, 1973.

Nicolaïdis, Kalpyso. "International Preventive Action: Developing a Strategic Framework." In *Vigilance and Vengeance: NGOs Preventing Ethnic Conflict in Divided Societies*, edited by Robert I. Rotberg. Washington, D.C.: Brookings, 1996.

Norton, Augustus R., and Thomas G. Weiss. "Superpowers and Peacekeepers." *Survival* 32 (May/June 1990), 212–220.

O'Brien, Conor Cruise. *To Katanga and Back.* London: Hutchinson & Co., 1962.

Owen, David. *Balkan Odyssey.* New York: Harcourt Brace, 1995.

Panteli, Stavros. *A New History of Cyprus.* London: East-West Publications, 1984.

Pearson, Frederic S., and J. Martin Rochester. *International Relations: The Global Condition in the Late Twentieth Century.* 3rd ed. New York: McGraw-Hill, 1992.

Polyviou, Polyvios G. *Cyprus: The Tragedy and the Challenge.* Washington, D.C.: American Hellenic Institute, 1975.

Posen, Barry R. "The Security Dilemma and Ethnic Conflict." In *Ethnic Conflict and International Security*, edited by Michael E. Brown. Princeton, N.J.: Princeton University Press, 1993.

Prins, Gwyn. *The Applicability of the 'NATO Model' to United Nations Peace Support Operations Under the Security Council.* UNA-USA International Dialogue on the Enforcement of Security Council Resolutions, paper no. 2. New York: United Nations Association of the U.S.A., 1996.

Reddaway, John. *Burdened with Cyprus: The British Connection.* London: Weidenfeld & Nicholson, 1986.

Regan, Patrick M. *Civil Wars and Foreign Powers.* Ann Arbor, Mich.: University of Michigan Press, 2000.

A Report on the Fifth Annual Peacekeeping Mission, November 2–11, 1995. New York: United Nations Association of the U.S.A., 1996.

Roberts, Adam, and Benedict Kingsbury (eds.). *United Nations, Divided World: The UN's Roles in International Relations.* 2nd ed. Oxford: Clarendon Press, 1993.

Rooney, John W., Jr. *Revolt in the Netherlands: Brussels—1830.* Lawrence, Kans.: Coronado Press, 1982.

Rosenau, James. *Turbulence in World Politics: A Theory of Change and Continuity.* Princeton, N.J.: Princeton University Press, 1990.

Rotberg, Robert I. (ed.). *Vigilance and Vengeance: NGOs Preventing Ethnic Conflict in Divided Societies.* Washington, D.C.: Brookings, 1996.

Ruggie, John Gerard. *The United Nations and the Collective Use of Force: Whither—or Whether*. UNA-USA International Dialogue on the Enforcement of Security Council Resolutions, paper no. 1. New York: United Nations Association of the U.S.A., 1996.

Sarkissian, A. O. *History of the Armenian Question to 1885*. Urbana, Ill.: University of Illinois Press, 1938.

Schelling, Thomas C. *Arms and Influence*. New Haven: Yale University Press, 1966.

Schmeidl, Susanne, and Howard Adelman (eds.). *Synergy in Early Warning*. Proceedings of a Conference, 1–18 March 1997, Toronto, Canada. Toronto: Centre for International Security Studies, University of Toronto, 1997.

Smith, Anthony D. S. *The Ethnic Origin of Nations*. Oxford: Basil Blackwell, 1986.

———. *Nationalism in the Twentieth Century*. New York: New York University Press, 1979.

Stedman, Stephen John. "Negotiation and Mediation in Internal Conflict." In *The International Dimensions of Internal Conflict*, edited by Michael E. Brown. Cambridge: MIT Press, 1996.

———. "Spoiler Problems in Peace Processes." *International Security* 22 (Fall 1997), 5–53.

Stedman, Stephen John, Donald Rothchild, and Elizabeth M. Cousens (eds.). *Ending Civil Wars: The Implementation of Peace Agreements*. Boulder, Colo.: Lynne Rienner, 2002.

Stojanovic, Mihailo D. *Great Powers and the Balkans: 1875–1878*. Cambridge: Cambridge University Press, 1939. Reprint. Cambridge: Cambridge University Press, 1969.

Strobel, Warren P. "The Media and U.S. Policies Toward Intervention: A Closer Look at the 'CNN Effect.'" In *Managing Global Chaos: Sources of the Responses to International Conflict*, edited by Chester A. Crocker and Fen Osler Hampson, with Pamela Aall. Washington, D.C.: United States Institute of Peace, 1995.

Summers, Harry G. *The New World Strategy: A Military Policy for America's Future*. New York: Simon & Schuster, 1995.

Sumner, B. H. *Russia and the Balkans: 1870–1880*. Oxford: Oxford University Press, 1937. Reprint. Hamden, Conn.: Archon Books, 1962.

Tellis, Ashley J., Thomas S. Szayna, and James A. Winnefeld. *Anticipating Ethnic Conflict*. Santa Monica, Calif.: RAND, 1997.

Trachtenberg, Marc. "Intervention in Historical Perspective." In *Emerging Norms of Justified Intervention*, edited by Laura W. Reed and Carl Kaysen. Cambridge: American Academy of Arts and Sciences, 1993.

Urquhart, Brian. *Hammarskjöld*. New York: Knopf, 1972.

———. *A Life In Peace and War*. New York: Harper & Row, 1987.

Ury, William L., and Richard Smoke. *Beyond the Hotline: Controlling a Nuclear Crisis*. Cambridge: Harvard Nuclear Negotiation Project, 1984.

Van Evera, Stephen. "Hypotheses on Nationalism and War." *International Security* 18 (Spring 1994), 5–39.

Walter, Barbara. "The Critical Barrier to Civil War Settlement." *International Organization* 51 (Summer 1997), 335–364.

Waltz, Kenneth N. "The Stability of a Bipolar World." *Daedalus* 93 (Summer 1964), 881–909.

———. *Theory of International Politics*. Reading, Mass.: Addison-Wesley, 1979.

Webster, Charles. *The Foreign Policy of Palmerston: 1830–1841*. London: G. Bell & Sons, 1951.

Woodhouse, C. M. *The Greek War of Independence*. London: Hutchison University Library, 1952.

Woodward, Susan L. "The Balkans and Europe: Euro-Atlantic Security and Values." In *Ethnic Conflict and Regional Instability: Implications for US Policy and Army Roles and Missions*. Edited by Robert L. Pfaltzcraff, Jr., and Richard H. Schultz, Jr. [Carlisle Barracks, Penn.:] US Army War College, n.d.

Zartman, I. William. "The Hurting Stalemate and Beyond." In *International Conflict Resolution After the Cold War*, edited by Paul Stern and Daniel Druckman. Washington, D.C.: National Academy Press, 2000.

———. "Negotiations and Prenegotiations in Ethnic Conflict: The Beginning, The Middle, and the Ends." In *Conflict and Peacemaking in Multiethnic Societies*, edited by Joseph V. Montville. New York: Lexington Books, 1991.

———. "Ripening Conflict, Ripe Moment, Formula, and Mediation." In *Perspectives on Negotiation: Four Case Studies and Interpretations*, edited by Diane B. Bendahmane and John W. McDonald, Jr. Washington, D.C.: Department of State, 1986.

Zartman, I. William (ed.). *Elusive Peace*. Washington, D.C.: Brookings, 1995.

———. *Preventive Negotiation*. Lanham, Md.: Rowman & Littlefield, 2001.

List of Titles in the SUNY series in Global Politics

James N. Rosenau, Editor

American Patriotism in a Global Society – Betty Jean Craige

The Political Discourse of Anarchy: A Disciplinary History of International Relations – Brian C. Schmidt

From Pirates to Drug Lords: The Post–Cold War Caribbean Security Environment – Michael C. Desch, Jorge I. Dominguez, and Andres Serbin (eds.)

Collective Conflict Management and Changing World Politics – Joseph Lepgold and Thomas G. Weiss (eds.)

Zones of Peace in the Third World: South America and West Africa in Comparative Perspective – Arie M. Kacowicz

Private Authority and International Affairs – A. Claire Cutler, Virginia Haufler, and Tony Porter (eds.)

Harmonizing Europe: Nation-States within the Common Market – Francesco G. Duina

Economic Interdependence in Ukrainian-Russian Relations – Paul J. D'Anieri

Leapfrogging Development? The Political Economy of Telecommunications Restructuring – J. P. Singh

States, Firms, and Power: Successful Sanctions in United States Foreign Policy – George E. Shambaugh

Approaches to Global Governance Theory – Martin Hewson and Timothy J. Sinclair (eds.)

After Authority: War, Peace, and Global Politics in the Twenty-First Century – Ronnie D. Lipschutz

Pondering Postinternationalism: A Paradigm for the Twenty-First Century? – Heidi H. Hobbs (ed.)

Beyond Boundaries? Disciplines, Paradigms, and Theoretical Integration in International Studies – Rudra Sil and Eileen M. Doherty (eds.)

Why Movements Matter: The West German Peace Movement and U.S. Arms Control Policy – Steve Breyman

International Relations – Still an American Social Science? Toward Diversity in International Thought – Robert M. A. Crawford and Darryl S. L. Jarvis (eds.)

Which Lessons Matter? American Foreign Policy Decision Making in the Middle East, 1979–1987 – Christopher Hemmer (ed.)

Hierarchy Amidst Anarchy: Transaction Costs and Institutional Choice – Katja Weber

Counter-Hegemony and Foreign Policy: The Dialectics of Marginalized and Global Forces in Jamaica – Randolph B. Persaud

Global Limits: Immanuel Kant, International Relations, and Critique of World Politics – Mark F. N. Franke

Power and Ideas: North-South Politics of Intellectual Property and Antitrust – Susan K. Sell

Money and Power in Europe: The Political Economy of European Monetary Cooperation – Matthias Kaelberer

Index